50 Hikes in the Maine Mountains

50 *Hikes*

In the Maine Mountains

Day Hikes and Overnights from
the Rangeley Lakes to Baxter State Park

Third Edition

CLOE CHUNN

Backcountry Guides

Woodstock, Vermont

AN INVITATION TO THE READER

Over time trails can be rerouted and signs and landmarks altered. If you find that changes have occurred on the routes described in this book, please let us know so that corrections may be made in future editions. The author and publisher also welcome other comments and suggestions. Address all correspondence to:

Editor, 50 Hikes™ Series
Backcountry Guides
P.O. Box 748
Woodstock, VT 05091

LIBRARY OF CONGRESS CATALOGING-IN-PUBLICATION DATA

Chunn, Cloe
    50 hikes in the Maine Mountains : day hikes and overnights from the Rangeley Lakes to Baxter State Park / Cloe Chunn.—3rd ed.
        p. cm.
    Includes index.
    ISBN 0-88150-499-8
    1. Hiking—Maine—Guidebooks.
2. Backpacking—Maine—Guidebooks. 3. Maine—Guidebooks. I. Title: Fifty hikes in the Maine mountains. II. Title.
GV199.42.M2 C58 2002
917.41—dc21   2001037527
                            CIP

Cover photograph by Paul Rezendes
Series design by Glenn Suokko
Trail overlays and non-topographical maps by Richard Widhu; new maps on pages 10, 81, 85, and 151 by Mapping Specialists Ltd., Madison, WI
Interior photographs by the author unless credited otherwise

Published by Backcountry Guides, a division of The Countryman Press, P.O. Box 748, Woodstock, Vermont 05091

Distributed by W. W. Norton & Company, Inc.
500 Fifth Avenue
New York, NY 10110

Printed in the United States of America

10 9 8 7 6 5 4 3 2 1

DEDICATION

For Ian, Skye, Curry, and Cory, and in reverence for this land of Maine, which has called me, held me, and made me its own.

50 Hikes at a Glance

HIKE	REGION
1. Tumbledown Mountain	Weld
2. Mount Blue	Weld
3. Little Jackson Mountain	Weld
4. Bald Mountain (Weld)	Weld
5. Angel Falls	Byron
6. Old Blue and Clearwater Brook	Andover
7. Bald Mountain (Oquossoc)	Rangeley
8. Mount Aziscohos	Rangeley area
9. West Kennebago Mountain	Rangeley area
10. Saddleback Mountain	Rangeley
11. Mount Abraham	Kingfield
12. Bigelow Mountain Loop	Stratton
13. Little Bigelow	Stratton
14. Cranberry Peak	Stratton
15. Poplar Stream Falls	Carrabassett Valley
16. Kibby Mountain	Eustis area
17. Pleasant Pond Mountain	Caratunk
18. Moxie Falls	The Forks
19. Moxie Bald Mountain	The Forks
20. Number Five Mountain	Jackman
21. Sally Mountain	Jackman
22. Boundary Bald Mountain	Jackman
23. Big Wilson Cliffs and Little Wilson Falls	Monson
24. Borestone Mountain	Monson
25. Barren Mountain	Monson
26. Gulf Hagas	Brownville

DISTANCE (miles)	DIFFICULTY	VIEWS	GOOD FOR KIDS	CAMPING	X-C SKIING	WATERFALLS	NOTES
5.5	3	★	★	★			swim, ice skate; mountain tarn
2.8	2		★				tower
6	2	★	★	★			view of mountain farm
3	2	★	★	★			interesting metamorphic rock
1.25	1		★		★		leisurely
10	3	★	★			★	variety of environments
2	1	★		★			popular short hike
3	2	★	★	★			remote
4.5	2	★	★	★			tower
10.2	4		★				swim, ski area (OK), open summits
8.25	4	★					open summits
12	5	★		★			challenging
12	4	★		★			great lean-to
6.4	4	★		★			well-known Maine mountain
4	3			★	★		swim, bicycle, x-c ski
5	4	★					remote, tower
2.5	3	★	★				swim, fish in pond
2.5	1		★		★	★	highest falls in New England
9.5	4	★					open summits
6	3	★	★				tower
5.8	3	★	★	★			swim, canoe trip
5.2	3	★	★				remote
3.5	3	★	★	★			good picnic spot
4	3	★	★	★			nature center, open summits
12.2	4	★					swim, remote
10	2	★	★	★	★	★	swim

50 Hikes at a Glance

DISTANCE (miles)	DIFFICULTY	VIEWS	GOOD FOR KIDS	CAMPING	X-C SKIING	WATERFALLS	NOTES
8	4	★					open summits
7	3	★					tower
4	3	★	★	★			canoe trip, tower
3	1	★	★		★	★	tower
4	3	★					tower
2.5	4	★	★				older kids (10+)
3.5	4	★					tower
4	4	★		★			open summits
9.8	5	★		★			older kids (10+)
11	5	★	★	★		★	older kids (10+)
6.6	4	★	★	★			open summits
2.5	1	★	★	★	★	★	swim
5.8	2	★	★	★	★		children, easy
6.4	4	★		★			avoid in rain
8.8	4	★		★			avoid in rain
6.6	4	★		★			wildflower plateau
6	3	★	★	★			swim
5.25	4	★	★	★			open summits
7.2	4	★		★			open summits
6	1		★	★	★	★	swim, pools and chutes
6	3	★		★			swim, the "ice chest"
14	4	★		★			open summits
12.6	4	★					glacial cirque
24.3	2		★	★	★		swim; solitude
40	2/3						swim; fish; moose; base camp

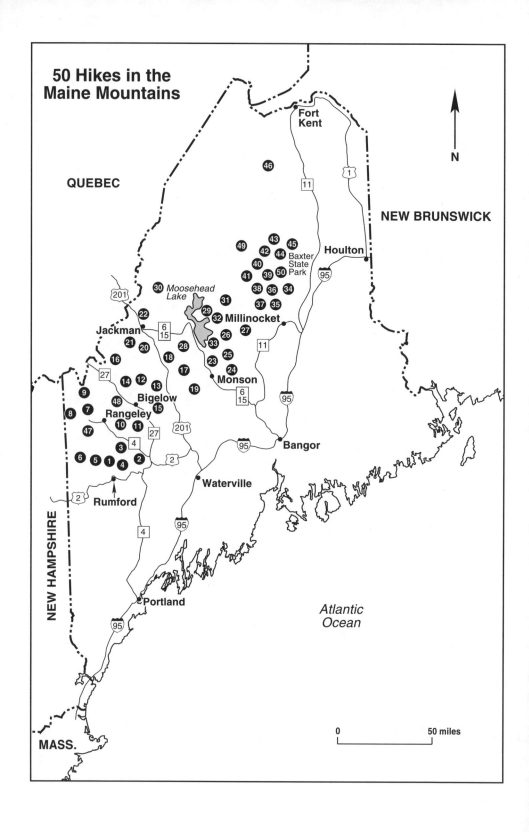

50 Hikes in the
Maine Mountains

CONTENTS

Preface to the Third Edition

After more than two decades of hiking Maine's trails, I am even more in love with this place than when I felt love-at-first-sight. Although the woods have changed—becoming more and more industrial—we still have them so far. Currently, debate is raging over clear-cutting; but whether we control our cutting with a ban or with stronger measures, we need to take better care of our woodlands. Forests, water, mountains—these make life sane. They offer physical and mental challenge, and they give peace and beauty. "In wildness is the preservation of the earth"—so said Henry David Thoreau, and it is a statement of truth and importance in my own life. In this age of a rapidly shrinking world, wilderness must be cherished and fought for with all of our might.

More than ever, we need to practice low-impact hiking, leaving no trace of our journeys or of ourselves when we hike. It is good to see more people hiking trails: These are the people whose experience in nature will make them care for it and see that others do too. However, increased foot traffic can adversely affect nature if we are not careful.

As Maine has acquired more public land over the last decade, more trails have been made, usually by volunteers. A recent development is the International Appalachian Trail/Sentier International des Appalaches, a trail of over 600 miles from Baxter State Park through Maine and New Brunswick to the Gaspé Peninsula of Quebec. About 115 miles are in Maine, including such choice climbs as Mount Chase near Patten and Mars Hill on the international border. This trail is usable for long-distance and also for day hiking.

I find myself walking more slowly and with more reverence, drawing and writing more, and looking around me more sharply as I hike these days. I have come to realize that my survival and my happiness depend on these quiet and high places, on trees and water. I invite you to hike these trails with loving feet and heart.

Acknowledgments

Without the help of some important people, this book would not have been as
much fun to write, and the result would
have been less than it is. I would like to
thank Charlie Gilman and Jean Hoekwater,
the friends I have met along the trail, and
the students in the hiking club at Gardiner
Area High School, who have been, and
continue to be, my loyal hiking partners on
many happy trails.

Introduction

Anywhere in Maine, hiking is a pleasure. In many places, it is also a challenge. The hikes and backpacking trips in this guide range from easy strolls to strenuous climbs. Some will be very popular, and on some you might not encounter anyone else.

Of the 50 hikes, 46 are day hikes and have been grouped into seven geographical sections. Each section offers a variety of hikes, from easy to difficult. Some are appropriate for getting into shape or for hiking with infants and young children. Many more offer a challenge to the hiker because of length, vertical rise, or ruggedness. You can estimate a hike's difficulty from the distance and vertical rise given at the beginning of each hike, as well as from the hike description. An eighth section contains four 2- to 5-day-long backpacking trips. These four backpacking trips—two in the western Maine mountains near Rangeley Lake and two in Baxter State Park—require that you be in good physical condition.

MAINE TRAILS

The trails described here are a sampling of those found in the northern and western parts of the state, up mountains, to waterfalls, and through forests. I have included hikes in the North Maine Woods, in Baxter State Park, and through holdings of The Nature Conservancy. Some trails incorporate sections of Maine's 280-mile-long stretch of the Appalachian Trail, and others traverse the state-owned Bigelow Preserve. On many trails, hikers are the guests of timber, pulp, and land companies: S. D. Warren, Champion, James River, International, Boise Cascade, (Irving) Great Northern, Seven Islands, Diamond, Plum Creek, Oxford, Brown, and Dead River. Regardless of ownership, all land deserves our utmost respect.

Maine's trails are always changing. Fire-tower trails become overgrown when towers are abandoned. Sometimes sufficient use maintains a trail; sometimes new trails are cut and maintained. Logging companies construct many new dirt roads in the deep forest each year, while numerous other old roads are in some stage of returning to forest. This dynamic aspect of Maine's woods roads and trails means that road approaches and the terrain you will hike may vary from the hike descriptions in this guidebook. These changing conditions are the most important reason for carrying topographical maps: Human-made features and even forest cover alter, but land contours, streams, ponds, and compass directions rarely change. Whenever possible, you should confirm hiking directions locally.

TOTAL DISTANCE, HIKING TIME, VERTICAL RISE, AND MAPS

Each hike description begins with a summary of location, total distance, hiking time, and vertical rise. These figures should help you judge the hike's difficulty and decide if a hike is within the limits of your ability and the amount of time you have to spend on the trail.

Total distance is the total number of miles you will hike on the suggested trails.

Each hike description clearly indicates if this distance refers to a circuit or loop, a return by the same route, or a one-way hike (where cars or bicycles are spotted at both the beginning and the end of the trail). If side trails to sites of interest are included in the totals, this fact is noted in the hike description.

Hiking time includes all time spent walking or climbing but does not include time for resting, picnicking, swimming, or simply enjoying the view. Times given are for a leisurely but steady pace, allowing for differences in terrain. If you pursue an alternate or side trail that is not included in the total distance, remember to adjust your hiking time. Allow yourself enough time for the special attractions of a hike, as well as enough time to cover the ground.

Vertical rise is the total distance climbed upward on a hike. The vertical rise may be more than the total gain in elevation if a trail often repeats an up-and-down pattern. On many hikes, especially strenuous ones, I have tried to indicate where along the trail you gain particularly significant amounts of the vertical rise.

In general, a difficult hike has a greater amount of vertical rise per mile, a longer total distance, and a longer hiking time than an easier hike. The vertical rise per mile is usually the best clue about how challenging a hike is.

Maps are suggested in each hike heading so that you can obtain supplements to the ones in this guide. The maps that accompany the hike descriptions are based on the appropriate United States Geological Survey (USGS) topographical sheets. Some of the areas hiked have USGS maps available in both 7.5' and 15' series. When both options are available I have listed the quadrangle names for each. The maps in this book give a good general idea of the trails followed but are less helpful if you are lost because, of necessity, they show less area than the originals on which they are based. It is always a good idea to carry USGS maps with you, both for a safer trip and for educational purposes. When using these maps, however, bear in mind that although land features remain relatively constant, the area may have been surveyed and mapped before the trail was cut, or the trail may have been relocated. The USGS maps, as well as a state index, price list, and pamphlet describing how to read the maps, can be obtained directly from the government by writing to the Distribution Branch, U.S. Geological Survey, Box 25286, Federal Center, Denver, CO 80225 (303-202-4700). The maps are also available at many sporting goods stores.

Maps other than the USGS sheets are sometimes listed in the summary headings. The Baxter Park Map refers to the free map you receive when you enter one of the Baxter State Park gates. It can also be obtained in advance when you make reservations. Steve Clark's detailed map and guidebook for Baxter Park can also be purchased at Park Headquarters, 64 Balsam Drive, Millinocket, ME 04462 (207-723-5140).

The *North Maine Woods Map* referred to in hike descriptions in the Monson to Moosehead and the Aroostook County sections is available for $2 postpaid from an association of paper, timber, and land companies by writing to North Maine Woods, Inc., P.O. Box 421, Ashland, ME 04732-0421.

The DeLorme *Maine Atlas and Gazetteer* is referred to simply as DeLorme. It is helpful for driving directions and for identify-

Bigelow from the northeast, seen from the inlet to Flagstaff Lake

ing landmarks. It is available from the De-Lorme Mapping Company, P.O. Box 298, Yarmouth, ME 04096.

And finally, the MATC maps refer to the strip maps published by the Maine Chapter of the Appalachian Trail Conference and included in its *Guide to the Appalachian Trail in Maine.* You can obtain this guide with its seven strip maps by writing to the Maine Appalachian Trail Club, Inc., Box 283, Augusta, ME 04330. This organization will also provide other information on hiking in Maine. The Appalachian Trail (AT) has gone through extensive changes in the last 10 years as both the National and Maine ATC have worked to achieve complete protection and have routed the trail away from roads as much as possible. Therefore, older AT maps and guides are of no use for many hikes now. The 1996 edition is up to date and will probably remain so indefinitely, because the trail is now stabilized for, we hope, a long while.

CLOTHING AND EQUIPMENT

Because many of these hikes are not heavily traveled, you should be especially prepared with your own first aid, warm clothing, rain gear, fire-starting equipment, food, water, and maps. A compass and this guidebook (or a photocopy of the hike you are following) should always be carried. Most trails are well marked and easy to follow, but on some of the rougher trails a compass is important for interpreting book directions.

When giving compass bearings, I have adjusted my compass for the declination appropriate for each hike. Declination is the difference between magnetic and true north. Maine's declination varies from 17 to 22 degrees, usually around 20 degrees for hikes in this book. To adjust your compass for the declination, rotate the compass so that north is 20 degrees to the right of the magnetic needle. Thus, the needle points to 340 degrees instead of 0 degrees, north.

Arranged in this way, the needle points, as always, to magnetic north, while the N points to true north, the north referred to in the book and designated on maps. Although the maps in this book are detailed, they can't show every twist and turn of the trail. The combination of landmarks, trail distances, and compass bearings at key points in the hike description should keep you on track.

For clothing, comfortable walking shoes should be your first consideration. Many of today's athletic shoes are sufficient for hiking and have the advantage of being lightweight. Sturdy walking shoes or Vibram-soled hiking boots are also desirable. Hiking in spring or after heavy rains sometimes calls for waterproof boots. Winter hiking demands insulated boots. Most important are fit and comfort.

For socks, wool is best, summer and winter. Wool does not absorb moisture and therefore does not lose its ability to cushion your feet. This is especially important in winter, when moisture will chill your feet quickly.

Other clothing choices are a matter of personal taste and your experience, as long as you carry enough. A rain jacket is necessary. In high winds, it can double as a wind shell for short periods. You should always tuck away a wool hat, mittens, and a wool sweater or shirt for unpredictable cold snaps and for use if you will be hiking above tree line. On a few hikes I suggest long pants. Otherwise, follow your own preference. Comfort should be the key.

Choose a day pack large enough to hold your gear. Other pack items include matches in a waterproof holder, a knife, insect repellent, and two liters of water. A flashlight and a small first-aid kit with moleskin added should be tucked away. Your compass should be accessible. In addition to your lunch and snacks, you should carry spare food for two meals. Many people enjoy taking a camera or fishing rod and license along.

Backpackers will need a sleeping bag, insulating pad, cooking utensils, matches (preferably the windproof type), and usually a tent and small stove. Supermarkets stock a variety of dehydrated foods. The backpack should be framed inside or out, should fit well, and should have a sturdy waist or hip belt.

Observing and learning about nature can enhance a hiking trip, so I suggest you also pack one or two field guides.

SAFETY

Maine weather is unpredictable. Always use caution. This is especially crucial above tree line, where weather changes suddenly and drastically, and where there may be no place to go for shelter. If you want to hike in bad weather, choose a forest trail to a pond, waterfall, or wooded mountain.

Winter is a time to use special caution. Snowshoe and ski travel require much more time than summer hiking, and days are shorter. Weather can change quickly. In general, choose shorter hikes with minimum vertical rise. Some hikes will be inaccessible by road in winter. When a trail is particularly good for winter hiking or cross-country skiing, I have noted that in the hike description and on the chart on pages 6–9.

Before setting out, study maps and guidebooks. Estimate the time needed for driving, hiking, eating, photography, and other activities. Inform a responsible person of your plans, where you will park your car, and when you expect to return. Carry a compass and enough emergency food and clothing so you can spend a night in the woods if necessary.

Getting lost happens to even the best of hikers. If you think you may be lost, the first step is to sit down and think rationally. You will probably remember where you missed the trail or took the wrong turn. Study your map and orient it with your compass. If you can figure out where you are, then you can find out where you should be. When you are really confused, find a stream to follow (downstream). If injured, build a fire if you can. Throw on green leaves and ferns as a smoke signal. And remember, if you left your itinerary with someone and you don't return when you are expected, someone will begin to search for you. For that reason, stick to your itinerary.

DRINKING WATER

Increasingly we hear about the illness giardiasis, which afflicts hikers and campers who have used water from a stream for drinking or washing dishes. It has been known to make hikers terribly ill, either within a week of the hike or many months later.

Giardiasis is an infection of *Giardia lamblia,* a protozoan carried in human or animal feces that can infest fresh water. Unfortunately, you never know if a *Giardia*-carrying animal has contaminated the water upstream. Beavers are often the culprits. A spring (source of groundwater) is usually pure and much safer than surface water (streams, lakes). The size of the spring (the smaller the better) and its location determine its safety. If it issues from a cleaved rock or falls from an inaccessible source, it is probably safe. But beware of surface water of all types. Symptoms of giardiasis include severe diarrhea, nausea, and chills, which can last several days or weeks. If you have these symptoms, see a doctor immediately for antibiotic treatment.

The best way to avoid *Giardia* is to carry water from home or a known safe source.

As this is not always possible or practical, the National Park Service recommends boiling drinking or dishwater for 1 minute, or using a filter for particles as small as 1 micron. Don't be misled by "granular charcoal" or "EPA registered" filters. Look for the filter size. They start at about $35. So far, the National Park Service does not recommend treatment with iodine tablets, as their effectiveness has not been proved.

ACCOMMODATIONS

Campgrounds and other accommodations are mentioned in the introduction to each section. Many, but not all, of the state parks offer overnight camping. To find out in advance, write to the Bureau of Parks and Recreation, State House Station 22, Augusta, ME 04333. Baxter State Park is a separate entity with its own regulations, which should be obtained in advance by writing to Baxter State Park, 64 Balsam Drive, Millinocket, ME 04462 (207-723-5140).

There is also a network of wilderness campsites approved and operated by the Maine Forest Service (MFS). The locations of these campsites are indicated in the DeLorme *Maine Atlas and Gazetteer* by the symbol for "Maintained Forest Campsites." Remote areas have many MFS campsites located singly or in pairs at a location. MFS sites permit fires in the proper fireplaces, are convenient to water, and usually have picnic tables. A very small fee is charged.

RESPECT FOR THE LAND

Rules and regulations are based on simple respect for land and property. Build fires only in authorized campsites; otherwise use a backpacking stove. If you camp in other than an authorized campsite, be sure to ask permission. In all cases, leave no sign that you were there. Trash should be carried out, not buried. Bodily waste should be buried at least 200 feet from any stream, spring, pond, or trail.

The various parks and forests have regulations of their own. Be familiar with them when you enter. By all means, be gentle with Mother Earth. She is our only home, a fact that many people ignore.

TAKING CHILDREN ALONG

Children are natural hikers, for they have limited needs and all outdoors is a toy to them. They are also easy to backpack when they are small.

In all hiking, the number one killer is a bad attitude. This single force is more powerful than bad weather, insects, heat, cold, getting lost, or a host of small inconveniences. When you are planning a hike with children, a few things to keep in mind will help your family preserve a good attitude.

Choose hikes with reasonable distances and reasonable vertical rises for your family's abilities. When in doubt, try the easier rather than the more difficult hike. If you discover you have attempted a hike that becomes too difficult, adjust your plans. Shorten the hike or take it more slowly. Allowing your child to walk ahead of you sometimes makes a remarkable change in attitude and enthusiasm. But always keep your child in sight, whether ahead of or behind you. Consider the ages of your children and how safe a trail is for them to walk or for you to hike while carrying them.

Babies up to two years old are easy to pack. They love to be carried, can sleep in a backpack, and enjoy the rhythm of hiking. There are several commercial child carriers on the market. You should be careful to choose one with a waist or hip belt. The belt transfers the load from your shoulders to your hips.

I prefer an old frame pack that has been converted into a child carrier. I cut and reinforced leg holes in the upper part of the pack bag, so the child sits in the top, facing backward, and the rest of the pack's compartments still hold cargo.

Two- and three-year-olds can walk part of the way and ride part of the way. Four-year-olds and older children can walk several miles if the pace is leisurely, and they enjoy carrying their own clothes, snacks, or lunch in a small pack. When a child is carried on an overnight trip, one adult needs to carry a pack with gear while another carries the child. Try to use lean-tos rather than tents whenever possible to lighten your load.

In general, spring, summer, and fall are the best seasons to hike with children. Clothing and equipment are heavier in winter hiking, and children—who are slower to complain than adults—can get very cold or wet before parents find out.

Pace your hike with frequent rest and snack periods. High-energy snacks like dried fruits, granola, nuts, and raisins are children's favorites anyway, and they are lightweight and easy to pack. Carry plenty of water; children are almost always thirsty. Children under two need only a few simple modifications in food. Nursing babies are the most convenient—no food or bottles are necessary at all. Older babies need a bottle or cup for powdered milk and simple foods such as bananas, apples (shaved or scraped with a knife), and cheese. For longer trips, a small plastic food grinder adds little weight and allows the baby to share the parents' food.

Have changes of clothes, shoes, raincoat, hat, mittens, and a warm jacket for each child. Tuck plenty of extra socks in the child's pack. For some hikes, sneakers might be good enough, but others may require waterproof boots or sturdy hiking shoes. Take disposable diapers for babies, the kind that can be burned.

Children (and adults) will be happier with good bug protection. Use one of several good repellents and in hot weather choose lightweight clothes that cover the whole body. A head screen can be made from a square yard of mosquito netting or other sheer material. Make a big circle by cutting the corners off the square. Turn under a small hem all the way around and run a piece of elastic through the hem. The elastic should fit a small child comfortably around the waist (protecting the upper body and arms), and an adult or older child around the neck. A hat with a brim will keep the netting away from your face.

Try to discourage children from bringing toys so they will notice the natural toys around them. Children love water, so it's a good idea to plan hikes with a swim or with other water features—falls, brooks, or ponds. Even a pot of water entertains a younger child. If children want to play in the rain, put their raincoats on them and let them play. If you are backpacking and fishing, your toddler will play with your catch of trout, put them to bed in the tent with washcloth covers, bathe them in a pan, and enjoy eating them for supper. Young children also need plenty of freedom as well as enough time to rest or nap. Older kids can learn to fish, practice orienteering (try a treasure hunt with compass and map or simple directions), experiment with photography, and help with camp chores. Remember that older children also need patient instruction—for example, in using a jackknife properly. Don't expect intuitive good sense or skill.

Help your children learn about nature by playing games with the objects of nature around you. Find hiding places,

identify wildflowers or animal tracks, or collect leaves or rocks. Imagine which animals would pick which tiny trees for their Christmas trees, or use acorn cups and saucers, or float leaves down brooks. The number of items that can be made from the large leaves of a striped maple is astonishing.

Planning for your family's safety and comfort should help children learn to enjoy, not detest, hiking. And as you try to interest your children in nature, you will find that their fresh outlook and unflagging curiosity will renew *your* interest in nature. You may recall the first time you stared into a bird's nest of tiny eggs, or saw a butterfly up close, or followed deer tracks. Wildlife sightings are much more exciting and memorable with children along. Wildflowers, too, are dear friends; it's easy to teach a child to stoop down to smell the flowers instead of picking them. Sunsets, mountains, toads and frogs, birds catching insects, woodpeckers pecking, waterfalls, and tiny brooks are all exciting for youngsters, as they should be for us. In the half hour it sometimes takes to get from here to 20 paces over there, we are reminded of the reasons we hike; what we lose in expectations of distance and accomplishment, we are repaid in enjoyment.

HIKING WITH YOUNG PEOPLE

As a high school and college teacher, I have enjoyed many trips—from one day to two weeks in length—with young adults. With their energy and enthusiasm they hike circles around me, and they can be eager to learn identifications of wildlife and edible plants. They learn quickly how to use map and compass, too, and can usually be depended upon for leading the group or helping "sweep" (bring up the rear). It is fun to pass around a group journal for everyone to write in each day. At the end of the trip, I make copies for all participants.

I use the buddy system, in which partners hike together and take care of one another. On longer trips I use a rotating buddy system so that everyone hikes with a different partner each day. This builds community solidarity and cooperation. Whenever possible, I use consensus decision making, which results in greater commitment and cooperation. However, I take command in cases of emergency. Not every decision affords time for consensus.

Still, whenever possible I let the leadership come from the group. Young people are full of good ideas and solutions. Several heads are better than one.

Attitude is everything. This is most important in bad weather. A tarp strung to trees, or a tent everyone can crowd into, can mean everything. A campfire cheers the spirit. Gathering firewood warms people even before the fire is built. Tasks keep people busy until the weather changes.

Hot chocolate and marshmallows to roast can save a rainy day. I always carry some "incendiary devices" in case a downpour makes starting a fire difficult. These can include waxed strips of cardboard, candles, G.I. fuel tablets, or a tube of fire-starting paste. Once a fire is going, even wet wood will burn.

If you know the members of your group, pay attention to them, and enjoy their company—and they know it—then you can look forward to a fun and satisfying trip with young people.

Key to Map Symbols	
——	main trail
•••	alternate or side trail
℗	parking
⇇	view
⚚	Appalachian Trail
⚕	campground
⋔	shelter

Mount Blue–Tumbledown Area

Introduction to Mount Blue–Tumbledown

The Mount Blue area is generally west of Farmington and just north of Rumford, occupying parts of Franklin and Oxford Counties. Weld, at the junction of ME 156 and ME 142, is the nearest village to Mount Blue, Tumbledown, Little Jackson, and Bald Mountains, while Byron on ME 17 and Andover on ME 5 are closest to Angel Falls and Old Blue. This area offers the earliest spring hiking in northern and western Maine, as well as the latest in fall, and provides the best winter access.

Weld and Byron are connected by Byron Notch Road, locally called Number Six because it is located in Township 6. The gravel road is used by logging trucks, but it is wide, well maintained, and safe.

Mount Blue State Park in Weld offers access to beautiful Lake Webb and has excellent camping. Campsites are easy to obtain; no reservations are necessary. The only other place where campfires are allowed is in Tumbledown Field at the Little Jackson trailhead (see Hike 3) off Byron Notch Road, but you must first obtain a fire permit from the Weld Maine Forest Service (MFS) office (207-585-2427) on ME 156 or the Weld General Store. Center Hill Picnic Area at Mount Blue State Park has a self-guiding nature trail that takes you to a dramatic outlook on Center Hill. The interesting information and the beautiful panorama are well worth the few minutes' walk.

While at the general store, you may also want to ask about directions and trail conditions for Blueberry Mountain, just a few miles up ME 142. Active logging operations have made the trail difficult to locate and to follow at the beginning. But with an update, you might be able to add this hike to the others described here for the Mount Blue area.

In Byron, be sure to stop at the Coos Canyon Rest Area at the junction of ME 17 and Byron Notch Road from Weld. Coos Canyon is a beautiful series of falls and chutes through pools scoured and polished over millions of years. There is no camping in the immediate Byron area, but 20 miles north on ME 17 you will find the entrance road to Rangeley Lake State Park on beautiful Rangeley Lake. No reservations are necessary, for the park usually has vacancies.

1

Tumbledown Mountain

Location: 5 miles north of Weld

Total distance: 5.5 miles (a circuit hike)

Hiking time: 4 hours

Vertical rise: 1,700 feet

Maps: USGS 7.5' Roxbury; USGS 7.5' Jackson Mountain; USGS 15' Rangeley; USGS 15' Rumford; DeLorme map 19

Tumbledown is Hike Number 1 for a reason. This is the hike to make you fall in love with hiking! The mountain offers an excellent variety of climbing experiences, culminating at a beautiful pond nestled among its three peaks. The Loop Trail to the summit provides easy trail walking, steep climbing, some boulder scrambling, and even some hand-over-hand on the rock faces just below the summit. An interesting, little-bit-of-everything kind of mountain, this is the trip I use to introduce people to hiking. It isn't as strenuous as Katahdin, and the experiences along the way are varied and exciting. And there is still trout fishing in Tumbledown Pond. Acid rain is beginning to affect this alpine tarn. Although it is not too acidic yet, if the trend continues, trout will no longer be able to live there. In the middle of this picturesque pond stands a little island that is fun to swim to in summer and skate to in winter.

How to Get There

Take the left (west) fork from ME 142 at Weld Corner, located about 2 miles north of Weld. Another fork is reached in half a mile. Stay to the right here. The gravel road meanders past the entrance to the Parker Ridge Trail and the path to Little Jackson Mountain (Hike 3) at 2.1 miles. Continue on and you'll reach the Chimney and Loop Trails on your right, just 3 miles beyond the Parker Ridge Trail sign at 5.1 miles. Stones and paint blazes mark the trail entrance. Park off the road out of the way of logging trucks.

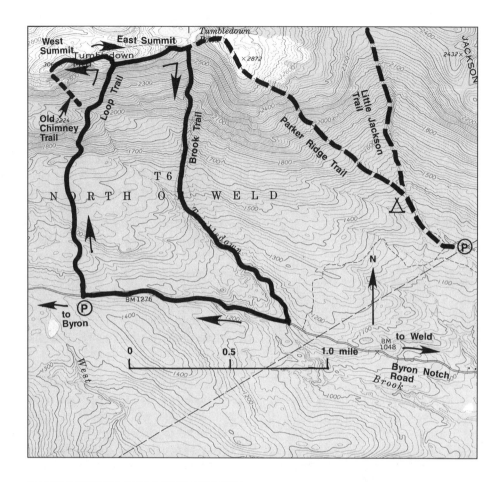

The Trail

Your climb to Tumbledown's West Summit begins from the north side of Byron Notch Road, where you immediately enter the woods. You follow the blue blazes almost due north from the road, passing through young hardwoods and traversing nearly level ground. You quickly walk over a low ridge. The trail then meanders across a brook and down into a boggy area.

Turning northeast, you begin the real ascent of the ridge below Tumbledown Cliffs. You pass a balanced rock on a pedestal at about 0.5 mile and a giant boulder at just under 1 mile. At the giant boulder, look

carefully for the blazed trail. Animal trails make this spot confusing. Be watchful as well for the next several minutes in order to notice the trail turn left to avoid an unscalable cliff.

Tumbledown probably got its name from the giant boulder field you now climb. The very steep ascent of the upper ridge will bring you, after a climb of about 0.3 mile, to the cairn where the Chimney Trail runs left and the Loop Trail goes to your right. Just below the cairn there are good outlooks to the south and west as you skirt the ledges. The old route to the West Summit, the Chimney Trail, is no longer in use and should not

The peaks of Tumbledown Mountain, behind Tumbledown Pond

be attempted. Rockfall at the top of the Chimney has made the area very dangerous and suitable only for those with rock-climbing skills. Turn right at the boulder, and head down through a depression to the east and northeast. After passing through the depression, the trail climbs steeply north over and through boulders to the ridge between Tumbledown's West and East Summits. Upon reaching the ridgeline, head left toward the West Summit. The views here are fairly open toward the southeast over Lake Webb, Byron Notch, and surrounding hills. From the West Summit, you can see Brush, West, and Walker Mountains ranging southward across the Notch.

Tumbledown and the Jacksons are part of the Smalls Falls Formation, which is Silurian metamorphosed sandstones and schists. This formation is part of the "country rock" of the Franklin County area, described in more detail in Hike 4, Bald Mountain. At the exposed summit you can see veins of quartz that filled cracks that formed when these mountains were thrust up, either by compressive buckling, by granite welling up from underground, or by a combination of both during the Silurian period 390 to 430 million years ago. It would be interesting to see what is inside this mountain!

Turning toward the east again, you retrace your steps along the ridge, pass the trail you ascended, and continue to the East Summit. Here you'll find beautiful little Tumbledown Pond, nestling in the col between Tumbledown and Little Jackson Mountains. The best views are just above the pond, and there are good spots to sit and have your lunch down by the water. From the pond you can also walk down the mountain via the Parker Ridge Trail (see map), which heads northeast over Parker Ridge. This trail will bring you out to Byron Notch Road 3 miles east of your car.

Your descent via the Brook Trail begins at the outlet, at the southeast edge of Tumbledown Pond. Tricolor Timberlands blazes lead you down, crisscrossing the brook. Don't take any side trails. Stay with the blazes along Tumbledown Brook, which, by the way, is sometimes panned for gold.

The trail is steep and requires careful footing until it eases onto an old logging road, still following the brook. About 1.5 miles down from the pond's outlet, the trail ends at Byron Notch Road. Turn right and walk 1.4 miles on the road to your car at the Loop trailhead.

2

Mount Blue

Location: 6 miles east of Weld

Total distance: 2.8 miles (a return hike)

Hiking time: 2½ hours

Vertical rise: 1,800 feet

Maps: USGS 7.5' Mount Blue; USGS 15' Dixfield; DeLorme map 19

Mount Blue looks the way a mountain should. Seen from high on the ridge west of Lake Webb, it's an elegant picture—a memory you'll always associate with Maine. Blue's nearly perfect, cone-shaped mass rises like a gumdrop east of Lake Webb and south of Pope and Hurricane Mountains. Mount Blue must be one of the most popular climbs in Maine, but, even on a summer day, the mountain is rarely crowded.

How to Get There

Head east from Weld on the paved road by the general store. Keep left at the first junction. The route shortly becomes a gravel road that winds eastward. Continue past the road (right) to Center Hill. Keep right at the next junction, arriving at a grassy parking area below the mountain about 6 miles from Weld. The road is well marked at all junctions.

The Trail

From the parking area, you walk east-northeast up a grassy fire road, which very shortly enters the woods. The lower west ridge and the higher reaches of the mountain rise before you as you start up. Once in the woods, you climb sharply east and northeast up the ridge. This is steady, steep going by anyone's standards, but not difficult once you get your rhythm.

As you climb rapidly, you'll hear a brook off to your left. A short side path takes you to this source of water at about 0.7 mile. At 1 mile, you pass the fire warden's cabin on your left, where there is a spring, and swing steadily upward toward the northeast. The

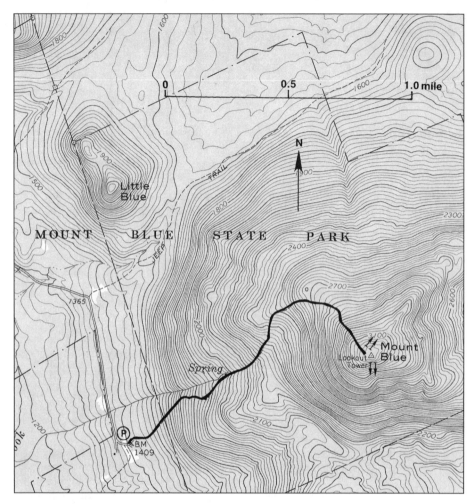

trail crests the north end of the lower ridge shortly, and you head east and southeast toward the summit. The grade becomes more comfortable for a short distance as you move toward the cone, but grows steep again as you turn nearly south for the final scramble to the top. Good views to the north and northwest begin to appear behind you here. The summit is reached at approximately 1.4 miles. The old fire tower is now loaded with microwave relay equipment complete with cold-weather deicing heaters. It's rather an odd experience to stand on the upper levels of the tower, listening to the wind and the bleep, bleep, bleep of the relays inside.

A good deal of western Maine can be seen from Blue. Looking to the northeast, the 4,000-foot summit of Mount Abraham (Hike 11) rises south of Black Nubble, Spaulding, and Sugarloaf Mountains (Hike 48). Saddleback in Rangeley (Hike 10) can be seen almost due north. The other major summits of the Weld region are to the northwest, Tumbledown (Hike 1) and the Jacksons (Hike 3), while the imposing shapes of Baldpate

Snowy trail up Mount Blue

and Old Speck in Grafton Notch rise to the southwest.

Geologically speaking, the bedrock of Mount Blue is a member of the Seboomook formation, which is Devonian metamorphosed sandstones, slates, and schists. This formation is part of the regional "country rock" of the Franklin County area, explained in more detail in Hike 4, Bald Mountain. Although Mount Blue does not afford many opportunities to view its bedrock, since the trail and summit are wooded, the stones along the trail will give you an idea of what the underlying bedrock is like.

The neatly manicured circle of grass lawn on the summit of Blue is a helicopter landing pad. The two dozen or so tanks of propane used to run the microwave deicers are flown in periodically. Not very romantic, but it keeps the relays open. Head down the way you came up for a muscle-crimping, quick descent.

3

Little Jackson Mountain

Location: 4 miles north of Weld

Total distance: 6 miles (a return hike)

Hiking time: 5 hours

Vertical rise: 1,800 feet

Maps: USGS 7.5' Roxbury; USGS 7.5' Jackson Mountain; USGS 15' Rangeley; USGS 15' Rumford; DeLorme map 19

How to Get There

The trail for Little Jackson Mountain is reached via Byron Notch Road from Weld Corner. Take the left (west) fork at Weld Corner about 2 miles north of Weld on ME 142. You come to another fork in 0.5 mile. Stay to the right here. The gravel road at 2.1 miles reaches the entrance to the Parker Ridge Trail and the path to Little Jackson Mountain. Both trails initially follow a gravel road leading past a camping area with plenty of room for parking. This camping area, called Tumbledown Field, is the only place an open campfire is permitted, but a fire permit must be obtained from the Maine Forest Service (MFS) station in Weld (207-585-2427) or from the Weld General Store. The road ends at a shelter where the Parker Ridge Trail runs left and west, while the trail to Little Jackson runs right up a logging road.

The Trail

Walk up the logging road through a luxuriant growth of wild berries. You are headed north and northwest. In 0.3 mile you pass through a large clearing once used for loading logs. At a fork a little beyond the clearing, keep right, climbing steadily due north. Watch for faded paint blazes on the rocky way. Behind you views of the valley can be seen.

You reach a second fork 0.2 mile above the clearing. Bear left here at an orange painted arrow. (The rocky logging road continues to your right.) After you pass a small, grown-up meadow—with views across the notch to Spruce Mountain behind you—your

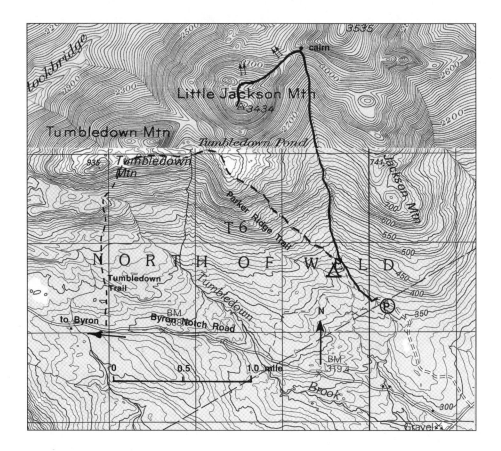

ascent grows steeper on a narrow path. Moose may be encountered here. The path, after being heavily overgrown with grass, shortly becomes rocky again and continues to rise steeply northward toward the col between Little and Big Jackson Mountains.

Be sure to avoid the many small, unused logging roads that meander off the main path. There are enough of them to confuse a saint. You climb up through spruce and fir, rising above the hardwood groves. Follow the arrows briefly west, then just as briefly north and northeast. The path enters a closely wooded section where birch and young beech parallel the pathway at approximately 1.5 miles from the trailhead. You

slab the extreme southwest ridge of Big Jackson for a short distance as you approach the col between the two peaks. A brook is crossed just below the col, at about 2.3 miles.

After crossing the brook, the trail runs briefly west and then north again through fine stands of brilliant white birch. The trail levels off momentarily and then climbs very steeply to the high point of the col on open ledges, offering fine views of the surrounding peaks.

Traveling briefly north to a prominent cairn, you then turn west for the summit. The trail is not well marked, and painted blazes must be carefully hunted out. The

The author's students on Little Jackson

route wanders erratically southwest and south from the col, reaching the summit in about 0.7 mile.

The excellent north–south views from the col are improved upon by the outlook from Little Jackson's summit. The Rangeley Lakes region is to the northwest, the imposing mass of Saddleback (Hike 10) is to the east of the lakes, and still more to the right you'll see the outline of Sugarloaf (Hike 48). The trailless summit of Big Jackson is immediately to the east with the three peaks of Tumbledown (Hike 1) lying over Tumbledown Pond to the southwest. Lake Webb shines below to the southeast.

When descending by the same route you followed in, watch carefully for the cairn on the col where the trail turns right and toward the south.

A description of local geology can be found in the texts of Hike 1, Tumbledown Mountain, and Hike 4, Bald Mountain.

Little Jackson Mountain

4

Bald Mountain (Weld)

Location: 5 miles south of Weld

Total distance: 3 miles (a return hike)

Hiking time: 1½ hours

Vertical rise: 1,400 feet

Maps: USGS 7.5' Mount Blue; USGS 15' Dixfield; DeLorme map 19

To get a good look at Lake Webb and its surrounding mountains from the south, you've got to climb Bald Mountain, which lies between Weld and Wilton on ME 156. The mountain is in Perkins Township: Find the right destination on a road map before you set out. Remember, there are eight mountains in Maine called "Bald."

This hike is short and relatively steep, but not too steep for most, from small children to Grandma. They will know they have accomplished something, but they will be able to make it.

How to Get There

The trail to the 2,386-foot summit begins on the south side of ME 156, just over 5 miles from Weld and a little over 8 miles from Wilton, 0.2 mile south of the Perkins and Washington Township line. There is a small clearing here for parking.

The Trail

A narrow signpost indicates the trailhead, but the sign is often missing. Walking south from the road, you quickly cross a brook and proceed gradually up through mixed hardwoods on a fairly well defined path. There are occasional blazes, but the trail bears close watching, particularly in its lowest section.

Climbing on a grade that is sometimes steep, you shortly emerge above the timberline into scrub and then onto the ledges. There is little protection from the elements above here on windy or stormy days, so dress accordingly—and if the weather gets

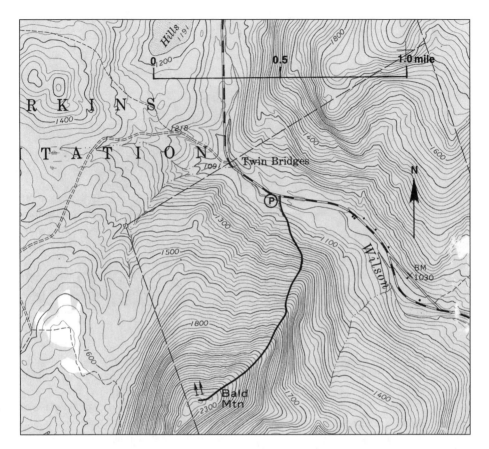

really vicious, head down. Cairns mark the remainder of the route, which rises at a comfortable rate to the summit, 1.5 miles from the trailhead.

Cherry Hill is immediately to your west, while the peak to the southwest is the higher, second summit of Bald, now renamed Saddleback Wind. A poorly maintained trail leads to this peak; the going is rough, and the walk is not recommended. Lakin Hill lies northeast of Cherry Hill, and you have a good view of Lake Webb between the two. Mount Blue with its tower (Hike 2) is due north over the waters of Hill Pond. Walker, West, and Brush Mountains are visible some distance to the northwest beyond the lake. Tumbledown (Hike 1), the

Jacksons (Hike 3), and Blueberry Mountain form the exceptionally beautiful north border of the area.

Bald Mountain is a granodiorite pluton, a mound of bedrock slightly darker than granite that welled up in molten form like a blister under the regional sedimentary rock that covered it. As it welled up, it heated and changed these overlying sedimentary layers into harder metamorphic rock, the surrounding "country rock" of slates and schists in this area. Solutions of quartz dissolved in water coursed through any cracks in the stretched layers over the blister, leaving veins of rock quartz when it cooled.

These metamorphic layers have begun to erode away from Bald Mountain, exposing its

Bald Mountain behind Hill Pond

granodiorite interior at the summit. However, the climb begins on country rock, the metamorphic shell still covering the lower reaches of the mountain. Examine the various stones in and along the trail. Some are chunks of granodiorite from above, and many are the metamorphic tailings that were clipped off by freeze-thaw actions and other weathering processes. Some of these metamorphic schist rocks contain staurolites, little cross-shaped minerals (or pieces of crosses) visible on the surface of the rock. These stau-

rolites tell us about the nature of metamorphism in this region, its underground temperature and pressure during mountain-building around 350 million years ago.

In late May and early June you will discover lady's slippers shyly nestled among rocks in the scrub growth of sheep laurel here and there over the broad summit.

It's an easy 35-minute walk down to the road from the summit. Take care not to miss the entry to the woods below the cairns on your return.

5

Angel Falls

Location: Halfway between Rangeley and Rumford, near Byron

Total distance: 1.25 miles (a circuit hike)

Hiking time: 1 hour

Vertical rise: 200 feet

Maps: USGS 7.5' Houghton; USGS 15' Oquossoc; DeLorme map 18

Not often does a hike as rewarding as Angel Falls require so little effort. The 70-foot cascade rivals Moxie Falls (Hike 18) in the largest-single-drop-in-Maine category (both make the claim, and both deserve it!). Originally named Mountain Brook Falls for its location, it has also been called Lost Falls.

How to Get There

The trail is in Houghton, which can be approached from several directions. You can drive south from Oquossoc, 18 miles from the junction of ME 4 and ME 17; or you can drive north from Byron, 4.2 miles from the rest area at Coos Canyon, a beautiful canyon cut and polished by natural scouring, located to the right (east) of ME 17 at its junction with Byron Notch Road to Weld. Byron can be approached from two different directions: north from Mexico on ME 17, or from Weld (ME 142) across 10-mile, unpaved Byron Notch Road to Coos Canyon at ME 17.

From either of these approaches, look carefully for a dirt road to the west off ME 17 that immediately crosses a bridge over the Swift River. A state highway marker at this turn is numbered 6102. About 0.2 mile after you cross the bridge, a small sign lets you know you are in Houghton; fork right at this sign. You are now driving on the old railroad bed that parallels Berdeen Stream northwest, with Brimstone Mountain ahead of you. Pass through a gate at 1.2 miles. At 2.5 miles from ME 17, pass a road to your left, and at 3.6 miles, park on the left.

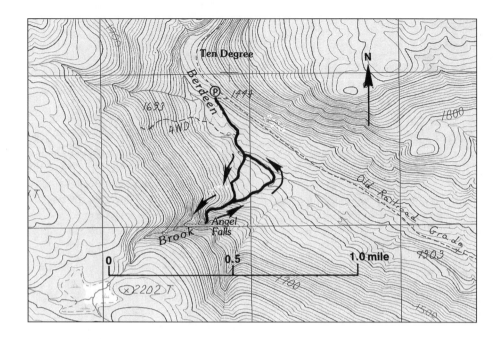

The Trail

Walk down to the bottom of a gravel pit (you may see red blazes). The half-mile trail begins from the gravel pit. Ignore the road straight ahead and begin walking on the grassy road to your left, crossing a washed-out culvert. Just ahead, you rock-hop across Berdeen Stream. From here, the trail is marked with red wooden arrows and old red paint blazes on trees.

After crossing the stream, turn left and walk downstream about 100 yards to where the trail divides, to your left along the stream, and to your right away from the stream. (You'll return by the trail on your left.) Bear right, rising briefly to a clearing where the trail angles slightly to your right through mature hardwoods with some grand old beech and maple. The diminutive fern growing on the forest floor is oak fern, and the lacy fern in circlets is spinulose wood fern.

After a 10- to 15-minute walk from the gravel pit, the trail crosses a faint intersec-tion a few yards before reaching Mountain Brook. (Remember this intersection be-cause you will go back on the trail that joins you here.) A few paces take you to a big slab of rock overhanging Mountain Brook. From here, the trail zigzags across the brook sev-eral times, following red paint blazes on rocks. This is an inviting glen, cool even on a hot day, adorned with ferns and mosses. Even if there were no falls ahead, this stream would be well worth the drive and the walk.

About half an hour from the start, after a turn to your left, you pick your way through boulders to the base of Angel Falls. The 70-foot metamorphic wall of phyllites, slates, and schists rises vertically in pyramidal and polyhedral slabs, while wispy plumes of spray resembling angel hair fall from Mount-ain Brook above. This is the end of the trail and a beautiful spot for lunch and a dip in the pool below the falls.

It is possible to scale the cliff to the left of the falls and get a bird's-eye view down the falls, but extreme care should be taken, both for personal safety and to avoid erosion of the steep cliff. A short walk above takes you past smaller cataracts. If you stop to picnic or climb to the top of the falls, you should lengthen the expected hiking time of this walk.

Waterfalls can result from a number of conditions usually associated with certain rocks or rock types being harder than an adjacent rock type in a stream. At the top of the falls, the metamorphosed sedimentary bedrock appears to have been tilted on its side during a folding event, heaving its bedding planes from their horizontal position when sedimented to a nearly vertical orientation. This vertical bedding position could account for the erosion-resistant quality of the bedrock at this point in the stream, adjacent to the steeply cut waterfall below it.

On the return trip to your car, begin by backtracking along the stream. When you've crossed it for the last time, watch for the trail intersection just into the woods. Instead of walking straight ahead on the trail you came on, turn right, paralleling Mountain Brook downstream, although it is not in view much of the way. Follow the red arrows backward, descending through yellow birch and maple in open, sunny woods. From the intersection, it is 0.5 mile to your car at the gravel pit, and you will cross Berdeen Stream at the same ford.

6

Old Blue and
Clearwater Brook

Location: 8 miles north of Andover

Total distance: 10 miles (a one-way hike)

Hiking time: 7 hours

Vertical rise: 2,300 feet

Maps: USGS 7.5' Andover; USGS 7.5' Metallak Mountain; USGS 15' Old Speck Mountain; USGS 15' Oquossoc; MATC map 7 (1993); DeLorme map 18

Old Blue, in the heart of the western Maine mountains near Andover, was trailless until 1979, when the Appalachian Trail (AT) was relocated over its summit. Before the relocation, few people climbed Old Blue as it had the reputation for being a tedious bushwhack. At 3,600 feet, it missed the "Hundred Highest" list by a few feet, so it was never a quarry for peak baggers, who might have found the thick undergrowth a challenge. Consequently, this fine peak is, for a time, unspoiled by hordes of humans.

The land you will hike is owned by the International Paper Company, the Brown Company, and Seven Islands Land Company. The Bates College Outing Club worked for two years clearing and preparing the trail's 4.5-mile-long relocation. Because the new section meets the old AT, now called the Clearwater Brook Trail, at the northern end of the mountain, this is one peak you can explore without having to backtrack.

Although also very enjoyable in spring and summer, this hike is especially scenic in fall, for it takes you up through mixed hardwoods, some very old, through spruce on Old Blue's summit, and back down the Clearwater Brook Trail through large mixed hardwoods. Except for the all-spruce summit, there is plenty of birch, maple, and other hardwood color, with some interesting fall wildflowers underneath. Since water is available only from brooks, you should take full water bottles with you.

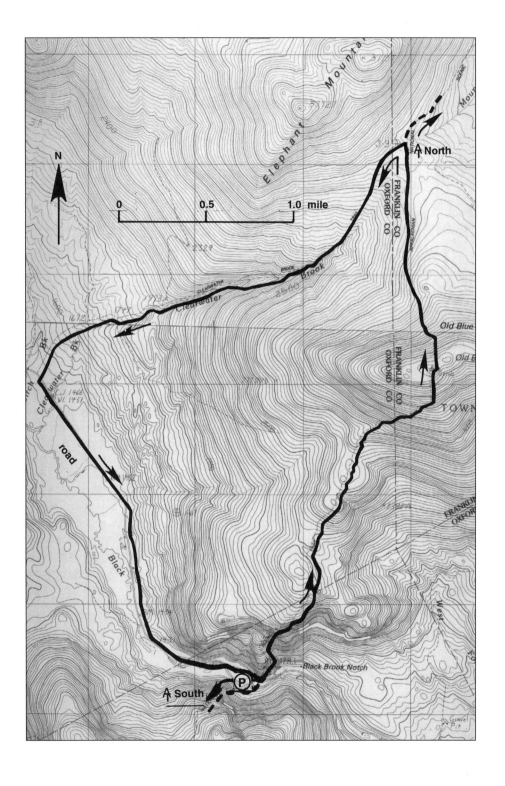

Lichen-covered granite surrounded by sheep laurel in bloom, a familiar sight in June

How to Get There

Travel US 2 to Rumford Point, west of Rumford, where you bear right (north) on ME 5 to Andover. Continue north 8.5 miles from the four corners in Andover on the road to South Arm, taking a left turn at 0.5 mile and another at 3.2 miles. The white blazes of the AT and the trail sign can be seen where the trail crosses ME 5 in Black Brook Notch.

The Trail

Your path leaves the road to the northeast, climbing steeply up the northeast side of Black Brook Notch. The first 0.6 mile rises over shelves of yarrow, asters, and other flowers; it gains 900 feet, making it one of the steepest sections of the AT in Maine. However, you soon reach the top of a cliff, after which the ascent is more gentle. While you catch your breath, the cliff offers views southwest to Sawyer Mountain with

Moody Mountain behind, both of which are on another recently relocated section of the AT on the way to Hall Mountain Lean-to. Southeast over Ellis Pond stands the white globe of the Andover Telstar Tracking Station.

From here the trail rises gradually through mixed spruce and hardwoods; some trees are very old and large with big burls. Beneath you is typical hardwood ground cover: wild sarsaparilla, ferns, asters, red berries of hobblebush and Solomon's plume (false Solomon's seal). Especially interesting is the doll's-eye (white bane-berry)—low plants with maplelike leaves whose spring white flowers turn in fall to white berries with a black dot, resembling a doll's eye with a black pupil.

You rise over four wooded knobs or "false summits," mounting the southwest shoulder of Old Blue. At the base of the main dome of the mountain, begin the

800-foot climb of the southwest slope, rising through spruce-fir duff and then sheep laurel, mountain ash, bunchberry, and scrub spruce to the open white granite summit. The 360-degree view is one of the best in western Maine: north to the two humps of Elephant Mountain with Bemis Mountain (Hike 47) behind, east to peaky Tumbledown (Hike 1) with Mount Blue (Hike 2) behind, southeast to Ellis Pond with Telstar behind, southwest to Baldpate, and beyond, Old Speck, the third highest peak in Maine. To the west over the west peak of Old Blue lie the Richardson Lakes and Pond-in-the-River (Rapid River).

From the summit, descend steeply at first and then gradually over soft ground through spruce-balsam woods. The farther you go, the bigger the trees become. Some of the red spruce have been dated to the 1620s by the University of Maine. Cross a spring brook and enter a forest of huge red spruce. The trees are almost all dead, probably from a spruce budworm infestation in the 1970s. Some clearings offer lovely vistas.

You will reach a junction where the relocation ends. (The AT continues to your right to Bemis Mountain, Hike 47.) Turn left onto the former AT, its blazes now painted blue as are those of the Clearwater Brook Trail. This former stretch of the AT is no longer maintained, and with time will return to nature. The trail is often wet, and in poor condition in places. In 0.3 mile, as you begin crossing and recrossing the headwaters of Clearwater Brook, the hardwoods, including some cherry trees, begin to return.

Cross Clearwater Brook where there is a pool of water deep enough to submerge yourself. The trail follows the widening stream through birch woods populated with partridge here and there. After passing vertical chunks of stratified bedrock on your left, cross back to the north side of Clearwater Brook. You pass a lovely set of cascades into a pool flecked with iron pyrite glinting gold. The rocks are stained red, and the freezing water tastes of iron. The trail leaves the brook and follows an old woods road through beech and birch, bears right onto a dirt road for 0.5 mile, and runs back out onto ME 5.

Turn left and walk 2.3 miles along the road back to your car. While walking, you can trace your hike over Old Blue's skyline on your left. You will pass a couple of mammoth birches on the roadside, as well as the fleecy, white down of fireweed in fall, goldenrod, yarrow, joe-pye weed, and the red berries of mountain ash. If you have two cars, you can eliminate this last road stretch by spotting one of the cars where Clearwater Brook Trail meets ME 4, 2.3 miles from the trailhead.

Rangeley Region

Introduction to Rangeley

The Rangeley region is famous for its lakes of all sizes, its fly-fishing, resorts, and downhill skiing. The town of Rangeley has restaurants, gift shops, sporting goods stores, and lodgings of varying sophistication. Between ME 17 and ME 4 on the south shore of Rangeley Lake, the state park is a good place for camping and recreation. No reservations are necessary, for the park usually has vacancies.

The drive up ME 17 from Rumford and Byron offers stunning views west over Mooselookmeguntic Lake of the western Maine and New Hampshire mountains. Sunsets are particularly thrilling from Height-of-the-Land, where the Appalachian Trail crosses the highway. Farther north, there are dramatic views east over Rangeley Lake of Saddleback, Sugarloaf, and Bigelow in the "4000-Footers" stretch of the Appalachian Trail.

Here in northern Franklin and Oxford Counties, you are also in snowmobile country, with a vast network of well-groomed trails reaching to Canada. Saddleback is one of the best downhill ski areas in Maine, offering many cross-country ski trails as well. The large lakes are a mecca for fly-anglers: the Richardson Lakes, Mooselookmeguntic, Rangeley, Aziscohos, and Parmachenee.

Hiking can be easy and civilized in this area, as with Bald Mountain on the peninsula separating Mooselookmeguntic and Rangeley Lakes, or solitary in utter wilderness, as with West Kennebago and Aziscohos Mountains or Mount Abraham. The Sabbathday Pond Loop is flat and interesting, while Mount Abraham is a climb of more than 3,000 vertical feet. There's a hike for everybody in Rangeley.

7

Bald Mountain (Oquossoc)

Location: 5 miles west of Rangeley

Total distance: 2 miles (a return hike)

Hiking time: 1½ hours

Vertical rise: 950 feet

Maps: USGS 7.5' Oquossoc; USGS 15' Oquossoc; DeLorme map 28

There's no better place to get the feel of the Rangeley region than along the short trail up Bald Mountain, right in the midst of it all.

Although a low summit, Bald Mountain in Oquossoc provides some of the best lake views in Maine. Nestled on an arm of land between Rangeley Lake and Mooselook-meguntic Lake, Bald delivers a satisfying perspective on both the waterways of the area and the dozens of mountains that surround them.

The little town of Oquossoc itself, by the way, wasn't always quite so remote. It was once served by rail and was the jumping-off point for city folks or "sports" who had come to rough it in the many fine hostelries that formerly dotted the area. Both Stan Plummer, the stationmaster, and the trains are long gone, but the land around Oquossoc is still beautiful, as a climb on Bald will prove.

How to Get There

Head west on ME 4 from Oquossoc. Slightly more than 1 mile west of Oquossoc center, you reach Haines Landing. The road bears left and south and can be followed another mile to the trail markers on the left side of the road, a short distance beyond the signs for Bald Mountain Camps. Park in the Bald Mountain parking area.

The Trail

Your pathway heads east from the road, and at first seems headed toward the ski slope on the north side of the mountain. Shortly

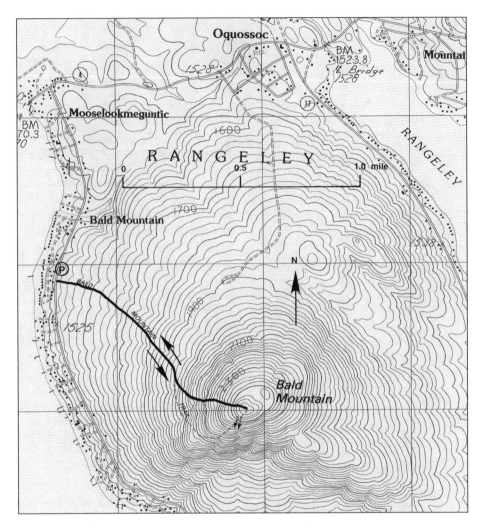

you reach a fork. Keep to the right and proceed more southeasterly toward the summit. The trail rises steadily on comfortable grades with occasional views over your shoulder to Stoney Batter Point on Mooselookmeguntic Lake. The grade increases during the last 0.2 mile, as the trail makes the final pitch below the summit, 1 mile above the road.

The best views are past the summit down to ledges on the south side. Immediately to the west are the upper reaches of Moose-lookmeguntic and, farther west beyond Sandy Cove, the long, slender arc of Upper Richardson Lake. The Richardson Ponds and Aziscohos Lake (hidden from view by the hills north and east of Observatory Mountain) lie north of Upper Richardson. Student's Island and Toothaker Island are off the point of land to the south, with the extensive waters of Rangeley Lake stretching to the south-southeast. Saddleback (Hike 10) is due east, with the Crocker Peaks (Hike 48) to the northeast.

This is certainly one of the finest lake and mountain viewpoints in Maine, and to attempt to praise it adequately would be about as futile as trying to describe the fishing in the Richardson Ponds.

Bald Mountain is a knob of Ordovician granite protruding from the surrounding "country rock" of metamorphic sandstones and schists. Its origins are thought to lie in a tectonic event that occurred 500 million years ago. At about this time, the North American tectonic plate collided with that of Europe and Asia, and the Appalachian Mountains were pushed up as wrinkles and corrugations, compressed between the continents. Our eastern seaboard was so corrugated and squeezed that molten magma from deep within the earth leaked out and oozed into the upper layers of the crust. This molten ooze formed blisters of granite, diorite, and gabbro under the "skin" or layers of sedimentary rock that had been laid down when Maine was covered by a shallow sea.

Some of the Appalachian Mountains are purely corrugations of sedimentary rock, now metamorphosed by mountain-building temperatures and pressures. Others are blisters or plutons of granite (Bald Mountain, this hike), diorite (Saddleback Mountain, Hike 10), or gabbro (Sugarloaf, Hike 48) that cooled and hardened over thousands of years underground. Some of these plutons have now been exposed by erosion. This is the case with Bald Mountain, a granite pluton that was exposed when the metasedimentary rock overlaying it was eroded away. We might well ask whether other mountains, like Bigelow, Tumbledown, and Abraham, hide similar granite, diorite, or gabbro plutons under their skins of slate, sandstone, or schist!

Return by the same trail.

8

Mount Aziscohos

Location: 2 miles from the New Hampshire border

Total distance: 3 miles (a return hike)

Hiking time: 3½ hours

Vertical rise: 1,700 feet

Maps: USGS 7.5' Richardson Pond; USGS 15' Oquossoc; USGS 15' Errol, New Hampshire; DeLorme map 28

The attractive Magalloway River rises in the highlands near the Quebec border in the northwest corner of Maine, feeds 13-mile-long Lake Aziscohos, and then flows over the dam near Wilson's Mills and on to the west and south. South of the lake and east of the river rises Mount Aziscohos, a fine specimen of a mountain with outstanding water views. For those who keep score of such things, roughly 15 lakes are visible from the summit of Mount Aziscohos when the weather is clear. Signs of the lumbering operations that took place here and there on the mountain in the early 1970s are now pretty much obscured by scrub, and most of Aziscohos remains densely forested and wild, with frequent signs of moose. Given its relatively isolated position west of Rangeley and Oquossoc, the mountain is never crowded, and it's rare to meet more than five or six people on the trail, even on a summer weekend. Aziscohos makes a good loner's mountain.

There were first two, then three trails up the mountain. The old route from the Aziscohos House up the west side of the rise is in disuse and grown up with brush. Another trail that climbs the mountain from the northwest just above the dam to the old fire warden's cabin has also become rather hard to follow. A third trail, the most direct route to the summit from the north side of the mountain, is described here.

How to Get There

The trailhead is along ME 16 at a point 1 mile east of Aziscohos Dam and about 2.3

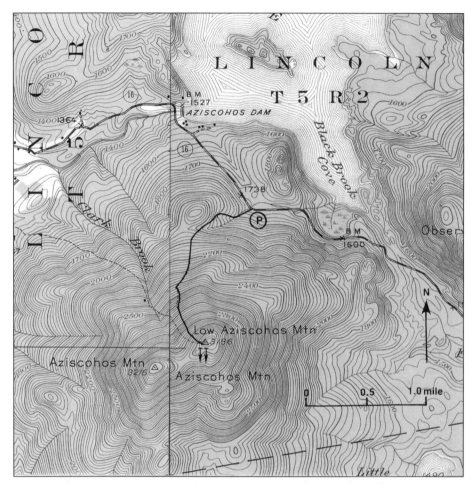

miles east of Wilson's Mills. The trail leaves the south side of the road by a good-sized turnout where there are small MOUNT AZIS-COHOS signs on a tree.

The Trail
Head into the woods, picking up the remnants of an old tote road on easy grades to the south-southwest and southwest. The road runs through a boggy area overgrown with spruce, young mountain ash, and a wealth of ferns: New York, sensitive, long beech, cinnamon, interrupted, and spinulose wood fern. In 0.2 mile, the route pulls

more to the right briefly, running over spots of bald ledge and through mixed growth.

Just under 0.5 mile from ME 16, the trail bears left onto another logging road after passing through a clearing. You continue south-southwestward here, in and out of the bed of the tote road, moving upward very gradually through stands of young beech and maple. Another, more prominent logging road is crossed at right angles about 0.8 mile from the highway. You then begin a brisk ascent of a low ridge, moving south through clusters of birch and into a jumble of blowdown. The going is rough and the trail easily lost in this tangled spruce and balsam. At the time of this writing, the trail was blazed with red ribbon. Watch for these markers and telephone wire particularly in this section.

Rising steadily, you cross a brook at 1 mile. A hundred yards beyond the brook, a dead end branches off to your left. Take the right (main) trail, following telephone wire and orange ribbons. There are views to the west here. The route continues upward and toward the south amid stands of attractive fir and more scattered blowdown. As with most of the trail, scrub and brush overlie the path and the going is sometimes obscure. Red spruce branches in need of trimming narrow the trail and scratch the legs. Long pants would be nice for this one stretch, but regrettable for the rest of the hike if the weather is hot. At 1.4 miles from the trailhead, you reach a junction with an old trail from the northwest. Bear left (southeast) and walk the remaining distance to the open east summit.

The broken remains of the fire warden's tower lie crumpled on the summit ledge. The bright mica-flecked granite is splotched with green lichen and dotted with blueberry bushes, sheep laurel, pin cherry, rhodora, and dwarfed spruce. As always, nature is the best gardener! For me, it is sad to see so many Maine Forest Service towers left abandoned, especially ones like this, rusting on the ground.

Tower or no, the views from the east peak are superb. USGS Oquossoc, Cupsuptic, and Rangeley quadrangles are useful to have along, as they will help you identify the beautiful circle of mountains and lakes that surround you. The water to the immediate north of the mountain is, of course, Aziscohos Lake, and above it lies small Parmachenee Lake. West Kennebago Mountain (Hike 9) is north-northeast. The Richardson Ponds and Upper and Lower Richardson Lakes are to the immediate east. Beyond them lie the broad expanses of Mooselookmeguntic and Rangeley Lakes, with Saddleback behind (Hike 10). From south to east, the Appalachian Trail runs from Old Speck over Baldpate, Old Blue (Hike 6), and Elephant Mountains. The long flank of Elephant nearly hides Tumbledown (Hike 1), barely in sight. To its left are Little Jackson (Hike 3), Big Jackson, and Blueberry Mountains. Southwest, past Umbazookus Lake, the Presidential Range rises in New Hampshire. Also in New Hampshire, Magalloway Mountain rises to the northwest.

To descend, carefully retrace your steps down the mountain. Use caution not to lose the trail in blowdown.

West Kennebago Mountain

Location: 10 miles south of Canada and 10 miles east of New Hampshire

Total distance: 4.5 miles (a return hike)

Hiking time: 3 hours

Vertical rise: 1,800 feet

Map: USGS 7.5' Kennebago; USGS 7.5' Little Kennebago Lake; USGS 15' Cupsuptic; DeLorme map 28

West Kennebago Mountain couldn't be better situated if it tried. The long ridge rises far back in paper company woodlands a good 10 miles from the blandishments of civilization (such as the nearest tarred road). Only 10 miles from Canada on its north side, the mountain is one of the eastern links in a long, horseshoe-shaped range of hills that runs down from Seven Ponds, through Upper and Lower Cupsuptic, and back up to Oxbow. The views are splendid.

How to Get There

Go first to the Maine Forest Service station at Toothaker Brook, 4.5 miles north and west of Oquossoc on ME 16. A good local map is available free here; it will help you navigate the timber road. Fire permits (if you're camping in an undesignated area) can be obtained here, too.

Proceed west from the station for 0.3 mile on ME 16. Turn right onto a gravel tote road. This route (Old Cupsuptic Tote Road) proceeds through former Brown Company timberlands for 2 miles, where you turn right. Continue on this right-hand gravel road for just over 2 miles, where you again bear right onto a wide, well-groomed gravel road that runs toward the northeast. Proceed eastward 7 miles, watching on the left of the road for a small sign that indicates the trail to the fire tower. Park your car well off the road—this is a route for heavy logging trucks.

The Trail

Your pathway follows a rough Jeep road toward the warden's camp, with both sides of

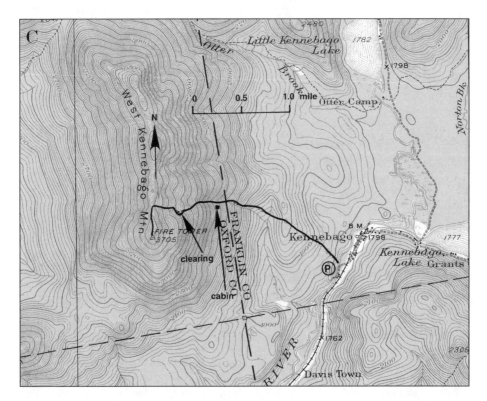

the road grown shoulder high with wild raspberry bushes. Berry picking and munching will inevitably slow you down a bit in this section, if the season is right (usually late July). Several turnouts are passed on your left as you ascend beyond 0.2 mile; turn gradually to the west-northwest and climb rapidly.

Just under 0.5 mile, you pass a final turnout (beyond which the road is impassable even for four-wheel-drive vehicles) and make a dogleg to your left, climbing steeply through young cherry trees. You shortly turn hard west again, ascend the first of two ridges, slab the second ridge past a large granite outcrop, and then traverse to the west through fragrant young balsam. At about the 1-mile point, you reach a brook. Continue over several small brooks as you climb south and southwest and, following

the signs, turn west again up a steep, pastured slope to the warden's camp at approximately the 1.5-mile point. There are excellent views south from the camp yard.

In the next 0.3 mile, the trail proceeds northwest above the warden's place, turns west soon, and rises through more fine stands of mature balsam to the height-of-land. The route then swings quickly over to the south as you ridge walk on an easy, grassy path just below timberline. The old telephone lines from the warden's camp to the tower run through the trees on your left. A cutover strip is passed with good views to the east and west, and the fire tower is reached after 2.25 miles of walking from the trailhead.

The West Kennebago tower is usually open to visitors when the warden is present. The views of uninterrupted wilderness and mountain terrain are first class. Kennebago

West Kennebago Mountain from the summit of Aziscohos Mountain

Lake is below to the east, while Cupsuptic Lake is nearly due south. Lincoln Pond (below Big Buck Mountain) and Aziscohos Lake are to the southwest. The ridge that forms West Kennebago runs to the north, and beyond it are Twin Mountains, Snow Mountain, and the range known as the Kennebago Divide. Burnt Mountain is the summit below to the southwest, while Cupsuptic Mountain rises to the west, opposite. If ever there were a series of views almost too painfully beautiful, certainly these from West Kennebago would be such.

When Ken Spalding was fire warden, my family had the pleasure of taking a winter trip with him to his cabin. We hiked on snowshoes and carried backpacks as far as the cabin, where we spent the night. In spite of January weather, the cabin was cozy with a fire in the woodstove that we kept roaring. The next day, we snowshoed to the tower and spent most of the day admiring the snowy winterscape from the tower and the cutover area.

When last on the mountain, I had the chance to see several spruce grouse in the brush around the summit, and I have seen a female marsh hawk soaring above the road below, searching for prey. As I said, it's a remote area.

Once you've savored that remoteness, return to your car by the route you came up.

10

Saddleback Mountain

Location: 5 miles east of Rangeley

Total distance: 10.2 miles (a return hike)

Hiking time: 7½ hours

Vertical rise: 2,900 feet

Maps: USGS 7.5' Saddleback Mountain; USGS 7.5' Redington; USGS 15' Rangeley; USGS 15' Phillips; MATC map 6 (1993); DeLorme maps 19, 29

Saddleback, from a distance, lies like a sleeping giant southwest of Rangeley. It is a great mountain with several open summits, two of which are more than 4,000 feet high. Its main summit is barren and exposed so that windy, wet weather on the mountain can be hazardous. Even on warm, calm days in the valley, the upper reaches of Saddleback above Eddy Pond can prove cold and treacherous.

Although a shorter trail reaches the summit from the ski area on the northwest side of the mountain, a far more interesting, if more lengthy, approach can be made via the Appalachian Trail (AT). This route affords a full day's hiking in attractive backcountry woodlands well populated with deer, moose, bear, and fox. I consider it, along with the circuit over Bigelow (Hike 12) and the long hike onto Mount Abraham (Hike 11), one of the best extended day walks in western Maine.

How to Get There

A substantial portion of the AT has, in recent years, been relocated southeast of Rangeley. The AT now leaves the north side of ME 4 at 9.5 miles east of the center of Rangeley and about 2.5 miles west of Madrid. A gravel turnout provides room to leave your car here at an S-curve in the road.

The Trail

From the road, you walk through a dense grove of fir and down a rib to the east. In minutes, you reach and cross the Sandy River,

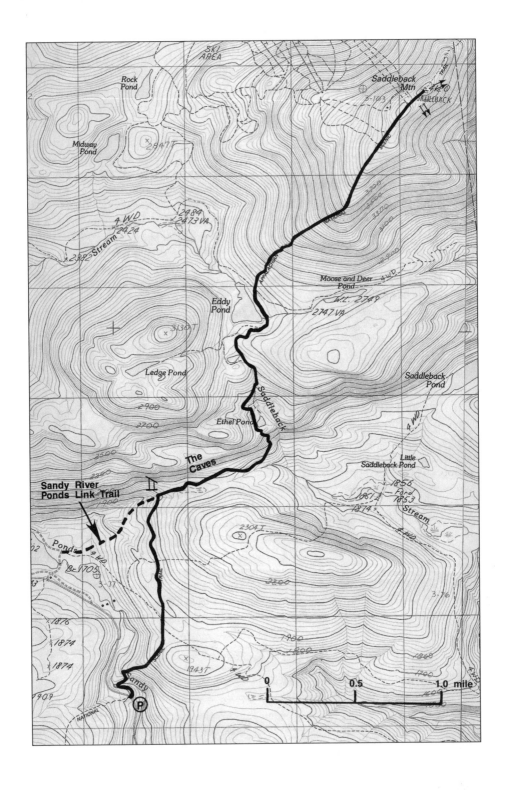

continuing uphill eastward over a low, recently logged ridge. The trail runs through a boggy area and shortly crosses a gravel tote road, running more to the north-northeast. You next walk on nearly level ground through an area marked by blowdown, past a cutover on your right, and then ascend north-northwest amid attractive, dense red spruce and balsam. These woods are rife with spruce grouse pecking about the underbrush, and you are very likely to see some.

Passing a couple of open spots on your left where you may glimpse the Sandy River Ponds, the trail crests a hummock and crosses a boggy area. You cross two barely discernible tote roads at right angles in a few moments and arrive, by a stream, at the junction of the old Sandy River Ponds link trail. On a recent trip along here, I nearly stepped on a large male fox who burst from the brush just in front of me and bounded ahead, his thick winter brush sailing along behind him.

You now walk to the east-northeast, with a high steep ridge to your left, and arrive at Piazza Rock Lean-to. A short side trail leads left to Piazza Rock, a great, hanging granitic outcrop. From the lean-to, 1.5 miles from the road, you continue northeastward, shortly passing another side trail to some rock slabs known as the Caves. The trail runs eastward and south of the ridge or bluff, then begins to climb the ridge steeply, thence dropping down to Ethel Pond, where you walk the length of the pond's boggy, rutted west shore. Boulders and blowdowns frequently mark the trail above the pond.

Past the pond, you climb easily toward the north and northwest over a moss-carpeted way among stands of balsam. Turning northeast, you cross Saddleback Stream, rise gradually through a series of boggy areas, pass a falls on your left, and soon come in sight of Mud Pond, also on your left. The going here is generally mucky, even in dry weather. You're likely to see moose tracks in the wet ground.

Swinging to the northwest on easy grades, you pass through stands of red spruce on a mossy, rock-strewn path, and arrive at a lookout above Eddy Pond. The southwest ledges of Saddleback are visible to the northeast. The steep climbing lies ahead. Walking to the east-northeast, you skirt the south end of Eddy Pond and pass through a mucky area grown up with bunchberries and young balsam. A grassy tote road is crossed, then the trail bears left and follows the east shore of the pond for a short distance. It is wet through here also, and you'll cross several small brooks. Don't be led astray by snowmobile trails. Stay on the white-blazed AT.

At 3.2 miles from the road, you bear to the northeast and cross another gravel tote road, reentering the woods immediately. You climb steadily here on a rooty, rocky path, ascending generally northeast and east toward the ledges. The trail runs through gradually thinning scrub with occasional views to the northwest and west.

Four miles from your car, you breach the timberline and, climbing steeply, emerge on the ledges. The walk is now completely in the open with the main summit of Saddleback visible ahead. Views to the east of Mount Abraham (Hike 11) open up here. You'll shortly pass a link trail on your left that runs to the ski slopes (in bad weather, descending to the ski area is the fastest, safest way off the exposed ridge). Dropping momentarily into a slump, the trail climbs briskly up the 4,116-foot main summit of Saddleback at just over 5 miles from your starting point.

It is worth taking along the four USGS quadrangles that cover this area, so fine are the views and so numerous the lakes and mountains seen from here (USGS 15' maps: Rangeley, Stratton, Phillips, and Kennebago Lake). Most striking is the long ridge of Mount Abraham to the east. The Horn, Saddleback Junior, and Poplar Ridge form the subsidiary summits immediately to the northeast.

Saddleback is a huge mound of Devonian granodiorite, similar to granite but slightly darker. It was formed underground, like an enormous blister, where it gradually cooled and hardened. Since then, millions of years of erosion have worn down its rock covering and exposed the granodiorite underneath. The flashy flecks are muscovite mica, which make Saddleback a sparkling gem on a sunny day.

Remember to carry extra clothing (waterproof) and food when making this ascent. Head down if high winds, rain, and clouds make finding the route difficult above tree line. Map 6 in the 1996 *Guide to the Appalachian Trail* in Maine is a useful companion on this walk.

11

Mount Abraham

Location: Between Sugarloaf and Saddleback Mountains

Total distance: 8.25 miles (a return hike)

Hiking time: 8 hours

Vertical rise: 3,050 feet

Maps: USGS 7.5' Mount Abraham; USGS 15' Kingfield; USGS 15' Phillips; DeLorme map 29

There is no mistaking Abraham. The mountain's bulldog brow peers boldly southeast over Kingfield, while its several summits run imposingly northwest toward Sugarloaf. No foothill, Abraham towers over 4,000 feet above sea level at its highest, and its subsidiary peaks are just under 4,000 feet. The barren and exposed rock field leading to the main summit might remind you of Mount Washington's cone. Because Abraham lies in timberlands well back from the road, you'll experience a variety of walking and climbing terrain before reaching the top.

How to Get There

Entry to the mountain is gained via Kingfield. Traveling on ME 16/ME 27, go north of the town center less than 0.3 mile, and turn on the paved road next to the JORDAN LUMBER COMPANY sign. Follow this road, unpaved after 2.8 miles, to the west and northwest. Continue straight ahead when the road divides at 3.5 miles. As of this writing, I've found the road to be roughest in this section. At 6 miles, the road turns left (west) and crosses Rapid Stream on a bridge. Park on the east side of the bridge.

The Trail

Follow the route of the logging road. On a slight rise, you walk west and northwest along the road, reaching a T-shaped junction at 0.5 mile. The trail continues west into the woods here (white sign). Moose range widely through the next 2 miles of trail.

Once in the woods, you climb briefly west-southwest for 50 yards on a boggy,

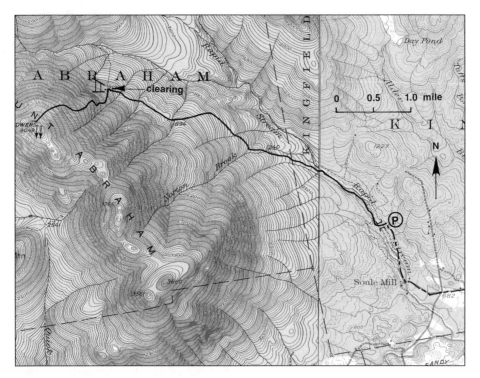

grassy road, cross Norton Brook, and rise easily through a corridor of thinned-out oaks to the northwest. Turning sharply to the north, you slab an abrupt ridge to your right, and then turn west again on higher ground. The trail winds through a cutover area of young oak, and continues north-northwest on a grassy road into denser woods.

Climbing very slightly, you soon pass a second cutover area and follow the trail through a mucky section that is usually a problem even in dry weather. As you enter a third cutover, the trail bears more toward the west again. The trail drops into a slight depression as you cross one of the feeder brooks of Rapid Stream. A short rise and descent brings you to another brook. Climbing more rapidly now, the path moves again to the west and northwest. It crosses three logging roads that run at right angles to the northeast, spans another attractive

brook with falls, and soon arrives at the old warden's cabin. The cabin has been used as a hostel of sorts in recent years and is not usually locked.

The ascent from the cabin contrasts with your travel thus far. The trail will climb nearly 2,000 feet in the next 1.5 miles. Your route lies southwest of the cabin. Shortly it turns more westerly, passing through two steep S-turns as it ascends the central cone. You pass up through dwarf spruce, young balsam, and clusters of bright red bunch-berries and bear around to the southwest again, reaching the boulder-strewn home stretch below the summits.

The views are as good here as anywhere in the Maine mountains. The overlook takes in the second highest peak in Maine, Sugarloaf (Hike 48), directly to the north. To its left looms the high shoulder of Spaulding Mountain. Burnt Hill, Owl's Head, and Black

Scree on the summit of Mount Abraham

Nubble form a ring to the northeast. In good weather, you can see beyond Sugarloaf to the great east–west ridge of Bigelow Mountain (Hike 12).

The trail continues 0.5 mile to the summit over the rock field. Follow the cairns and downed telephone line to the old tower site. Because this is an extremely exposed position, caution is necessary in wet, cold weather. At the summit, a cave has been hollowed out of the scree. In bad weather, you can find shelter inside.

One weekend in early May, a friend and I hiked up Mount Abraham and spent the night in the cave at the summit. It is no glamorous accommodation, but someone had placed planks inside, which kept us off the ice underneath. While lying in our sleeping bags, we cooked our "Macaroni Massacree" by candlelight on a mountain stove between us and spent a pleasant evening talking. The next day, we had all day to explore the 4 miles of Abraham's summit before climbing back down. The summit is a long ridge of scree, broken rock rubble that was once part of the mountain's bedrock. Abraham, like its neighbor Bigelow, is metamorphic sandstone, schist, and slate, but its entire ridge appears greenish because the rocks are covered with lichen.

Note: The lower section of this trail is wet and slowed by blowdowns. The steep upper section is frequently blocked by blowdowns, and extra time should be allowed for getting through.

Follow the same route on your descent.

Mount Abraham is also accessible from a 1.7 mile side trail off the Appalachian Trail, one mile west of the Spaulding Mountain lean-to, between Saddleback and Sugarloaf. However, it is not easily accessible for a day hike.

Bigelow, The Forks, to Jackman

Introduction to Bigelow, The Forks, to Jackman

Between ME 27 and US 201 in northwest Maine, a large area untracked by tarred roads offers some of the state's best hiking and adventuring. Its wildness and remoteness make it one of my favorite areas for hiking. Mostly in Somerset County, this is the westernmost region of Maine above Rangeley. The area is remote enough to assure sightings of moose, deer, and possibly black bear. Feathered wildlife live here in abundance, including the rare spruce grouse, a protected cousin of the ruffed grouse, with its characteristic red eye. Its nickname, fool's hen, is derived from its habit of standing on a branch or on the ground while you walk up to it. The protective law also results from this trait.

At the southwestern end of this section, the many peaks of Bigelow rise in challenge from the Carrabassett River Valley near ME 27, a scenic river drive. The Bigelow Range begins in Stratton and includes Cranberry Peak (Hike 14); the Horns, West, and Avery Peaks (Hike 12); and Little Bigelow (Hike 13). This range overlooks Flagstaff Lake to the east, whose history is described in Hike 14. Farther north on ME 27, the Cathedral Pines Campground offers camping on the shore of Flagstaff Lake. Still farther north, past Snow Mountain, lies the beautiful Chain of Ponds, which Benedict Arnold's army did not consider all that beautiful when trying to negotiate them by bateau in winter. There are some private campgrounds at Chain of Ponds.

The Bigelow area also offers lots of cross-country skiing on groomed trails in the Carrabassett Valley, and Sugarloaf provides downhill skiing on Maine's second highest mountain, as well as cross-country trails. The Sugarloaf gondola, which carries skiers to the top of the mountain, operates in all seasons. It makes an excellent ride during fall foliage season, and it offers an easy alternative way to climb Sugarloaf (Hike 48). Using the Mount Abraham hike (Hike 11) and the Appalachian Trail (AT), you could plan a large traverse using the Sugarloaf gondola, hiking the AT to Mount Abraham, and hiking down to Kingfield. With some imagination, the gondola could be part of an adventure in any season.

The Forks is named for its location at the fork of the Kennebec and Dead Rivers north of Wyman Dam on US 201. The AT passes through this area over Moxie Bald Mount-ain (Hike 19) and Pleasant Pond Mountain (Hike 17), in the heart of white-water canoeing and rafting country. Along US 201 you'll see the headquarters of the different rafting companies, which usually require reservations. Raft trips are guided regularly through the wild and deep Kennebec Gorge, the exciting Dead River, and the challenging West Branch of the Penobscot. For white-water canoeing, inquire at Ed Webb's store on US 201 in The Forks. At Webb's you can camp behind the store, rent canoes or kayaks, and hire transportation to canoe the lower Dead River, famous for its nearly continuous white-water Class III and IV rapids, dropping more than 400 vertical feet in 15 miles. As campgrounds are small and limited in this area, the Maine Forest Service (MFS) wilderness campsites will be useful.

Jackman, at the northern end of US 201, grew up as the last railroad station before the Quebec border. Now the town offers a variety of outdoor pursuits: fishing, guided or unguided; deer, moose, and bear hunting; snowmobiling and cross-country skiing; lots of four-wheel driving on a vast network of logging roads; and some hiking and canoeing. Jackman's famous canoe trip, the Bow Trip, is a 3- to 4-day flatwater paddling trip through a circuit of lakes with very little portage. From the Bow Trip, you can climb Sally Mountain (Hike 21) and make some climbs that have otherwise difficult access. For wildness, you can't beat Number Five (Hike 20) and Boundary Bald (Hike 22) Mountains.

There are numerous camps and cabins for rent but no state parks in the Jackman area, so don't go there without your DeLorme *Maine Atlas and Gazetteer* for locating MFS wilderness campsites.

12

Bigelow Mountain Loop

Location: Just north of Sugarloaf and east of Stratton

Total distance: 12 miles (a circuit hike)

Hiking time: 7½ hours

Vertical rise: 2,850 feet

Maps: USGS 7.5' The Horns; USGS 15' Stratton; MATC map 5 (1993); DeLorme map 29

Bigelow must rank as one of Maine's greatest mountains for its size, ruggedness, beauty, and challenge to the hiker. A wild and unspoiled mountain (it was saved from heavy resort development by concerted citizen opposition), Bigelow constitutes a range of six major summits nearly 9 miles in length, running west to east. The range is more than 12 miles in length if you include connected Little Bigelow Mountain, with its three lower summits. Views over beautiful Flagstaff Lake north to Canada, and to the many mountains that lie to the south and west, make Bigelow one of the two or three best vantage points in Maine. This hike takes you on one of the less-traveled routes to Horns Pond and to the Horns, West, and Avery Peaks. It runs over the rerouted Horns Trail from Stratton Brook Pond.

How to Get There

Head in on a dirt road that runs east from ME 16/ME 27, about 3.3 miles north and west of the Sugarloaf Mountain Road and 4.5 miles east of Stratton. Though rough in places, the road can be driven the 1.8 miles to a parking area near Stratton Brook Pond. Park off the track here.

The Trail

From the clearing, walk northeast and north on a gravel road around the bog above Stratton Brook Pond. In 1 mile you will reach the junction of the Horns Trail and the fire warden's trail. Keep right here, as the old Horns Trail route is not in use and provides an unreliable approach to the ridge.

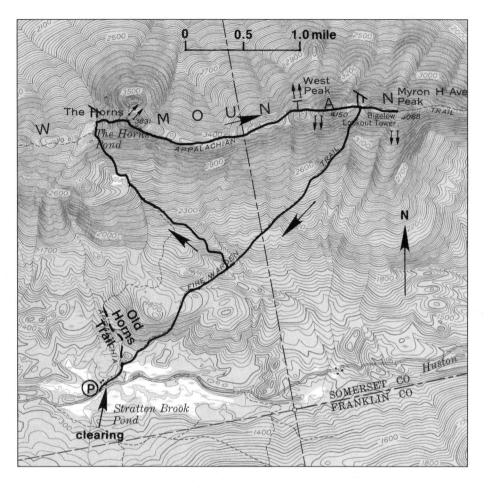

Follow the fire warden's trail to your right as it runs on a distinct logging road to the northeast through stands of pretty, tall birches and red oaks. You soon bear more to the east, cross a seasonal brook, and slab briskly up a ridge.

In minutes you ascend a ledge to the northeast and then walk over a series of low rolling ridges. The trail levels off briefly and then descends through birch and balsam groves to a gully bisected by a small brook. Moving up out of the gully, you continue on a logging road to the northeast, arriving at a trail junction 1.2 miles from the clearing where you parked. (Watch carefully for signs

here; they are posted rather high up on the trees and are easily missed.)

The new Horns Pond link bears left here and runs northwest through an attractive area of second-growth forest, which is at its most colorful in autumn. The blue-blazed trail begins its ascent of a series of ridges to the northwest, rising gradually into stands of balsam, birch, and maple. The trail soon joins another woods road, and you walk more steeply northwest, crossing several brooks. A side trail is passed shortly above the most prominent brook. The trail leads to good views over Sugarloaf and Crocker Peaks (Hike 48). Still ascending northwest,

The many peaks of Bigelow (left to right): Cranberry Peak, the two Horns, West Peak, and Avery Peak

you cross several more brooks, and pull abruptly left off the road and over a boggy hummock. The trail follows the south side of a marsh here, and there are open spots where you can see up to the South Horn.

Passing a second outlook to your left where there are further views across to Sugarloaf, you walk northwest again through dense, low balsam and mossy ground cover. The trail rises steadily to a junction with the Appalachian Trail (AT) 4 miles from your starting point. Bear right here, and in a few moments arrive at the Horns Pond shelters. The two lean-tos and several tent platforms offer good camping, but the facilities are heavily used in high summer, and finding space may require an early arrival. A trail behind the northernmost of the two shelters leads, in a few yards, to the shore of strikingly beautiful Horns Pond.

From the clearing around the shelters, you head northeast and east on the AT, climbing steadily through balsam and red spruce. The going is often muddy in this section. As you ascend, you'll have occasional views back to Cranberry Peak west of the pond. The northernmost of the two Horns comes into view shortly, and you momentarily pass the connector trail to your left, arriving on the summit of the South Horn. The views here to the east, south, and west are superb. Horns Pond lies like a small mirror in the col to the west. Canada jays, gray-and-white robbers, will land and eat from your hand if you share your lunch with them.

The trail now dips several hundred feet into a depression as it runs eastward through spruce and balsam scrub, and then it gradually ascends the ridge again on increasingly steep grades to Bigelow's West Peak. This is the highest summit on the range at 4,150 feet, and there are spectacular views to the north over the long, thin strip of Flagstaff Lake, northeast toward Katahdin (Hike 35), and south and west to Sugarloaf (Hike 48) and Saddleback (Hike 10). West Peak gets the full brunt of the cold Canadian winds, so pack extra clothing, particularly if you're hiking Bigelow in the autumn.

Once off West Peak, you descend sharply eastward to the Myron H. Avery tent site just below Avery Peak. The caretaker's cabin and a spring are nearby. From here, you climb Avery Peak to the east over steep grades, arriving on the summit in 0.4 mile. Splendid views to the east are the rule here, especially over the widest section of Flagstaff Lake and Little Bigelow Mountain (Hike 13), immediately below.

To descend, retrace your steps down to the Avery Lean-to, turning left, or south, on the fire warden's trail. The route turns more to the southwest shortly, descending steeply over a series of ladders, rock steps, and terraces. You'll lose about 1,500 feet of elevation in about 1.2 miles. The grade slackens abruptly, and you continue southwest, crossing several barely discernible woods roads as you proceed downward through young beech and maple. The trail isn't well marked in this section, but it is easy to follow. Just under 2 miles from Avery tent site, you pass the Horns Pond link to your right that you followed on your ascent. Continue straight on to the southwest here. The trail meanders in

and out of a prominent logging road. Watch carefully for the point where the path abruptly leaves the road and runs more to the southwest. This turn can be missed easily at dusk.

The trail then descends a series of grassy ridges, crosses a brook, and continues southwest in the boggy depression you walked through on your way up. The logging road is regained shortly, and you stay with it to the southwest and to the clearing where you parked.

Much of your walking on this loop is in sheltered areas. The main ridge, including the Horns, West, and Avery Peaks, is dangerously exposed and, as I suggested earlier, tends to collect inclement weather from the northwest. A mild, sunny day down on the road will give little warning that high winds and near-zero chill factors may prevail on the peaks. Because this is a long route, fatigue also becomes a consideration as you walk over the summits. You should carry extra clothing, including rain gear, and plenty of food and water. A flashlight may come in handy. If you're climbing in September, October, or November, it'll probably be dark before you reach the road on the final leg of the loop.

13

Little Bigelow

Location: 10 miles east of Stratton

Total distance: 12 miles (a circuit hike)

Hiking time: 8 hours

Vertical rise: 2,000 feet

Maps: USGS 7.5' Little Bigelow Mountain; USGS 15' Little Bigelow Mountain; MATC map 5 (1993); DeLorme map 29

Little Bigelow, in Dead River Township, rises from the southeast end of Flagstaff Lake in the wilderness of Somerset County. It is the easternmost of the six peaks in the 17-mile-long Bigelow Range. A circuit hike using 6 miles of the Appalachian Trail (AT) across Little Bigelow's ridge, the 1.5-mile Safford Brook Trail descent at the west end of the ridge, and 4.5 miles of dirt road along the shore of Flagstaff Lake (no views of the lake) allows you to explore this well-known Maine mountain. To avoid the 4.5 miles of shore road, a car or bicycle can be spotted where the Safford Brook Trail joins the shore road, a few yards past the driveway to the Bigelow Lodge.

How to Get There

Travel on ME 16 northwest from North Anson or southeast from Kingfield to North New Portland. At the North New Portland Post Office and General Store, leave ME 16 and drive north on Long Falls Dam Road for 17.6 miles and turn left at a group of marked mailboxes onto Bog Brook Road (dirt). At 18.3 miles take the left fork, and at 18.5 miles you can see on your left the white paint blazes of the Appalachian Trail where it crosses the road. Back up a few yards and park in the clearing. (If you wish to spot a car at the end of the Safford Brook Trail, continue another 4.5 miles on the road and park in the gravel pit opposite the driveway to Bigelow Lodge.)

The Trail

Pick up the AT as it crosses the road to your left and rises gently through young hard-

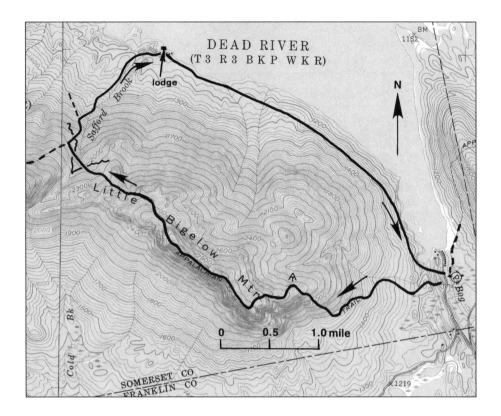

woods and some large old cedars. A wide variety of terrain and viewpoints make the first mile and a half very interesting.

At 1.4 miles, the lean-to can be reached by a 0.1 mile side trail. Built in 1986, it was the first shelter in Maine designed to hold 8 people. "The Tubs" in the brook are a great place to soak a weary body in ice cold water.

At 1.9 miles, the trail takes you over boulders and then climbs steeply up through a boulder-filled ravine, almost a grotto. Use caution here, especially if the rocks are wet. Shortly after climbing out of the grotto, you reach the first open ledges and are rewarded with bunchberry, blueberries, and views north over Flagstaff Lake. The ascent is more gradual beyond, following cairns through open ledges with blueberries, sheep laurel, and reindeer lichen, and duck-

ing into thick spruce and fir forests. On the ground you can find leaves and berries of wintergreen (teaberry) to chew.

At 2.9 miles, you reach Little Bigelow's summit (3,040 feet), with views northwest to Avery Peak on Bigelow (Hike 12), over the Carrabassett Valley southwest to Sugarloaf with Crocker Mountain on its right (Hike 48), south to Mount Abraham (Hike 11), and southeast to Stewart Mountain.

Continue walking the ridge northwest toward Bigelow. The trail is rough and passes over a series of knobs on the long crest of Little Bigelow. At 4.2 miles, the trail begins a long, gradual descent, winding in and out of ledges—some with views north, others with views south. Wood sorrel, Canada mayflower, wintergreen, and spinulose wood fern grow along the way, as well as starflower, asters, clintonia lily, sarsaparilla, and bunchberry. The descent steepens and is slippery and dangerous when wet. You cross a tributary of Safford Brook and descend through maple and white birch, crossing the brook again on the remains of an old bridge. Shortly, at a huge cedar, two forks of the brook converge into the main stream of Safford Brook.

At 6 miles, turn right onto the 1.5-mile-long Safford Brook Trail. (The AT turns left, uphill to Avery Peak.) A side trail to Safford North campsite passes beneath huge boulders. The Safford Brook Trail soon crosses the brook on an old bridge and runs onto an old tote road, the old "Dead River Route" that was part of the Appalachian Trail in the 1930s before Flagstaff Lake was formed in 1949. The road descends gradually through beech and maple and runs into a gravel pit. Unless you spotted a car here, turn right and walk the dirt road east 4.5 miles, past the driveway to Bigelow Lodge (locked gate) on your left and back to the trailhead where you parked.

Before returning on the dirt road, you may want to follow the Safford Brook Trail left from the gravel pit to the shore of Flagstaff Lake. Along the shore to the west is a field where a round barn used to stand. Only the stone foundation remains, but the field is still called the "round barn field."

In June 1976 a 10-year battle climaxed between developers who wanted to make Bigelow an "Aspen of the East" and conservation groups led by the Friends of Bigelow, the Maine Appalachian Trail Club, the Natural Resource Council of Maine, and the Appalachian Mountain Club. A petition drive overrode the legislature and forced a referendum vote, which, by a narrow margin, established the Bigelow Preserve, a 35,000-acre wilderness protecting the entire Bigelow Range and a buffer zone around the mountain's base. Long-term management of the preserve is yet to be settled, and the threat presented by the Bigelow Lodge still kindles many a debate.

14

Cranberry Peak

Location: The trail starts in Stratton

Total distance: 6.4 miles (a return hike)

Hiking time: 4½ hours

Vertical rise: 2,100 feet

Maps: USGS 7.5' Stratton; USGS 15' Stratton; MATC map 5 (1993); DeLorme map 29

Cranberry Peak is the westernmost peak of the 17-mile-long, east–west Bigelow Range, south of Flagstaff Lake. It makes a pleasant half-day hike with rewarding close views of the Horns of Bigelow and a 360-degree panorama of the western Maine mountains.

How to Get There

The most direct trail to Cranberry Peak is the Bigelow Range Trail, which begins at ME 16/ME 27 in Stratton. At 0.6 mile south of the junction of ME 27 and ME 16, signs indicate the start of the trail. Take a sharp turn east onto a dirt road and continue 0.1 mile to a sandy opening to park.

The Trail

Your pathway heads east on a gravel road following blue blazes 0.4 mile to a smaller area where it is also possible to park. In this smaller opening, the trail leaves the road to the left, following blue blazes uphill, downhill, and up again to an old lumber road at 0.7 mile. Turn left onto the old road and ascend more easily, following the blue blazes at any forks.

The woods are a mixture of tall spruce, birch, and hemlock. On the ground are purple wake-robin, clintonia lily, wild sarsaparilla, and Indian cucumber. At 1.5 miles, a spring on your left (last water) is a good place to fill canteens. From the spring, the trail climbs steeply through very large white and yellow birch; rock, red, and striped maple; some large ash; asters; Solomon's plume; long beech fern; and spinulose wood fern. At its

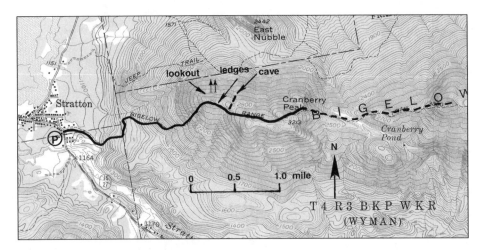

steepest part, the trail ascends through huge, stately red and white pines. These trees used to be the climax forest growth in Maine, giving it the nickname the Pine Tree State. Now most of the pines are gone from logging and fires, and in their place are faster-growing spruce and balsam fir.

Past the big pines is an overlook with views west to East and West Kennebago Mountains (Hike 9). Below is Stratton, where Flagstaff Lake begins at the North and South Branches of the Dead River. Return to the trail, and continue climbing steeply through more openings. At 1.9 miles you pass Arnold's Well on your right, a deep cleft in the ledge, sometimes holding stagnant water at the bottom. Do not drink the water. Benedict Arnold's route in 1775 followed the Dead River, which has since been dammed into Flagstaff Lake. Even though he did not cross the Bigelow Range, Arnold's Well is named after him. Bigelow Mountain and the Bigelow Range are named after Major Timothy Bigelow, a member of the Arnold expedition who climbed the mountain to look for Quebec.

From 2.1 to 2.3 miles, step carefully over the Cranberry Ledges, which offer views of Stratton, Flagstaff Lake, and Sugarloaf to the southeast. Up here among the spruce cliffs, gray Canada jays are residents, and hawks soar above and below you. At 2.3 miles, a short side trail leads left to the Cave, an interesting overhanging granite slab. Continue walking through open ledges where sheep laurel and Labrador tea grow and through moist wooded sections dotted with sphagnum moss and Indian pipe. The final ascent through scrub blueberries, scrub spruce, and birch takes you at 3.2 miles to bare, conical Cranberry Peak (elevation 3,213 feet). From here you will turn around and retrace the trail to you car.

From the summit, to the east rise the two Horns of Bigelow. Behind the South Horn, the cap of West Peak is visible, Avery Peak with its tower is farther right, and the long loaf of Little Bigelow (Hike 13) sweeps to the right of Avery. Southeast, Sugarloaf (Hike 48) is easy to spot with its ski trails and communications building. To the south and behind Sugarloaf is contiguous Spaulding Mountain. From here look south to Crocker Mountain (also Hike 48), whose south peak is hidden behind the north peak. Southwest is East Kennebago Mountain, with West Kennebago Mountain behind (Hike 9). Northwest rises Snow Mountain, and north over Flagstaff Lake you can see three-peaked Boundary Bald Mountain (Hike 22) far on the horizon and the pointed peak of Coburn Mountain to the north-northeast. East-northeast it is possible to see the Carry Ponds, through which Arnold's army struggled with their 300 bateaux.

Cranberry Peak is a good lunch spot. Mountain cranberries grow in the rock crevices, a welcome addition to lunch. If you walk to the next ledge, several yards farther ahead on the trail, you can look down on Cranberry Pond, beyond which the Appalachian Trail comes into the Bigelow Range Trail for the ascent to Horns Pond, the Horns, and Bigelow's summit.

Flagstaff Lake was formed in 1949 when the Central Maine Power Company built Long Falls Dam on the Dead River (the West Branch of the Kennebec), so named because many of its twists and turns were dead water. The Dead River Valley was changed from a series of farming communities to a 22-mile-long storage lake. The former villages of Dead River and Flagstaff now lie under the lake. Their inhabitants had to relocate, and it took crews two years to excavate the dozen cemeteries in the villages. Occasionally, when the lake is drawn down, old bridge abutments, roadbeds, foundations, and other signs of the old valley settlements are visible proof that humans once lived and worked below the present lake's water level.

15

Poplar Stream Falls

Location: Carrabassett Valley near Sugarloaf

Total distance (round trip): 4 miles

Hiking time: 2 hours

Vertical rise: 240 feet

Maps: USGS 7.5' Poplar Mountain, DeLorme map 29

Poplar Stream Falls, which is located between the Carrabassett River and Poplar Mountain near Sugarloaf Ski Area, is the perfect place to spend a hot, humid day. Without expending much effort, you can have a cool, refreshing dip in a pool beneath a cascading waterfall. In fact, you can enjoy two waterfalls on this hike.

How to Get There

To find the trail, drive ME 27 roughly 9 miles north from Kingfield and turn right on Carriage Road, 3.9 miles north of the Kingfield/Carrabassett Valley town line and 2.4 miles north of the Carrabassett Valley Rest Area. This turn is 0.3 mile south of the Chamber of Commerce information building and is also the road to the Carrabassett Valley Town Office. After crossing the Carrabassett River on a bridge, drive straight for 0.3 mile until the road turns to dirt. Park off the road here and begin walking. You could drive a bit further on this road, which is a snowmobile trail in winter, except there is no place to turn around when the road becomes too rough for an automobile.

The Trail

Start walking the dirt road, which parallels Poplar Stream through beech, birch, ash, and maple. The road rises steadily above the stream, leaving it entirely after 0.5 mile. You might hear the "Teacher, teacher teacher!" call of the tiny ovenbird, the loudest voice in the woodland forest.

After 1.5 miles, the trail forks, left to Bigelow and Stratton, and right toward

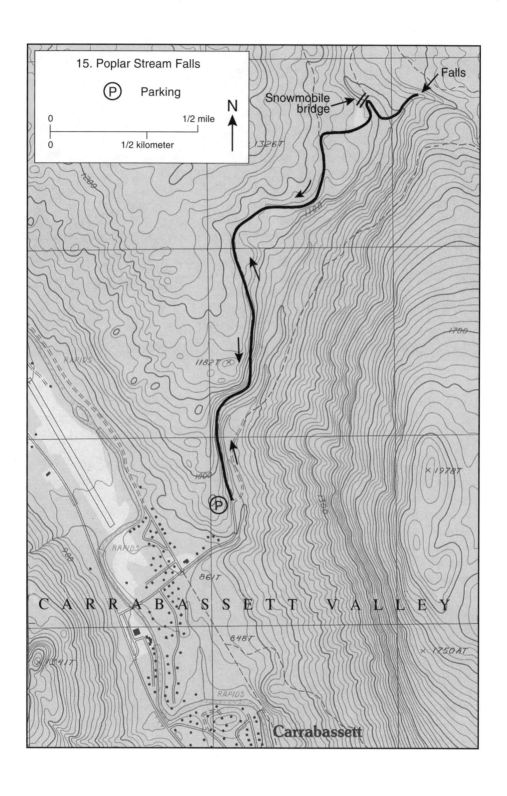

15. Poplar Stream Falls

Ⓟ   Parking

N

0   1/2 mile

0   1/2 kilometer

Falls

Snowmobile
bridge

C A R R A B A S S E T T   V A L L E Y

Carrabassett

The lower falls at Poplar Stream Falls

Poplar Mountain. Take the right fork, which trends gradually downhill through more open woods with tall maples, into a clearing growing up with young poplar. Keep walking straight through the clearing and you will hear the falls ahead. A footbridge (snowmobile bridge) crosses Poplar Stream.

To get close to the top of the falls, cross the bridge and climb down to the right on a tiny trail next to the falls. To reach the pool below the falls, backtrack across the bridge and turn immediately onto a small side trail which runs downhill to the stream. Here you can sit and admire the 24-foot falls from rocks that form a partial dam and a good swimming hole. Violets, grasses, ferns, and meadow rue grow from rock islands, which taper downstream into the chutes and pools of a smaller set of falls. Even at dry times of year, these falls have enough water to be beautiful and musical, and their cool cascades feel so good on a hot summer day!

To find the higher 51-foot falls, pick your way downstream, first on the right bank (facing downstream) until you pass the vertical block walls of rock on the left bank. As soon as you can, cross to the left bank, hug a cedar (to avoid falling into the stream), and walk downstream for less than five minutes, listening for falls on your left. When you hear them, cut left through the woods until you see them. Although the falls are higher, the pool beneath is very shallow and not as good for swimming. This waterfall is on South Brook, just before it flows into Poplar Stream. The path to the high falls has an amazing diversity of ferns in its short stretch, among them spinulose woodfern, oak fern, long beech fern, and silvery spleenwort.

You have been hiking on the Carrabassett Formation, a series of interbedded sandstones and shales that were metamorphosed under huge pressure and high temperature during the Devonian period approximately 400 million years ago. The result of the metamorphism left some rock harder and more resistant to erosion than others, thus creating the highs and lows that give us waterfalls.

I found this place a haven for thrushes. On one day in June, I listened to wood thrush, hermit thrush, Swainson's thrush, and veery. These birds are some of the sweetest singers in our forests.

To leave, retrace your path to the first falls and return to your car on the snowmobile trail. I have also found this trail fun on a mountain bike and on cross-country skis. If you decide to ski the trail, remember that snowmobiles have the right-of-way; get off the trail when you hear them coming.

If you haven't had your fill of swimming, as you drive out, there is good swimming in the chutes and pools in the Carrabassett River under the bridge on the upstream side.

16

Kibby Mountain

Location: Boundary Mountains north of Eustis

Total distance: 5 miles

Hiking time: 3½ hours

Vertical rise: 1,250 feet

Maps: USGS 7.5' Kibby Mountain, DeLorme map 39

Kibby Mountain stands sentinel at the western border of the United States and Canada. Its summit is less than four miles from the border, and the trail begins about three miles from the border. It stands in Maine's industrial forest amid clear-cuts of various stages of regeneration, offering varied habitats for plants and animals. From the observation tower on the summit (the remains of a former fire tower), you can survey much of western Maine into Quebec province bordered by its guardian Boundary Mountains.

How to Get There

Start in Eustis, above Kingfield and Stratton in Franklin County. From The Pines Market, drive north on ME 27 along the North Branch of the Dead River. At 11.5 miles, pass Sarampus Falls Rest Area, and at 12.9 miles, turn right onto a dirt logging road known as the Gold Brook Road. Zero your mileage here. On weekdays, huge logging trucks thunder down this road. You may ask, "Do they think they own the road?" In truth, they do. Give them the right-of-way, and drive carefully. Drive 9.3 miles on the Gold Brook Road, and then turn right onto a wide road. Go 0.4 mile and park at a turn around on your left. The trail is a small jeep track almost hidden by fir trees, leading to the left from this parking place.

The Trail

The first mile ascends slightly and descends as much, mostly feeling like a flat walk. The narrow corridor through balsam fir and white

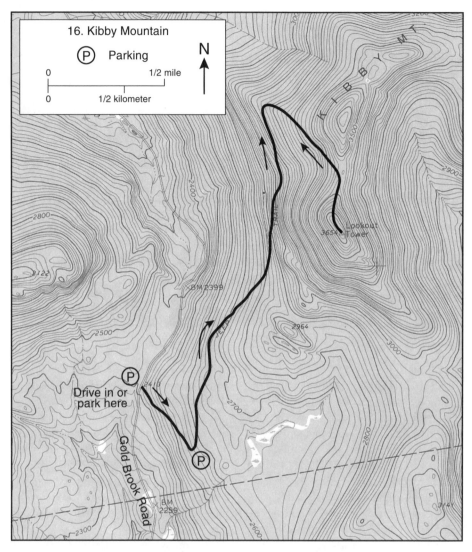

16. Kibby Mountain

Ⓟ Parking

N

0   1/2 mile

0   1/2 kilometer

Ⓟ
Drive in or
park here

Ⓟ

Gold Brook Road

Lookout
Tower

birch is little used by hikers, more so by people on ATV's and snowmobiles, and most of all by moose, bears, and other animals. Their tracks and scat are ample evidence. Prominently displayed scat, often topping a rock in the middle of the trail, is left by coyote (larger diameter) or fox (smaller diameter). Usually tracks and scat are our only evidence of the mammals living in an area.

Sightings of the animals themselves are rare, so I have learned to get excited over these clues of their presence.

During this pleasant walk, you may hear the cheery, buzzy "Beer, beer, beer, BEE?" of the black-throated blue warbler, or the sweetly fluted notes of hermit thrush or veery.

At 1 mile, take the right fork in the trail, and get ready for some climbing. The trail is

November snow on the Kibby Mountain Trail

much steeper from here to the summit. As it gets higher in elevation, the birch and fir get shorter and shorter due to exposure to extreme temperatures and winds. At 1.7 miles, the trail flattens out, opens up, and curves nearly 180 degrees to the right on the northwest shoulder of Kibby. From here on, keep looking behind you at the views.

At 2 miles, the trail climbs sharply, lined on both sides by clintonia lily and spinulose woodfern. In less than half a mile, a narrow corridor of dwarf fir leads you to the truncated tower on the 3,654-foot summit. Look southeast (over the stairs) to Bigelow (Hike 12) behind Flagstaff Lake; due south to Saddleback, the Horn, and Saddleback, Jr. (Hike 10); southwest to East Kennebago, Snow Mountain, and Chain of Ponds; northwest to the Boundary Mountains of Canada; north to Boundary Bald (Hike 22); northeast to Number Five Mountain, the mountain with the tower (Hike 20); east to Coburn Mountain.

Like a patchwork quilt, clear-cuts in various stages of regeneration surround Kibby in all directions. Nowadays it is extremely rare to find hikes with views that do not look down on extensive cutting of the industrial forest. Sometimes only a "beauty strip" remains along highways to hide vast timber cuts.

Return by the same trail, taking care on the steep part of the descent. One late June day, as I was returning on the trail, I surprised a mother dark-eyed junco and her chicks. They surprised me, too, as the mother ordered the babes to scatter, and they half flew, half ran in all directions like fuzzy, little Ping-Pong balls bouncing out of sight into the bunchberry and bracken fern.

17

Pleasant Pond Mountain

Location: 16 miles north of Bingham in Caratunk

Total distance: 2.5 miles (a return hike)

Hiking time: 2 hours

Vertical rise: 1,230 feet

Maps: USGS 7.5' The Forks; USGS 15' The Forks; MATC map 4 (1993); DeLorme map 30

Pleasant Pond Mountain in Caratunk rises over Pleasant Pond just south of The Forks, where the Upper Kennebec and the Dead Rivers join to become the Kennebec River. From the summit, which is in The Forks, you can look down on the pond and see many of the high western Maine mountains. The steep climb will make you thirsty, so carry water.

How to Get There

Drive US 201 to Caratunk, 16 miles north of the junction with ME 16 in Bingham. Turn right on the Caratunk Road, drive 0.3 mile to the post office and general store, and turn right at the intersection. Follow the road along Pleasant Pond Stream to the pond. Fork left at the pond on a road that soon turns to gravel, and drive 1.8 miles to the north end of Pleasant Pond, where you will see an Appalachian Trail (AT) sign. Park here.

The Trail

The AT crosses the parking spot. Follow it to the right (east) onto the northbound AT. After crossing two dry brooks, begin the steep ascent up gabbro outcroppings in a forest of red pine and large cedar. As the trail climbs, views open through the trees to your right (southwest) over Pleasant Pond. The forest changes to a variety of large hardwoods and spruce, with thin striped maples interspersed. On the ground are wild sarsaparilla, Canada mayflower, starflower, trillium, asters, and spinulose wood fern.

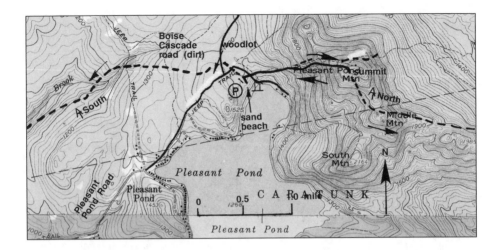

The trail climbs at a steep grade, gaining 1,200 feet in the 1.2 miles to the summit. Parts of the path are severely eroded. The trail climbs through mature hardwoods and softwoods, with various mushrooms living on fallen dead trees. The hardwoods end abruptly as you ascend into conifers: spruce, red pine, white pine, and balsam fir. A steep scramble up eroded bedrock takes you into a beautiful garden of young spruce of perfect form, like miniature Christmas trees. On the ground, their red needles alternate in a checkerboard pattern with patches of green haircap moss.

The trail ascends steeply again through magnificent spruce, crests a rise, and drops down to a trail junction. From here, the old AT heads east, downhill to Moxie Pond and Moxie Bald Mountain (Hike 19). Turn right on the new AT that continues 0.2 mile to the summit of Pleasant Pond Mountain. Two hundred feet up the trail you'll find a small spring on your right, beyond which lie the charred ruins of the fire warden's camp. The trail then rises over the open gabbro summit through dwarfed spruce and sheep laurel, which is beautiful in July, and ends at the un-

derpinnings of the fire tower that used to stand on the 2,480-foot peak.

Views are perfect in all directions if you walk around the summit. To the northeast, Mosquite Mountain sits like a gumdrop over Moxie Pond, and behind it Big Moose (Hike 28) rises over Moosehead Lake. Look east over Moxie Pond to Moxie Bald Mountain (Hike 19) and south to the large wooded hulk of Moxie Mountain. Southwest beyond Pleasant Pond are the many peaks of Bigelow (Hike 12), with Sugarloaf (Hike 48) and Mount Abraham (Hike 11) to their southwest. To the northwest is Coburn Mountain.

Return by the same trail, which will be much easier going down. On your return, you will probably want to walk to the lakeshore to see the Pleasant Pond Lean-to. If it's especially hot, you can dip in the icy waters of Pleasant Pond at the sandy beach just past the lean-to. The water is always exhilaratingly cool, even on the warmest summer days.

At the Kennebec River in Caratunk, you are just east of the Carry Ponds, named for the difficulties Benedict Arnold and his

A swim in Pleasant Pond after climbing Pleasant Pond Mountain

troops had when carrying their 300 bateaux from East to Middle to West Carry Ponds and then to the Dead River. Not only was the portage difficult, but also the army was near starvation and freezing from the wintry October of 1775. The AT partly follows Arnold's trail from the Kennebec River west to Flagstaff Lake.

Pleasant Pond Mountain

Moxie Falls

18

Moxie Falls

Location: 2 miles east of The Forks

Total distance: 2.5 miles (a return hike)

Hiking time: 1 hour

Vertical rise: 40 feet

*Maps: USGS 7.5' The Forks; USGS 15'
The Forks; DeLorme map 40*

Moxie Falls, in Moxie Gore, near The Forks, rewards hikers with startling beauty for little effort. The 89-foot falls have been rated the highest in New England, and the setting, a gorge carved through slate, is equally dramatic.

How to Get There

Travel US 201 to The Forks, 48 miles north of Skowhegan and 23.4 miles north of the junction of ME 16 and US 201 in Bingham. At the bridge over the Kennebec, turn east onto Moxie Pond Road on the south side of the river. At this turn, there is a picnic area with tables and public facilities. Follow this road 1.8 miles to a parking area with a MOXIE FALLS sign.

The Trail

Your pathway is fairly level and takes you through lovely woods to a boardwalk leading to Moxie Stream, where you will find the introductory upper falls to your right and the dramatic lower falls to your left. The upper falls are a series of step falls coursing through pyramidal slabs of Devonian slate and schist. There is no trail upstream, but you can make your way up the bank.

The boardwalk follows the bank left and downstream to the 89-foot lower falls. Be careful if you walk out onto the falls! Not even Vibram soles will grip wet, water-polished rock. The falls roar down into a gorge walled with schist and rimmed with rock fern on sphagnum moss. Cedar and spruce grow from vertical walls, and more mature cedar surrounds the rim. The trail

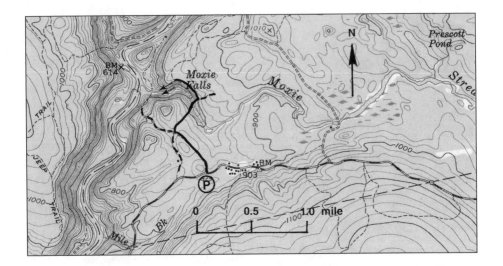

skirts about a quarter of the rim, arriving at a beech and birch knoll, the best vantage point for viewing the falls. Some of the older trees are hung with old-man's beard lichen. In spring you'll see the white blossoms of Canada mayflower and bunchberry, and in later summer and fall their red berries. In summer, you can find the tiny yellow blooms of the northern honeysuckle. The only vertical rise is encountered when you retrace the trail to your car.

Winter is my favorite time to visit the falls. Besides the advantages of no people and no bugs, the scene is a fairyland. Most of the trees are evergreens, and the snow is beautiful against the dark spruce and the rusty green of the cedars. The trail I leave with my snowshoes is embroidered with tracks of rabbit, red squirrel, deer, grouse, and an occasional moose. The step falls are invisible under snow-covered ice, but mink tracks leading from hole to hole reveal where the ice remains open. The high falls appear frozen at a standstill, but you can hear the rushing of the unseen water underneath. The falls are different every winter: sometimes hung with long tresses of icicles, sometimes frothy and white, sometimes topaz or aquamarine. It is an easy hike on properly maintained snowshoes.

19

Moxie Bald Mountain

Location: 12 miles east of The Forks

Total distance: 9.5 miles (a return hike)

Hiking time: 5 hours

Vertical rise: 1,650 feet

Maps: USGS 7.5' Moxie Pond; USGS 15' The Forks; USGS 15' Bingham; MATC map 4 (1993); DeLorme map 30

Moxie Bald Mountain, southeast of The Forks, is a 4-mile ridge running north–south above Moxie Pond. On maps, Moxie Bald is often designated simply "Bald Mountain," but because it is near Moxie Mountain and Moxie Pond and to distinguish it from the seven other "Bald Mountains" in the state, general use is gradually accepting the woodsmen's designation, Moxie Bald. Extended ledges and open crests make it a panoramic climb to the summit in good weather. The trail also passes through uncut spruce, fir, and hardwoods, using the Appalachian Trail (AT). Water on the trail is not dependable and should be obtained in advance. Moxie Bald is not a good place to be in bad weather. Even on warm summer days it can be cold on the exposed summit. Be prepared.

How to Get There

The road approach begins at The Forks, 48 miles north of Skowhegan and 23.4 miles north of Bingham. Turn right off US 201 on the south side of the Kennebec River at a picnic area, onto the paved road to Moxie Pond and Indian Pond. Drive 5.3 miles, passing the trail to Moxie Falls (Hike 18), to the dam on Moxie Pond. This used to be Lake Moxie Station when the Maine Central Railroad ran from Bingham to Lake Moxie (now called Moxie Pond). Turn right (south) and follow the lakeshore on a Scott Paper Company road, which used to be the Maine Central Railroad bed. The rutted road makes driving very slow. Partway down the lake, AT blazes come in from your right, and the AT follows the road for a short distance.

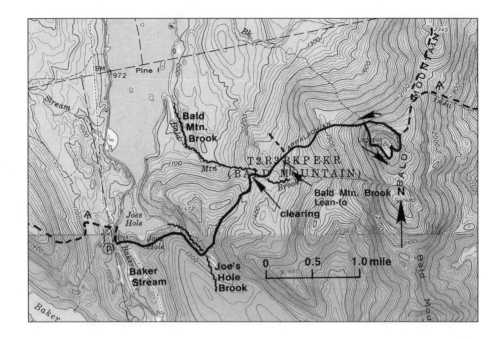

You can see Moxie Bald rising over the south end of the lake.

At 7.9 miles, a signpost on your left indicates where the AT leaves the road to the east. Park on the right side of the road and begin walking the trail east at the signpost.

The Trail

Begin by crossing Baker Stream, the inlet of Moxie Pond. There used to be a cable for crossing at high water, but it has been removed. Across the stream, the trail passes through birch and marsh fern to a power-line cut at 0.3 mile. The cut reveals slate outcroppings and boulders, sheep laurel and blueberries; then the trail reenters woods of tall spruce. Mosses, trailing arbutus, bracken fern, and wintergreen line the sides of the trail, but the spruce are so thick that the ground below has no undergrowth, only spruce duff.

The trail then rises into a beech-maple forest with typical hardwood ground cover:

Canada mayflower, starflower, bunchberry, trillium, asters, clintonia lily, violets, wild sarsaparilla, and Indian cucumber. Shrubs are striped maple and hobblebush. Maine woods have two common species of trillium: painted trillium, which has three leaves with three white petals that appear to have been "touched up" with red paint, and purple wake-robin, which has three leaves and three dark red to purple petals and is sometimes called stinking Benjamin. Both varieties are found in these woods in late May and early June, with purple wake-robin in greater abundance. Moose tracks, too, usually mark the trail.

At 1.1 miles, you cross Joe's Hole Brook. Across the brook, the trail continues up an old logging road through mixed growth into spacious, open beech-maple woods and through a beaver bog, rising gently for the next 1.5 miles.

The woods change to tall black spruce, and at 2.5 miles you cross an old lumber camp clearing, now a grassy field. Cross Bald Mountain Brook and enter another clearing beyond with tent sites. In another 200 yards, a side trail to your right takes you to the Bald Mountain Brook Lean-to.

From here, the trail begins the ascent of Moxie Bald. Just beyond the brook and clearing, you enter a former campground, where the old fire warden's trail comes in on your left from an abandoned boat landing on Moxie Pond. Follow the white blazes across the campground and to your right, where the trail enters mature beech, birch, and maple, some of grand size.

Cross a dry brook and ascend more steeply into spruce, with reindeer lichen and mica on the rocky ground. From here, the trail alternates between stands of spruce-fir and stands of hardwoods, as it rises more steeply. Notice how the thin layer of topsoil has eroded to granodiorite bedrock on the trail. This shows the importance of staying on the trail, so that the rest of the woods will not erode.

The trail rises through a garden of sheep laurel and spruce, and levels briefly. Rising steeply again, the trail widens through red spruce, mountain ash, and sheep laurel, until you can see the summit above you on your right. At 4.2 miles, the blue-blazed summit bypass trail turns left and can be used to avoid the open summit in bad weather. It rejoins the AT half a mile later, north of the summit. If the weather is very inclement, however, you should turn around and head back to Joe's Hole and your car.

At the eastern end of the summit bypass is the site of a former fire warden's cabin. Its front yard is a slight depression moist enough to perpetuate growth of some delicious chives planted by a fire warden in days gone by.

To continue to the summit, bear right on the AT, which leads in 0.6 mile to the open, central (main) summit. This is the steepest part of the hike, through a corridor of slab caves, young red spruce, and bunchberry over an outcrop of tabular granodiorite. To reach the summit, the trail climbs up switchbacks. Sheep laurel landscapes the bare summit at an elevation of 2,630 feet.

From the former tower site, a 360-degree panorama surrounds you. Northwest, Mosquito Mountain is the gumdrop mountain over Moxie Pond. Close by is the north peak of Moxie Bald, which you can reach via a ¾-mile side trail from the AT. Beyond the north peak are Coburn and Boundary Bald (Hike 22) Mountains near Jackman. North is Moose Mountain (Hike 28), and northeast are Big Spencer (Hike 31), White Cap (Hike 27), and in the distance Katahdin (Hike 35). In closer range, the West Branch of the Piscataquis winds its beginning path through the marshland that nurtures it. Eastward lies Bald Mountain Pond and behind it, Blue Top. To the south is Moxie Bald's south peak, and southwest is Bigelow (Hike 12) with its two sets of twin peaks. To the west, South, Middle, and Pleasant Pond (Hike 17) Mountains rise left to right, with Sugarloaf (Hike 48) and Mount Abraham (Hike 11) in the distance.

To vary your descent, proceed north on the AT. In 0.3 mile, you will see the blue-blazed summit bypass trail on your left. Use this trail for your return. A spring is located shortly down it.

Before you return, you might want to explore the north peak by continuing north on the AT and taking a side trail to your left. Add 3 miles (round-trip) to the distance and 1 hour to your walking time.

20

Number Five Mountain

Location: 15 miles south of Jackman near Parlin Pond

Total distance: 6 miles (a return hike)

Hiking time: 4 hours

Vertical rise: 1,360 feet

Maps: USGS 7.5' Holeb; USGS 7.5' Tumbledown Mountain; USGS 7.5' Spencer Lake; DeLorme maps 39, 40

Number Five Mountain, named for its location in Township Number Five, stands sentinel over miles and miles of flat land, the remains of an ancient lake bottom following the glaciers. The center of this 30-mile-diameter lake bottom is still wet, comprising Number Five Bog with Bog Pond in its interior. An old fire tower still stands on the summit of its peak, and its ladder is in good enough condition to climb. Views north and west reveal the wilds of Quebec extending the wilds of Maine, where you can wander for days and encounter only coyote, moose, bear, and French-speaking loggers.

How to Get There

The lengthy logging road through Plum Creek timberlands begins between Jackman and The Forks on US 201. Drive 14.2 miles north from the bridge at The Forks, or 19.3 miles south from the junction of US 201 with ME 6 and ME 15 in Jackman. Here, 0.2 mile north of the Parlin Pond Rest Area, turn west onto a dirt road with a sign to Hardscrabble Lodge. The road is smooth and wide for easy travel, but it is used by huge, fast logging trucks, so be cautious; they have the right-of-way. Stay on the main road. Miles are posted. At 5 miles, you can see Number Five with its tower on your right in the distance. At 12.2 miles, pass the left turn to Hardscrabble Lodge, and at 17 miles, notice the trailhead on your right beside a gravel pit (one of a dozen on the road). Park beside the gravel pit.

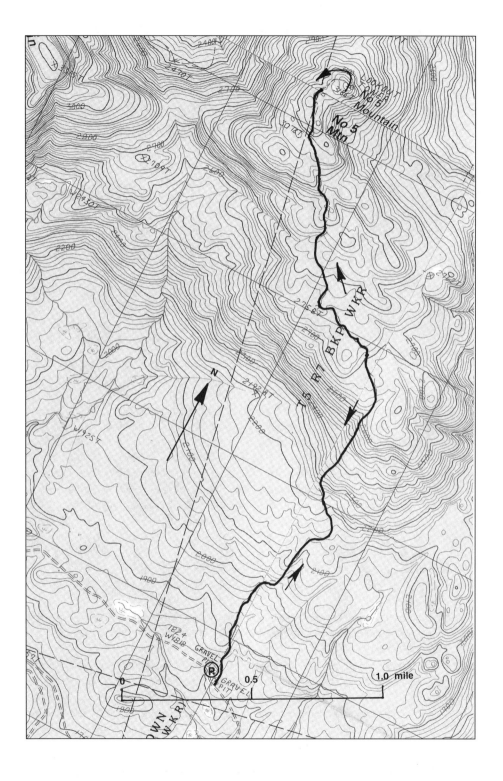

Number Five Mountain as seen from the Moose River

The Trail

A small sign on a white birch marks the trail, which starts on a grassy road, now maintained as a snowmobile trail. Begin hiking the snowmobile trail, which is the former fire warden's trail up Number Five. You walk through the cool shade of striped maple and poplar. At 0.4 mile, cross a brook and continue, rising steeply through maple, beech, and birch woods, opening into bracken fern and then back into spruce, fir, and striped maple. When you start seeing moose droppings, proceed quietly, and you might come across a moose.

After about 0.8 mile the trail passes through a small clearing of asters, blueberries, bunchberry, and bracken fern. I have flushed partridge (ruffed grouse) in this area. The trail levels out for the second mile through a narrow, muddy corridor of dense spruce and fir. If you look carefully, you might notice the former fire warden's cabin

site on your left in the dense growth. Only a rusty bed frame remains.

As you walk through wetter spots, you might notice the lush, broad, green leaves of false hellebore, an herbaceous plant sometimes confused with skunk cabbage. Its ribbed leaves spiral down its stem in a counterclockwise whorl. Although the plant is poisonous if eaten, a garden of false hellebore growing along the trail is beautiful to look at.

This part of the trail has a few large mud puddles to skirt, and then it brings you to a clearing where an arrow on a tree tells you to circle left around a sphagnum bog. This is the end of the snowmobile trail, and the last 0.75 mile of this hike is on a tight, brushy trail over some boulders that a snowmobile could not negotiate. While scrambling up rocks, notice the wood sorrel (Oxalis) under the fir and spruce. About 0.25 mile from the tower you can see remnants of old telephone wire as the trail levels out near the summit. One more climb up open ledges brings you to the top of a world of wilderness with a 360-degree panorama. The tall tower is a bonus for views, but I prefer to enjoy them from the top steps of the ladder and not from the platform, which does not look safe to stand on.

To the north, close up, is Attean Mountain behind Number Five Bog, with Sally Mountain (Hike 21) close behind and to its right. Behind Sally and to its left in the distance stand the three rolling peaks of Boundary Bald Mountain (Hike 22), 8 miles from Quebec in a northerly direction. On Number Five, you are a mere 12 miles from Quebec to the west, looking past close-up Number Six Mountain to Lac Megantic and Megantic Mountain. To the southwest is Kibby Mountain, and beyond it Snow Mountain near Coburn Gore. To the south are Spencer Mountain and, to its left, Spencer Lake. Far to the south is Sugarloaf behind the Horns of Bigelow, and the other peaks of Bigelow (Hikes 12 and 13) trending southeast, with the Crocker Peaks (Hike 48) peeking from behind Cranberry Peak (Hike 14). To the east is Coburn Mountain.

From the tower, the lay of the land is obvious. From east to northeast, a huge flat expanse shows evidence of a prehistoric, postglacial lake that covered the area from Number Five to Jackman. Number Five Bog, and Bog Pond at its center, is the lowest part of this depression and is still wet today. You will recall the 18 miles of sand and gravel you drove through on the road in to this trail—you were driving across the ancient lake bottom. The Moose River braids its way through this lake bottom and bog, and makes a wonderful 3-day (or more) canoe trip when combined with Attean and Holeb Ponds. To find out more about this special trip, you can inquire at the chamber of commerce information office in Jackman.

21

Sally Mountain

Location: Jackman

Total distance: 5.8 miles (a return hike)

Hiking time: 4 hours

Vertical rise: 1,000 feet

Maps: USGS 7.5' Attean Pond; USGS 15' Attean; DeLorme map 39

Sally Mountain is named for Sally Holden, daughter of Captain Samuel Holden, who was the first settler of the Jackman–Moose River area. It rises above the town of Jackman between its two principal lakes, Wood Pond and Attean Pond. Its long ridge extends northeast to southwest, and a Maine Forest Service fire tower once stood on the central summit.

How to Get There

If you are traveling by canoe on Attean Pond, from Attean Landing follow the right (east) shoreline about 1.5 miles to the second beach campsite. In back of this campsite, climb up onto the railroad track and turn left. A 10-minute walk will take you to the trailhead, a trail to your right with painted tree blazes opposite Central Maine Power pole #3112. Leave the railroad track and begin walking this trail 1.2 miles to the summit. This shortens the total round-trip distance to 3.4 miles.

To reach the trailhead by automobile, drive north on US 201 to a point south of Jackman Station where ME 6/ME 15 turns east and Attean Road turns west by signs to Attean Lake Resort. Turn left (west) on Attean Road, which soon turns to dirt and is paralleled by a power line. At 1.4 miles, opposite power pole #31, turn right onto another dirt road and drive 50 yards to a locked gate at the Canadian Pacific Railroad track. Park off the road.

The Trail

Walk left onto the railroad track, as the first 1.7 miles of the hike follow the track southwest over the Moose River, which connects Wood and Attean Ponds, and along the northwest shore of Attean Pond. Cross the Moose River on a railroad bridge, from which you can see on your right one of the northeast summits of Sally Mountain over Wood Pond. A power line parallels the railroad track, which rises gradually from boggy land and cattails through birch and aspen, grasses, bracken fern, and pearly everlasting.

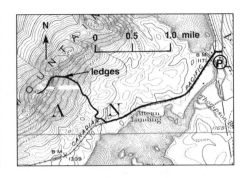

At 1 mile, Attean Pond becomes visible through the trees to your left. This northeast corner of the pond has a large beaver lodge near shore. At 1.7 miles, a few paces beyond power pole #3112, turn right (northwest) and enter the woods on a path. There is no sign, but this is the former fire warden's trail, which leads 1.2 miles to the northeast summit. The trail is blazed with green paint on trees as it runs through dense small birch, balsam fir, and maples. One hundred yards up the trail, cross a small, spring-fed brook from which the fire warden used to pipe water. Pieces of pipe run along the trail as far as the old cabin site, which is now obscured by underbrush The trail ascends gently into larger trees, with purple wake-robin, Canada mayflower, starflower, clintonia lily, and wild sarsaparilla on the ground. The trees are predominantly large white birch, striped maple, and several very large aspens.

After 0.3 mile, the trail steepens. The 1,000-foot vertical rise of this hike is nearly all gained in the last mile to the summit. Various flowers and ferns grow on the steep bank: asters, violets, partridgeberry, white baneberry (doll's-eye), Solomon's plume, northern honeysuckle, New York fern, sensitive fern, long beech fern, and large circlets of interrupted fern. Watch for a small clearing with a spring, but don't depend on it as it is hard to see.

After you pass a large balancing boulder on your left, the trail steepens considerably. Here especially you can see some large specimens of Solomon's plume, also called false Solomon's seal and false spikenard. The single stem of 1 to 2 feet has alternating oval pointed leaves and frothy white flowers on the end in spring, which become mottled pink berries in late summer and ruby red in fall.

The trail climbs between massive granite outcroppings up onto open ledges looking southeast over island-dotted Attean Pond. To the east you can see where Wood and Attean Ponds join, and a cut through the trees shows where the railroad skirts the shore of Attean Pond. The last 0.2 mile crosses open ledges through sheep laurel, lowbush blueberries, and reindeer lichen. From late July to September the blueberries are plentiful. Several mountain ash trees have white flowers in summer and red-orange berries in late summer and fall. The trail curves southwest following cairns to the underpinnings of the former fire tower, where the 360-degree panorama sweeps many peaks of northwestern Maine and Quebec Province and looks down on the lakes of the Jackman area.

To the north, Mud Pond lies to the right of Burnt Jacket Mountain, and behind them part of Little Big Wood Pond is visible. Look north-northeast over Wood Pond to Jackman

The view from Sally Mountain: Attean Pond, with Coburn Mountain in the background

with Boundary Bald Mountain (Hike 22) behind. To the northeast is the northeast summit of Sally Mountain, and below it to the right are the twin Gothic spires of Saint Anthony's Church, Main Street, Jackman. East-northeast beyond Long Pond, Mount Kineo (Hike 29) rises in the distance. East, close by, unnamed hills fill the view, and southeast, Catheart Mountain rises over Attean Pond, with Coburn Mountain behind it to the right. South beyond Bog Pond runs the Moose River, and beyond it are two peaks of equal elevation, Hardscrabble (left) and Hardwood (right) Mountains. Southwest close by is Attean Mountain, and behind to its left are Number Five Mountain (Hike 20) on the left with a tower and Number Six Mountain on the right. To the west behind an unnamed hill are Holeb Pond and Birch Island, behind which are the mountains of

Quebec. Sally Mountain is in view for most of the famous Bow Trip, a canoe circuit of the Moose River: Attean Pond, carry to Holeb Pond, Holeb Stream, and the long Moose River return to Attean Pond.

From the fire tower site, the trail continues 3 miles, not included in this hike, southwest into a saddle and back up to the southwest peak of Sally Mountain. From there it goes down the mountain to a logging road and crosses the railroad track at the west end of Attean Pond. Unless someone is picking you up by boat or you enjoy an extra 4 miles of railroad track walking, you should return the way you came.

Throughout the hike, you can hear loons calling on the lakes. They are an endangered species in some places but flourish in these ponds. Even at the summit, their cries are clear, a reminder that you are in wilderness.

22

Boundary Bald Mountain

Location: On the Quebec boundary north of Jackman

Total distance: 5.2 miles (a return hike)

Hiking time: 4 hours

Vertical rise: 1,800 feet

Maps: USGS 7.5' Boundary Bald Mountain; DeLorme maps 39, 47

Boundary Bald Mountain rises in the wilds of northwestern Maine approximately 8 miles from the wilds of Canada at the Quebec border. Although there was a fire warden's trail many years ago, the summit has long been inaccessible and thus seemed all the more tantalizing. Recently, local hikers reblazed the trail to the fallen tower, and it is well worth the climb to see so much untracked, unsettled country from this mountain's summit.

How to Get There

The jumping-off point for this climb is Jackman, an hour north of Skowhegan on US 201, and west of Greenville on ME 6/ME 15. In the town, you can purchase the topographical map at Bishop's Store and pick up information at the chamber of commerce information booth on US 201.

Following US 201 north from Jackman, cross the bridge over the Moose River into the town of Moose River. Driving mileage is from this bridge. At 7.2 miles, you will pass "The Falls" Rest Area on your right; at 7.6 miles, turn right onto a dirt road that may have a small bald mountain trail sign. Skidders have muddied the road in places, so be careful not to get stuck. If necessary, you can park and walk the last part of this road.

From the beginning of the dirt road, it is 2.3 miles to a bridge over Heald Stream at Heald Falls, with a campsite on your right. Stay on the main dirt road, taking no turns. At 3 miles, pass Mud Pond on your right, and at 4 miles cross a bridge over a small

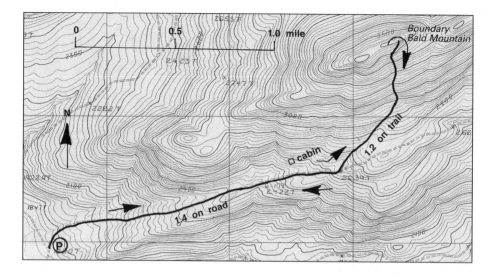

stream. At 4.1 miles, the road forks; right is Bald Mountain Road, and left is Notch Road and the correct way to this trail. At 4.3 miles, Notch Road forks. You should park on the right fork, off the road.

The Trail

Begin by walking 1.4 miles to the trailhead. You could attempt this 1.4-mile section by vehicle, but only if you have four-wheel drive and high clearance. It is better to walk.

Walking the road is interesting because you can see numerous patches of coltsfoot, with its irregular leaves that look a bit like rounded, webbed duck feet. You will also see joe-pye weed, mountain ash, fireweed, pearly everlasting, and goldenrod. At 1.2 miles, you pass the former fire warden's camp on your left, and at 1.4 miles, the trail takes off to your left at a sign that says BALD MOUNTAIN.

From the trailhead it is 1.2 miles to the summit. The trail begins in a "rain forest" of meadow rue, thistle, cow parsnip, and mountain ash. The day after a rain, this first part of the trail is a brook, and its upper reaches are waterfalls. The narrow trail rises steeply through fir and mountain ash following blue blazes on trees. Halfway up, pieces of old fallen telephone wire run through wood fern, sphagnum, bunchberry, and little white aster.

The second half of the trail is much steeper, sometimes a waterfall, following old wire and blazes up a couple of ladders. The first open views are from the southwest ledges of scrub spruce and fir, overlooking Heald Pond (large, on your left) and Mud Pond (small, on your right). Behind Heald Pond lie Wood and Attean Ponds and the Moose River.

Still following wire, you reach the 3,640-foot summit on fins of weathered, whitish slate. Even though the tower is lying down, views are superb because the scrub growth is no taller than knee-high, pruned by harsh alpine conditions. From the tower looking southeast, you can see Fish Pond connected to Muskrat Pond. Behind them are Luther Pond on your left and Mud Pond on your right. In the distance to the south is Long Pond. Southwest is Heald Pond, with Big Wood Pond and Attean Pond behind it. Farther southwest is Little Big Wood Pond.

The author on the summit of Boundary Bald Mountain

Facing north, from the other side of the mountain, look northeast to Trickey Bluffs, which look like three gumdrops. If you look hard, you can see Iron-bound Pond between you and the gumdrops. North is Jones Pond, with Canada 8 miles from you. West is bumpy Sandy Stream Mountain.

If you are interested in history, you might have noticed the three different decades of telephone wires used on the fire warden's trail.

To return to your car, follow the same trail in reverse, taking care to turn right onto the dirt road when you come off the trail. This will take you, in 1.4 miles, to your car.

Boundary Bald Mountain

Reaching the top of Boundary Bald was call for quite a celebration. For me, it was an 18-year dream come true: I had admired the three rounded peaks of Boundary Bald from many other mountaintops and lakes, and I was finally on top of the mountain that had eluded me for so long. The friend who hiked to the summit with me reached her goal of climbing all of the Bald Mountains in Maine—of which there are eight. Even without those celebrations, we had a rewarding wilderness trip—one I plan to take again soon.

Monson to Moosehead

Introduction to Monson to Moosehead

Moosehead Lake, the largest lake east of the Mississippi within one state, lies partly in Somerset County but mainly in Piscataquis County in north-central Maine. It is surrounded by many other lakes of all sizes. Greenville is the town at the southern end of Moosehead, and Monson is about 15 miles south of it on ME 6/ME 15. This section also includes three hikes to the east, near Katahdin Iron Works off ME 11.

Monson, the slate capital of the Northeast, has several operating slate quarries, although slate is in less demand these days due to competition from other building materials. Monson is also the first opportunity for south-bound Appalachian Trail (AT) hikers to buy food, receive mail, and find amenities of civilization after hiking the Hundred Mile Wilderness from Baxter State Park to Monson.

Hikes 23 through 27 are located in the Hundred Mile Wilderness. Hikes 26 and 27 can be reached by traveling to Katahdin Iron Works off ME 11 north of Brownville Junction (see Hike 26 for directions and a description of the ironworks). The Gulf Hagas hike (Hike 26) takes you through the Hermitage, a virgin stand of huge white pine protected by The Nature Conservancy, worth seeing even if you don't take the hike.

Accommodations in the Monson area are few. The Maine Forest Service (MFS) Little Wilson Stream Campsite is the only place to camp. Shaw's Boarding Home is a friendly bed & breakfast for hikers. If you stay here, you'll meet the Shaws and some AT hikers, many on their way from Maine to Georgia or vice versa. The only state park in the area, Peaks-Kenny near Dover-Foxcroft, has overnight camping.

Katahdin Iron Works has a large number of campsites along the West Branch of the Pleasant River, White Brook, and other locations here and there in the wilderness.

The Moosehead Lake area has numerous private accommodations, including camping. Your DeLorme atlas will show you MFS wilderness campsites in the area. Lily Bay State Park on the eastern side of the lake offers overnight camping, as does Brassua Lake Campground west of Moosehead on ME 6 and 15.

This country is rich in history: the Native American–guided travels of Henry David Thoreau, the log-driving years, the World War II prisoner-of-war camps hidden here and there in the wilderness (see various hikes for descriptions). It is also rich in wildlife and other natural wonders. You could spend a lot of time getting to know this country.

23

Big Wilson Cliffs and Little Wilson Falls

Location: 8 miles north of Monson

Total distance: 3.5 miles (a circuit hike)

Hiking time: 2 hours

Vertical rise: 800 feet

Maps: USGS 7.5' Barren Mountain West; USGS 15' Sebec Lake; MATC map 3 (1993); DeLorme map 41

This hike in the area southeast of Moosehead uses the Appalachian Trail (AT) part of the way. You make an easy tour of slate cliffs for views and finally reach a dramatic set of slate falls. The only water available on this hike is surface water, so you should begin with a full canteen.

How to Get There

Drive 0.5 mile northwest from downtown Monson on ME 6/ME 15, and turn right onto Elliottsville Road. Drive 7.7 miles, almost to Big Wilson Stream; just before you reach the bridge, turn left onto a woods road and drive 0.7 mile to Little Wilson Campsite, which is maintained by the Maine Forest Service.

The Trail

Your pathway begins at the site of a washed-out bridge over Little Wilson Stream. Pick your way across slate falls to the opposite bank of the stream. Look for violets and other surprises growing from cracks in the slate.

After crossing, turn left on a gravel road. After 0.1 mile, you pass on your right a blue-blazed side trail that runs (northeast) into the woods toward Jim Whyte's Lookout and Big Wilson Cliffs. This trail used to be the AT, but the latter has been rerouted in the aftermath of logging operations. With the obliteration of this old trail, the way to Jim Whyte's Lookout is lost, along with the first trail to Big Wilson Cliffs.

Continue walking the gravel road approximately 1 mile, rising steadily past slash from logging operations. At 1 mile, the road

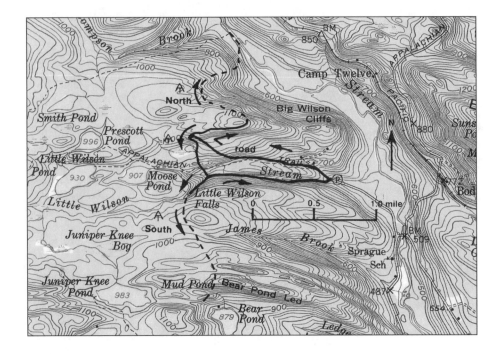

levels and begins to descend slightly. You will meet the current AT (white blazes) when the road reaches a gravel pit on your right. Directly across from the gravel pit, the AT turns left (sign AT SOUTH). You will follow the AT South to Little Wilson Falls after you have returned from Big Wilson Cliffs. But first, keep walking up the road, following the white blazes of the AT North for 100 yards, until the white blazes turn right, leaving the road and leading you uphill through the woods. The trail shortly levels and begins to take you east across an open slate cliff. Borestone Mountain (Hike 24) is always ahead of you. Follow the trail over the slate ridge as long as it runs east toward Borestone Mountain. After 0.5 mile on this ridge, the AT turns north and away from the slate ridge. This is the turnaround point. The ridge runs another 0.5 mile to Big Wilson Cliffs, but skidders have wrecked the area and left it nearly impassable.

The cliffs here lie in an east–west direction, an unusual orientation for Maine. Because of the direction of bedrock folding in Maine, most ridges run from north to south or northeast to southwest. The gigantic upheaval of bedrock that forms these cliffs forced local drainage patterns to change direction in order to skirt the land mass. This abrupt change in direction and bedrock hardness caused the uneven topography and the numerous rapids and falls in Big Wilson and Little Wilson Streams.

From the cliffs, retrace your steps on the AT back to the gravel road. At the road, follow the AT 100 yards to its turnoff south (right). From here it's 0.5 mile to Little Wilson Falls. The trail passes a small pond and beaver dam.

Soon the trail arrives at Little Wilson Stream, where step falls pitch over slate slabs. Pin cherry overhangs the top of the falls, covered with white blossoms in spring. Beside the stream is a natural garden of jack-in-the-pulpits, which bloom in late May.

Follow the white blazes across the stream. The trail parallels the left bank of the stream, passing more series of falls and pools, and arrives in 0.3 mile at the top of spectacular, 60-foot Little Wilson Falls. Massive slate walls enclose the falls, supporting the growth of ferns, mosses, and grasses. This is an excellent place for a picnic, a shower in the falls, or a swim in the pool below—or to camp overnight.

From the falls, return to the Little Wilson Stream crossing. From here, you can retrace your steps on the AT back to the gravel road, turn right, and walk back down the road to your car. But if you would prefer to return to your car a different way, you can follow Little Wilson Stream back down to the campsite where you parked. The distance is 1 mile, but the going is slow since the rough fishermen's trail crisscrosses the stream from bank to bank. In warm weather, it's fun to walk in the stream, avoiding the deep pools (unless you feel like taking a dip). There is also a large pool in the stream at the campsite for cooling off after a hot hike. Either return takes about 45 minutes.

For two more hikes in the area, see Hike 24, Borestone Mountain, and Hike 25, Barren Mountain.

24

Borestone Mountain

Location: 10 miles north of Monson

Total distance: 4 miles (a return hike)

Hiking time: 3½ hours

Vertical rise: 1,150 feet

Maps: USGS 7.5' Barren Mountain West; USGS 15' Sebec Lake; MATC map 3 (1993); DeLorme map 41

Like a sparkling gem in the Hundred Mile Wilderness area of the Appalachian Trail (AT), Borestone Mountain offers astounding views and an education in nature with a hike of relatively moderate effort. Until the 1970s, Borestone was private property, but a generous gift from R.T. Moore and his heirs has resulted in a well-kept road, trail, and nature center open to the public and managed by the National Audubon Society as a sanctuary since 1984. In 1984, the north side of the mountain was donated by Dr. John H. Lewis.

The nature center, halfway up the mountain, is operated from June 1 through October 31, when a fee of $1.50 for adults and $1 for students is charged for using the trail. At other times of the year, the hike is gated off but can be hiked without benefit of the nature center. The only water on this hike is surface water, so you should begin with a full canteen. The forest of Borestone Mountain, uncut for a century, is mixed hardwoods and softwoods—beech and birch at the bottom grading into spruce and fir toward the top. You'll see some huge "old-timers" on this hike.

How to Get There

Borestone (sometimes shown as Boarstone on some maps) is located in the Monson area near Hike 23, Big Wilson Cliffs and Little Wilson Falls, and Hike 25, Barren Mountain. To find the trailhead, drive ME 6/ME 15 north from the center of Monson for 0.5 mile, and turn right (northeast) onto Elliottsville Road. Continue 7.8 miles to Big

Wilson Stream, cross the bridge, turn left, cross the Canadian Pacific Railroad tracks at 8.5 miles, and at 8.6 miles you'll see the trailhead to Borestone Mountain on your right. Park off the road, taking care not to block the gate in case the ranger needs to drive up or down the trail.

The Trail

Your pathway follows the auto road, beginning with a gentle rise through mature beech and birch with smaller moosewood (striped maple) trees scattered throughout. The typical hardwood forest floor is open with wild sarsaparilla, trillium (red and white), and numerous ferns. You can walk the road all the way to the nature center or take a few shortcuts following the trail under the telephone wire.

At 0.6 mile, a side trail leads 200 feet to your right to Little Greenwood Overlook, with a view to the south of Little Greenwood Pond with Greenwood Mountain, 1,100 feet high, behind it to the left. At the right time of summer, you'll find blueberries and blackberries on the ledges. The ledges themselves, made of schist, are scraped in parallel grooves trending south toward Little Greenwood Pond. These grooves are striations gouged by debris at the base of a glacier pushing southward a million years ago.

As you continue up the auto road, the woods change to predominantly spruce, fir, and pine, with sheep laurel and bracken fern in sunny spots like garden shrubbery. At 1.3 miles, you'll see the Robert T. Moore Visitor Center on Sunrise Pond. A little time spent studying the exhibits in the nature center will enhance the rest of your trip. You'll learn that hundreds of plants and numerous animals inhabit these slopes, one of which, the peregrine falcon, is a recently reintroduced resident. You can also see a map of the

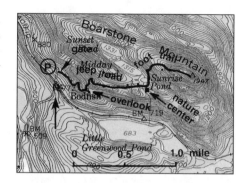

Onawa Pluton and its effect on the geology of the Borestone area.

Sunrise Pond is the first in a series of three ponds, including Midday and Sunset Ponds, named according to the time of day the sun shines on them. The trail leaves the road, curves past the nature center, and makes a quarter circle around the pond. Abruptly, it leaves the pond for a steep spurt of 0.5 mile through mixed woods, then spruce and fir, then over open ledges, to the barren summit. You will need to use your hands to scramble up some of the rocks, and you'll cross two false summits before reaching the 1,947-foot summit.

At the top, iron pins remain as evidence of the former fire tower erected in 1914. To the north runs the impressive Barren-Chairback Range, traversed by the AT. From north to northeast, the peaks are Barren, Fourth, Third, Columbus, and Chairback Mountains. Below you, Lake Onawa spreads north and east, nearly bisected by a delta and dotted with tiny islands. Southward lies Big Greenwood Pond, and west you can see Midday and Sunset Ponds, beyond which the land falls precipitously to Big Wilson Stream Valley.

In the nature center, an exhibit on the local geology reveals an interesting story about the formation of Borestone and its surrounding area. Borestone is part of the massive Onawa Pluton, which encompasses the

---

Lake Onawa area. During the Devonian period, between 390 and 345 million years ago, most of Maine's mountains were built by molten magma either shooting up through the crust (volcanoes) or pushing up huge blisters beneath the crust without bursting the crust. The second method results in granitic mountains such as Borestone, which is granodiorite, slightly darker than granite.

The Onawa Pluton was a "blister" of molten magma that welled up under the surrounding crust or "country rock" of sedimentary rock, mostly shale. Heat from the liquid granite baked the surrounding shale "country rock" into very hard and durable slate and schist (the process of metamorphism). The baked slate and schist, resistant to erosion, remain standing as the Barren-Chairback Range, Big Wilson Cliffs, and other mountains in the Onawa area; and the liquid magma that cooled and hardened into granodiorite remains as Borestone Mountain and part of Barren Mountain. Granite and granodiorite are less-resistant rock. Lake Onawa lies as proof that much of the pluton (the blister) has eroded away.

Why, then, is Borestone still standing? At the summit you will notice that the rock is striped with white vein quartz, a result of contact metamorphism between the Onawa Pluton and overlying country rock. This durable metamorphic "cap" on Borestone has withstood weathering, glaciation, and erosion; it preserved the mountain, while the rest of the pluton eroded away around it.

Your trail down is the same as your trail up. Watch your footing carefully. Hiking down is more dangerous than hiking up.

25

Barren Mountain

Location: 12 miles north of Monson

Total distance: 12.2 miles (a return hike)

Hiking time: 8 hours

Vertical rise: 2,260 feet

Maps: USGS 7.5' Barren Mountain West; USGS 7.5' Barren Mountain East; USGS 15' Sebec Lake; MATC map 3 (1993); DeLorme map 41

Barren Mountain, the highest and westernmost peak of the Barren-Chairback Range, looms over Elliottsville Plantation north of Monson. Barren is the last peak in the Hundred Mile Wilderness of the Appalachian Trail (AT) from Abol Bridge south to Monson, which is 12 miles north of Guilford and 14 miles south of Greenville on ME 6/ ME 15.

How to Get There

Take ME 6/ME 15 north from the center of Monson for 0.5 mile, and then turn right (northeast) on Elliottsville Road. Continue 7.8 miles to Big Wilson Stream, cross the bridge, and turn left. At 8.5 miles, cross the Canadian Pacific Railroad track and pass the Borestone Mountain Trail; 10.7 miles from Monson you come to Bodfish Farm, a wide flat expanse. Bear left at the next fork (10.8 miles); the gravel lumber road you follow for the final 1 mile cuts through Long Pond Stream valley and Bodfish Intervale. Park at the next fork.

The Trail

Begin walking on the right fork over a rotting bridge across Vaughan Stream. Follow the road, which is washed out in several places beyond the bridge, for 0.5 mile to the AT crossing. Turn right, leaving the road, and follow the white-blazed Appalachian Trail. At 0.6 mile (not long after you leave the road), you cross Long Pond Stream at a ford, normally knee deep, and follow the east bank. At 1.2 miles (0.7 mile from the road), you enter Slugundy Gorge and pass Slugundy

Falls. Here, Long Pond Stream has cut sharply into slate bedrock forming the gorge.

A steep ascent then leads uphill through wood sorrel, wild sarsaparilla, and rosy twisted-stalk in mature hardwoods. Cross a dry brook and enter younger growth with some very big rock (sugar) maples. On the ground are foamflower and starflower.

At 1.5 miles you come to a trail junction. (To your left, 0.6 mile away, is Long Pond Stream Lean-to.) Turn right (south) and follow the white blazes toward Barren Ledges. The 1-mile ascent to the ledges steepens as you mount the Barren-Chairback Range. Giant rock maples tower over younger maples and beech, with hobblebush and Indian cucumber beneath. At its steepest, the trail climbs water bars, log steps placed to slow erosion. At the higher reaches, spruce begins to predominate, and you come shortly to slate outcroppings.

The trail corners sharply onto more outcrops, the trees thin, and views open to the north of the Gulf Hagas Mountains (Hike 26). Immediately, the trail curves south and levels out at the crest of a ridge, still heading south. At 2.6 miles, a side trail leads right 250 feet to an overlook of Barren Slide. Views left to right from the slide are south to Lake Onawa with Borestone Mountain (Hike 24) behind, southwest to Bodfish Intervale (the flat floodplain of Long Pond Stream), and close under the slide to Otter Pond. Beyond are Bodfish Farm and Big Wilson Cliffs (Hike 23). West is Big Moose Mountain (Hike 28).

Shortly beyond the slide, the trail takes you out onto Barren Ledges, which offer dramatic views of Borestone Mountain rising over Lake Onawa. Beyond the ledges, the trail levels and cuts a hairpin curve through bracken fern, bunchberry, clintonia lily, Canada mayflower, and blueberries, rising gradually for 1 mile. Moose tracks mark the trail through the gently sloping wooded corridor. Then you ascend sharply 0.5 mile up the granite cone of Barren Peak, and at 4.4 miles reach the tower at the 2,660-foot summit. The entire length of Barren Mountain is a granodiorite hulk rising above a countryside entirely of slate. (For a description of local geology see Hike 24, Borestone Mountain.) The fire tower wasn't erected on Barren Mountain until 1951. Until then fires were scouted from the Borestone tower, which was established in 1914.

Views from the Barren summit and the tower rank with the best in the state. To the north, beyond Long Pond, the AT eventually crosses Gulf Hagas Mountain, West Peak, and Hay and White Cap Mountains. Beyond White Cap (Hike 27), Katahdin (Hike 35) is visible on a clear day. To the east, the AT follows Barren Ridge to Cloud Pond (out of sight) and to the rest of the Barren-Chairback Range: Fourth, Third, Columbus, and Chairback Mountains. To the south is Lake Onawa, and behind it, Sebec Lake. Southwest are Borestone and Bodfish Intervale, and west is Big Moose (Hike 28). To the north are Big and Little Spencer Mountains (Hikes 31 and 32).

From the tower, continue east on wooded Barren Ridge, losing very little elevation, for 1 mile through balsam fir and bunchberry. At 5.4 miles, a blue-blazed side trail leads right 0.2 mile to Cloud Pond Lean-to. Cloud Pond's 2,409-foot elevation is only 250 feet below the summit elevation of Barren Mountain. This lean-to is one of the nicer places to spend the night on Maine's AT. It is in remote wilderness on Cloud Pond, shielded from wind in a grove of trees. Loons call on the pond, and when it mirrors blue sky and white clouds, you understand why it was named Cloud Pond. Or was it because at 2,409 feet, the pond is up among the clouds? If you plan to spend

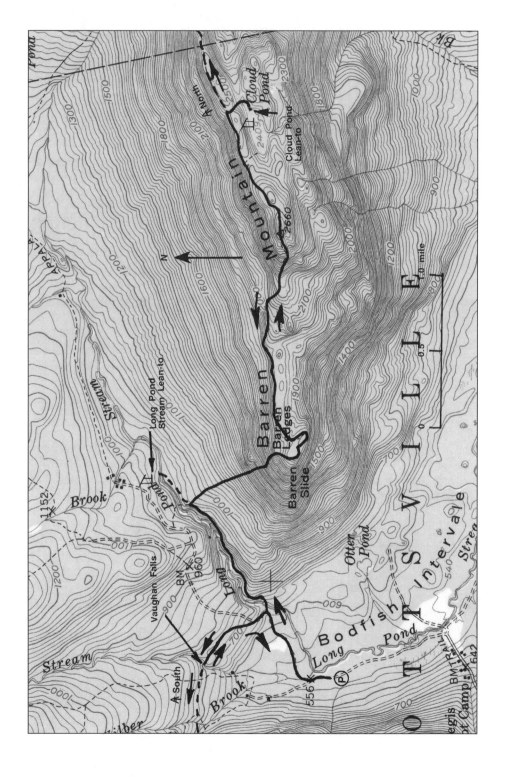

the night at the lean-to in summer, it may be filled with hikers. In spring and fall you are more likely to be alone.

Return to the white-blazed AT, turn left, and retrace the trail over Barren's peak and ledges, back through Slugundy Gorge to the road on which you started.

To end on a dramatic note, instead of returning straight to your car, follow the AT south as it leaves the road to your right (west), and walk 0.5 mile to Vaughan Stream. It is an easy walk and well worth the time to see the 20-foot Vaughan Falls. Time and mileage for this side trip have been budgeted into the hike.

From Vaughan Falls, return on the Appalachian Trail the way you came, half a mile back to the road. Turn right on the road, and walk 0.5 mile back to your car at Vaughan Stream.

26

Gulf Hagas

Location: Near Katahdin Iron Works north of Brownville

Total distance: 10 miles (a circuit hike)

Hiking time: 7 hours

Vertical rise: 600 feet

Maps: USGS 7.5' Barren Mountain East; USGS 15' Sebec Lake; MATC map 3 (1993); Diamond Company Map; DeLorme map 42

Gulf Hagas, known as Maine's miniature Grand Canyon, is hidden in the Hundred Mile Wilderness of the Appalachian Trail, which extends from Monson to Abol Bridge. This scenic gorge is 7 miles west of historic Katahdin Iron Works, which is several miles northwest of Brownville and Brownville Junction. The West Branch of the Pleasant River has carved a slate canyon of sheer narrow walls up to 400 feet high, with numerous waterfalls and curious rock formations. The stream drops 500 feet through the 2.5-mile-long canyon, tumbling and frothing most of the way.

Old Pleasant River Road, used in lumber operations a century ago, offers access to the Gulf from the east. The lands surrounding the Gulf are held by the Champion Paper Company and Diamond International Corporation. In 1968 Gulf Hagas was declared a Registered Natural Landmark in order to preserve its natural beauty.

The hike begins at the Katahdin Iron Works, a Maine State Historical Memorial with history and diagrams of the iron industry detailed on display boards. Although the area is now mostly uninhabited woodlands, in 1843 the settlement of Katahdin Iron Works was a thriving village with several hundred people, a hotel, and later a railroad. Iron ore was mined from Ore Mountain, a ridge 1.5 miles west, and carried by rail to the ironworks for the roasting separation process. Several brick beehive charcoal ovens, of which one remains, prepared the charcoal used in the massive blast furnace, which still stands.

Although this hike is continually following water, there is no spring on this trail. You should begin with a full canteen.

How to Get There

Heading north on ME 11, turn left (west) 4 miles north Brownville Junction at the KATAHDIN IRON WORKS sign, and drive 6.5 miles down a gravel road to the ironworks. After you register with the caretaker and pay a day-use or camping fee, you are provided with a Diamond Company map and admitted through the gate and across the bridge over the West Branch of the Pleasant River. (The USGS map is of limited usefulness here.) Beyond the bridge, take the right fork (stay on the widest road), bear left at the fork in 3.4 miles, and recross the West Branch of the Pleasant River. At 7 miles, the Appalachian Trail (AT) crosses this road at a bridge over a brook. Park in the AT parking area.

The Trail

Follow the white blazes north. (Directly opposite, the AT going south leads to Chairback and Columbus Mountains.) You parallel the brook through a generally young beech and maple forest. At 0.7 mile, ford the West Branch of the Pleasant River. Use caution on the slippery rocks. A stick will help you balance. In winter there is no problem on the frozen river; in early spring the water is likely to be too high to cross. As in all stream crossings, your backpack should be unbelted for quick removal in case you fall. Across the river, you begin walking through the Hermitage, a famous grove of beautiful white king pine, some 130 feet tall, now preserved by The Nature Conservancy of Maine. At 1 mile, you encounter Old Pleasant River Road. Turn left (west) where a sign points to Screw Auger Falls. Shortly, you

leave the Hermitage and walk in mixed woods, mostly beech and maple. A variety of wildflowers dot the ground, including clintonia lily, Canada mayflower, bunchberry, painted trillium, purple wake-robin, and wild sarsaparilla.

At 1.1 miles, in a clearing, the blue-blazed 5.2-mile circuit trail to Gulf Hagas takes off straight ahead (north) while the white-blazed AT corners to the right (east) toward White Cap (Hike 27) and Gulf Hagas Mountains. Cross Gulf Hagas Brook on the blue-blazed trail to a boulder on which a 1968 bronze plaque names Gulf Hagas a Registered Natural Landmark. From the boulder, a side trail leads 0.2 mile left to Screw Auger Falls, 26 feet high by 4 feet wide. The falls have worn and polished the rock into the shape of an S. This side trail should not be missed. Backtrack to the blue-blazed Gulf Hagas circuit trail, which continues north on Old Pleasant River Road for 0.5 mile to an intersection marked by a painted rock where you turn left downhill. (The circuit trail will bring you back to this point, from which you return to your car the way you came.)

The trail drops south toward the West Branch of the Pleasant River, with a side spur 0.2 mile south to Hammond Street Pitch. Peering down from this 90-foot cliff of slate and sheep laurel, you will find it difficult in summer to see through the trees to the bottom of the gorge. Retrace the side spur back to the circuit trail and pull uphill past a couple of open viewpoints to Indian Head, the craggy profile of an Indian jutting out of the canyon wall. This rock is on one side of the Lower Jaws, where a Native American log driver was killed in a logjam in May 1882. Above, at the Main Jaws, the channel was only some 7.5 feet wide until a blast widened it to 26 feet. On the opposite south canyon wall, you can see white

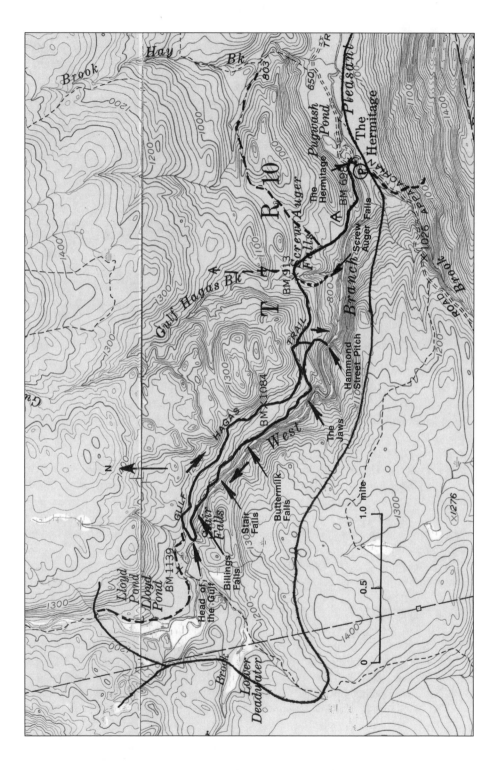

A relaxing swim at the "Head of the Gulf" on the Gulf Hagas Trail

flowers of Labrador tea blooming in June and mountain ash's white flowers in June and its red berries in July and August. Beyond, four short spur trails provide downstream views of Lower and Main Jaws and upstream views of Upper Jaws.

Farther, 0.3 mile above the Jaws, a side spur leads to a pool at the base of Buttermilk Falls, an appropriate name for the frothy, foaming water. The trail stays near the northern edge of the canyon for the next 0.5 mile, taking you past Stair Falls and Billings Falls, whose three bridal veils fall into a semicircular pool.

Gulf Hagas was carved by the West Branch of the Pleasant River, aided by river drivers' dynamite, out of rock known as the Carrabassett Formation. This rock type consists of shales, slates, and schists of the Devonian period, about 350 million years ago. The various falls occur where the river

could not erode the rock away; thus, they stand as stumbling blocks impeding the river's course. It's a shame we can't see such extraordinary beauty in all of life's stumbling blocks!

Shortly you reach the Head of the Gulf, where the river divides around an island and cascades toward you in step falls on both sides. This is the last overlook before the trail leaves the river and circles clockwise away from the Gulf and back to Old Pleasant River Road. You will pass on your left a road up the West Branch of the Pleasant to Lloyd Pond (where it crosses a main road, should you wish to spot a car there) and on to Little Lyford Ponds. The trail takes you through dense spruce, marsh fern, jewelweed, hobblebush, and some large old maple, beech, and birch. The return trail is much faster, taking you past the painted rock, back to the side trail to Screw Auger Falls, and onto the white-blazed Appalachian Trail again, which you retrace to your car.

An important factor affecting the walking time of this hike is the ruggedness of the trail. Although there is not much measurable vertical rise during the 2.5 miles that the trail runs along the Gulf, every step you take is either up or down. There is no easy stride. The numerous spur trails to observation points add uncounted mileage to the hike. And you will want to stop, perhaps to photograph and most definitely to admire the wonders of Gulf Hagas. Be sure you allow yourself ample time.

27

White Cap Mountain

Location: In the wilderness between Brownville and Greenville

Total distance: 5.2 miles or 8 miles (both are return hikes)

Hiking time: 4½ hours or 6 hours

Vertical rise: 2,200 feet

Maps: USGS 7.5' Hay Mountain; USGS 7.5' Big Shanty Mountain; USGS 15' First Roach Pond; USGS 15' Jo-Mary Mountain; MATC map 2 (1993); DeLorme map 42

White Cap is in the Hundred Mile Wilderness of the Appalachian Trail. At 3,644 feet it is the trail's highest point between Katahdin and Bigelow and is the highest peak in the Moosehead Lake region.

This is one of two hikes in the book that describe two trails to the summit (the other is Katahdin, Hike 35). The White Brook Trail (5.2 miles, 4½ hours) is approached from Brownville Junction in central Maine. The West Branch Pond Trail (7.2 miles, 6 hours) begins closer to Greenville in western Maine. Although both trails meet on top of White Cap, their trailheads are half a day's drive apart. Not only can White Cap be climbed on a trip with Hikes 25 and 26, but it can also be climbed in a unit with Hikes 28 through 31 if you are spending time in the Moosehead Lake area.

I. WHITE BROOK TRAIL

How to Get There

Drive on ME 11 to a point 4 miles north of Brownville Junction. The sign KATAHDIN IRON WORKS indicates the 6.5-mile gravel road to the remains of the ironworks, which you take. (For a description of the ironworks, see Hike 26, Gulf Hagas.)

After you register with the caretaker and pay a day-use fee, you are provided with a Diamond Company map and admitted through the gate and across the bridge over the West Branch of the Pleasant River. Beyond the bridge, take the right fork, cross a smaller bridge, and pass Silver Lake on your right. Pass a right turn 2.3 miles from

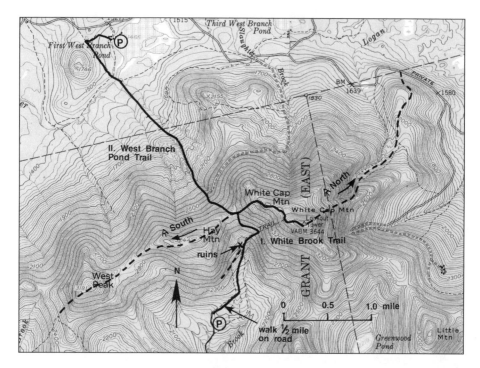

the gate at Katahdin Iron Works. At 3.5 miles, bear right at a fork, and at 5.9 miles cross High Bridge over White Brook. At 6.1 miles pass a left turn to Gulf Hagas and the Hermitage, and at 7.3 miles take the left fork. The last leg is rough going, and you may need to park and walk if your car hasn't enough clearance. The road is firm on a gravel base, so there is no danger of becoming stuck; however, rocks or washouts may be a problem. At 9.6 miles the road crosses through a gravel pit, and at 9.9 miles a series of gullies will put a stop to your progress. Park off the road.

The Trail

Begin walking, following blue blazes. In about 0.5 mile, the gravel road ends, and the White Brook Trail continues to your left between two cairns at a trail sign. From here it is 2 miles to the summit of White Cap. You hike through a cutover area giving good open views. The young second growth offers prime moose habitat, verified by copious moose sign. Remnants of telephone wire along the trail show the former use of White Cap as a fire-tower peak. The trail soon leaves the cutover area and rises more steeply through spruce and fir. Half a mile from where you left the gravel road, the trail crosses the headwaters of White Brook in a beautiful glen where cascades keep the rocks wet, so be careful when crossing. Uphill from the brook, you reach a trail junction and the ruins of the former fire warden's cabin. Take the trail that goes straight ahead. You are climbing through spruce and fir about 50 years old, but notice the size of some of the stumps of trees that were logged. Some stumps are 10 times the size of the present growth!

Half a mile up from the cabin ruins, you crest the ridge between White Cap and Hay Mountains at a junction with the

---

White Cap Mountain

The misty summit of White Cap Mountain

Appalachian Trail (AT). To your left is Hay Mountain with Gulf Hagas beyond. Turn right, following the white-blazed AT for 1.1 miles to White Cap's summit. (Refer to the second hike description of White Cap for a summary of views from the summit.) To return to your car, hike the same trail in reverse.

II. WEST BRANCH POND TRAIL

How to Get There

The western route to White Cap is approached from Greenville, on ME 15 at the southern tip of Moosehead Lake. From the blinking light in town, drive 17.8 miles north on Lily Bay Road (also known as Ripogenus Road) to a dirt road 1 mile south of Kokadjo. (You will pass Lily Bay State Park.) The dirt road is Frenchtown or First Roach Pond Road and is marked with a sign to the West Branch Pond Camps. Turn right and drive carefully 10 miles to West Branch Pond Camps, passing many campsites along the shore of First Roach Pond. The Stirlings, who own and run the camps, can confirm road conditions. Looking southeast over First West Branch Pond, you can see your destination: White Cap is the highest peak. To its right are Hay Mountain, West Peak, and Gulf Hagas Mountain on the Appalachian Trail, none of which is on this trail to White Cap. Parallel marks evident on the mountainsides are burns and skid roads, the results of logging operations.

From the West Branch Pond Camps driveway, continue driving east on Roach Pond Road, which now becomes B Pond Road. At 0.8 mile from the camps, fork right, passing Second West Branch Pond on your left. At 1.4 miles, fork left (actually, it's the fork straight ahead) onto a smaller road, still

B Pond Road. At 2.4 miles, fork right and drive (or walk) 1 more mile to a washed-out bridge over Logan Brook. Park at the brook.

The Trail

Cross the brook on rocks and keep walking down the road. The Appalachian Trail crosses this road 0.5 mile beyond the washed-out bridge. Turn right onto the AT and follow white blazes 3.1 miles to the top. (Logan Brook Lean-to and Falls are 1.7 miles up the trail, 1.4 miles from the top.)

The trail runs along White Cap's ridge, dipping into a sag and back uphill through blueberries, bunchberry, Labrador tea, pale sheep laurel, and low scrub spruce. Mountain cranberry creeps over the summit rocks.

The tower is no longer standing on the slate and schist summit. Views from the summit are thrilling. You must walk a circuit of the summit to get the views in all directions. The north ledges are best for views. To the north lie First, Second, and Third West Branch Ponds with Second and Third Roach Ponds behind. To the northeast, look over Big and Little Boardman Mountains to Katahdin (Hike 35). In the east, the highest mountain is Jo-Mary Mountain, standing big and round behind B Pond. Behind Jo-Mary, the AT runs through the famous lake country and then turns north to Katahdin. Southeast lies large, long Saddleback Mountain (Hike 10). Look south over Big Spruce Mountain to Chairback and Columbus Mountains, eastern peaks of the Barren-Chairback Range. From Chairback to the right are Columbus, Third, Fourth, and Barren (Hike 25) Mountains. Long Pond lies in front of Barren. To the west is Hay Mountain with Baker Mountain behind. Northwest are Number Four Mountain (Hike 33) and First Roach Pond, beyond which are Little Spencer Mountain (Hike 32), shaped like a whale, and Big Spencer Mountain (Hike 31), shaped like a box.

Return by the same trails to the West Branch Pond Camps. If you have made a supper reservation, a pleasant evening awaits you in the dining cabin. I once spent a lovely summer evening at supper here. A storm gathered, darkening the sky and shrouding mist over White Cap and its nearly identical but smaller unnamed companion pinnacle. Fish were rising to flies on First West Branch Pond, surrounded by blue flag iris in luxuriant bloom around the shore. A few raindrops began to fall, gathering to a brief but thorough summer shower and then tapering to clearing before the meal was over. The evening air was sweet and fresh after the rain.

28

Big Moose

Location: On Moosehead Lake in Greenville

Total distance: 7 miles (a return hike)

Hiking time: 4 hours

Vertical rise: 2,000 feet

Maps: USGS 7.5' Big Squaw Pond; USGS 15' Greenville; DeLorme map 41

Big Moose Mountain, formerly known as Big Squaw, rises majestically over Moosehead Lake northwest of Greenville. It offers an aerial view of the lake from its summit, where the abandoned fire tower stands on the site of the first fire lookout in the nation, established in 1905. The mountain was originally named for Maquaso, wife of the legendary Chief Kineo, who left him because of his wickedness and died on the mountain. Moose Mountain Ski Area, now owned by the state of Maine, is on the east side of the mountain, but none of it can be seen from the summit or the hiking trail.

How to Get There

Drive 5.2 miles northwest from Greenville on ME 6/ME 15. Just before the road crosses Moose Brook, a sign on your right marks the Maine Forest Service Moose Brook Campsite, which is open to the public. Immediately after the highway crosses the brook, turn left at a sign onto a Scott Paper Company gravel road. One mile down this road is a turnaround space on your left for parking.

The Trail

Across from the parking space, your pathway (an old woods road) enters the woods to the southwest. There are no blazes, but the trail is worn and wide, rising only gradually. In July, near the beginning where the trail may be wet, blue flag iris grow among grasses in the center of the trail. Other summer flora are buttercups, cinquefoil, hawk-

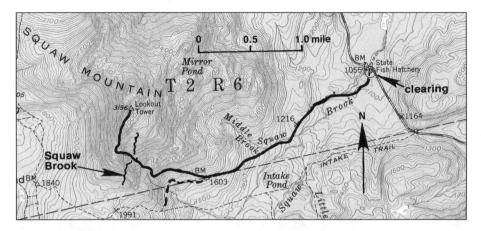

weed, meadow rue, self heal, wood sorrel, marsh fern, spinulose wood fern, and sensitive fern. Fauna on this trail are also abundant: families of partridge, red squirrels, songbirds, and tracks of moose. The first half of the trail runs through mixed hardwoods, mostly beech and maple. When the trees become taller and the woods more open, you will see a stream on your left. The woods road ends as the trail angles left (west), crosses the stream, and heads uphill. As you rise higher, more birch and spruce appear among the maples, until soon the predominant growth is spruce, birch, and balsam fir.

At 2.5 miles you reach the empty warden's cabin, its dooryard filled with New York fern and long beech fern. One hundred yards farther, you cross Moose Brook and climb steep, set-in stone steps, following the brook a short distance. The trail soon leaves the brook, swings north and then northeast, ascending more gently the last 0.5 mile to the summit through mature spruce and a forest floor of wildflowers. Note that the vegetation on top of the mountain, which has a shorter growing season, can be very different in timing from vegetation at the lower reaches. While summer flowers are in full

bloom below, spring flowers such as Canada mayflower, trillium, and clintonia lily may still bloom at higher elevations. Later, fall flowers such as asters will bloom earlier above, while summer flowers are completing their longer cycle below.

The trail follows the exposed spine of the ridge the last few yards to the 3,196-foot summit. If you explore the summit, you might find garnets or black tourmalines. The west side of Big Moose has large sheet deposits of mica.

The views from Big Moose are famous for their variety. Spreading north and east are the hundreds of bays of Moosehead Lake, the largest lake east of the Mississippi within the boundary of one state. In Moosehead to the north, Mount Kineo (Hike 29) rises on a peninsula, and to the northeast you can see Big Spencer (Hike 31) and Katahdin (Hike 35). To the east White Cap (Hike 27) and the Gulf Hagas Mountains form a citadel. Little Moose Mountain stands close to the south. Southwest rise the horned peaks of Bigelow (Hike 12), and west is Coburn's gumdrop shape. Northwest beyond Moose's ridge lies Brassua Lake and, behind it, Boundary Bald (Hike 22).

Big Moose Mountain as seen across Moosehead Lake from Little Spencer

From the tower a short trail leads north, past a large clump of Labrador tea on your right, to a ledge with a view over Mirror Pond, a tarn high on the northeast spur of the mountain. Near the ledge you'll see more Labrador tea, whose clustered white flowers bloom in June and early July. The small, green oval leaves with brown fuzz underneath can be picked, dried, and used for tea. In large enough quantities the tea is a laxative.

Return to the fire tower, where you retrace the trail past the warden's camp and down to your car.

At the time of this writing, new trails were being developed on and around Little Moose Mountain, just south of Big Moose Mountain. Little Moose is now a state recreation area owned by the Bureau of Public Lands. You might want to investigate these new hikes.

29

Mount Kineo

Location: In Moosehead Lake near Rockwood

Total distance: 4 miles (a circuit hike)

Hiking time: 2½ hours

Vertical rise: 800 feet

Maps: USGS 7.5' Brassua Lake East; USGS 15' Moosehead Lake; USGS 15' Brassua Lake; DeLorme map 41

Mount Kineo is a cliffhanger of a hike up a mountain in the middle of Moosehead Lake. It stands on a peninsula that is almost an island, projecting from Moosehead's eastern shore across North Bay to within 1 mile of the western shore at Rockwood. Views from the restored Maine Forest Service tower on the summit sweep all of Moosehead Lake, the largest lake within the boundary of a single state east of the Mississippi. There are no public roads to Mount Kineo; the only approach is from the water. If you do not have your own canoe, you can rent one from any of several places in Rockwood.

How to Get There

Rockwood is 30 miles east of Jackman and 20 miles northwest of Greenville on ME 6/ME 15. In Rockwood, turn north off ME 6/ME 15 on the only road that turns north down to the lakeshore and Rockwood Village. This road passes Whitten's Store, where you can rent a canoe, and the post office. From the post office, turn onto a dirt road and drive a few yards to the public boat launch on the lake. A parking fee is sometimes charged.

The canoe trip should be made only in good weather; a gale on a lake as large as Moosehead can resemble a storm at sea. Paddle northeast toward Mount Kineo. You can beach and leave your craft anywhere along Kineo's south shore and intersect the shore path as it skirts Kineo. However, the hiking mileage will start at the dock at Kineo Cove, which you reach by skirting the shore around to your right and entering the cove by the Mount Kineo Hotel. From the cove you can see the sheer east face, below which is the deepest place in all of Moosehead Lake, the 250-foot Kineo Deep Hole.

The Trail

From the Kineo Cove dock, walk the dirt road past the eastern edge of the golf course, staying left at any forks and passing open fields that used to be sheep pastures, until you reach the path at the water's edge on the south shore. Walk the shore path westward through alder and birch, under towering cliffs of Kineo flint and past the remains of an avalanche, to the southwest point of land, 0.6 mile from the dock. Here you leave the lake. There is no water on the mountain, except an intermittent spring near the top.

The Indian Trail leaves to your right, straight uphill northeast into a grove of red pine. There is no sign, but the trail is worn, and there are occasional blue blazes. Ascend stratified layers of sandstone, shale, and quartzite almost like steps. When you reach the top of the first cliff, you pass a side trail that leads back toward the hotel. In spite of all the cliff-climbing, no handholds are necessary on this hike. You walk above the avalanche remains that you saw from below, along bearberry-covered cliffs, and then ascend into woods of red oak and maple.

When you come back out onto ledges again, views are southeast to the hotel, golf course, and fields where sheep once grazed. This southeast end of Kineo is volcanic Kineo rhyolite. The mountain was formed from a contact of volcanic rhyolite and sandstone, shale, and quartzite. The trail alternates between sheer cliffs and woods. The last time you leave the open cliffs, at 0.9 mile, notice a trail that drops into the woods on your left as you enter the woods. There is no sign. This will be your return circuit; it is the Bridle Trail.

After passing the Bridle Trail on your left, you ascend to the top of a rise and descend into a small valley of spinulose wood fern, bracken fern, Canada mayflower, bunchberry, and wood sorrel. The change from cliffs to woods is extreme. Suddenly you could be in the middle of the Maine woods instead of in the middle of a lake.

Ascend gradually northeast to a fork in the trail. (To your right the trail runs a few yards to the former fire warden's tiny, decrepit emergency shelter.) Bear left and walk a few yards to the tower on the wooded 1,789-foot summit. The tower, restored in 1993, offers spectacular views in all directions.

Look south over Moosehead Lake to Big Moose (Hike 28), southwest to Long Pond, closer southwest over the shoulder of Kineo to Blue Ridge, the only sharp hill across the lake in Rockwood, and beyond to the right to Coburn Mountain. To the west, the Moose River flows east out of Brassua Lake, past Rockwood, and into Moosehead Lake. To the northwest, Boundary Bald Mountain (Hike 22) rises above Jackman only 8 miles from the Quebec border. To the north, Moosehead ends in Seboomook Cove and northeast at Northeast Carry. Look east-northeast over Little Kineo Mountain to Lobster Mountain, and east over Little Spencer (Hike 32), shaped like an inverted kettle, to Big Spencer Mountain (Hike 31). Southeast beyond Cowan Cove is Spencer Bay, backed by Number Four Mountain (Hike 33) and the Lily Bay Mountains.

From the tower you can trace the entire Moosehead Lake traverse made by Henry David Thoreau on July 25, 1857, detailed in *The Maine Woods*. Starting in Greenville near Big Moose Mountain, Thoreau and his Native American guide paddled 40 miles across the lake in a 16-foot birch-bark canoe with about 1 foot of freeboard (clearance above water). It took them 8 hours to paddle the 20 miles to Kineo, a trip that takes most people two days. They stopped overnight, climbed Mount Kineo, and continued from there 20 more miles to Northeast Carry.

You are also looking at most of the watershed of the upper Kennebec River. Another interesting feature is the route taken by the quaternary (the most recent) glacier through this area. Blue Ridge to the southwest and Little Kineo Mountain to the northeast are in perfect alignment, with Kineo at the center. These three mountains form one straight ridge. All are smooth-sloped on their northwest faces, the side from which the glacier approached and pushed against the long ridge. Correspondingly, all three have a vertical southeast face that resulted from the back-eddying (known as plucking or quarrying) of the glacier as it tumbled over the peak. Thoreau described the east face of Kineo on an earlier trip in 1853: "The celebrated precipice is so high and perpendicular that you can jump from the top, many hundred feet, into the water. . . . Probably it will be discovered that some Indian maiden jumped off it for love once, for true love never could have found a path more to its mind."

Native American lore is rich with legends concerning Mount Kineo. The mountain was named for Chief Kineo, a wicked Native American leader who was exiled by his tribe and lived on the mountain. One legend claims that the mountain is the petrified body of a moose killed by Glooskap, from Native American mythology. The word in Abnaki means "sharp peak."

Leave the tower and retrace 0.3 mile of the trail. Just before the trail emerges onto

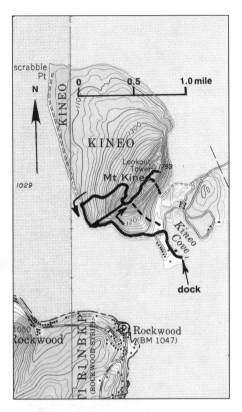

the first open ledges, the Bridle Trail (no sign) drops into the woods away from the cliffs, first through spruce and fir, and then through maple, white and yellow birch, Canada mayflower, clintonia lily, rosy twisted-stalk, club moss, purple wake-robin, wild sarsaparilla, and white aster. The trail descends to the former fire warden's cabin on the lakeshore, turns left behind the cabin, and runs out onto the shore path. From here, follow the shore path south back toward the hotel. In 0.3 mile you pass on your left the Indian Trail, which you climbed up the mountain. From here it is 0.6 mile back to the hotel.

(The shore path extends north beyond the fire warden's cabin just over 1 mile to Hardscrabble Point, where there is a state-authorized campsite.)

A view of Moosehead Lake from the cliffs of the Indian Trail

Kineo has long held two positions: summer tourist haven and overseer of logging operations. Kineo has stood watch over two centuries of logging and log driving. Logging hit its record high in the 1890s and ended with the Last Log Drive in the summer of 1976, when log driving by water was declared illegal.

As a tourist center, Kineo was visited in the 19th century by summer people who came with steamer trunks and horses to the two or three hotels and often stayed for two months. They arrived by the Somerset Railway from Bingham, or by buckboard, and finally by lake steamer. The *Katahdin* is the last of these steamers, later used by the Scott Paper Company to tow logs, and it is now a pleasure cruise boat. The hotels often burned down and were rebuilt. From 1900 into the 1920s, Kineo was in its heyday of summer activity, complete with fishing guides, boating, golf, and elegant hotels. Recent years have seen changes. In the 1960s Kineo became a private club with 48 lots and owners. Before many of the plans to build had materialized, the 1973 energy crisis ended the endeavor to develop Kineo, and the future of the peninsula has been in limbo ever since.

30

Green Mountain

Location: Deep in the north woods near Quebec province, 20 miles north of Moosehead Lake

Total distance: 3 miles (a return hike)

Hiking time: 1½ hours

Vertical rise: 600 feet

Maps: USGS 7.5' Foley Pond; USGS 15' Penobscot Lake; North Maine Woods Map; DeLorme map 48

Green Mountain, northwest of Moosehead Lake and near the Canadian border, is appropriately named. It is forested with large, old hardwoods, predominantly rock (sugar) maple. Except during the fall blaze of color, the trail is canopied with lovely green leaves of tall maples. This hike is especially beautiful in spring, around Memorial Day, when the entire trail is carpeted with wildflowers. Mr. Ray Hearn, former fire warden, for many years kept the trail immaculately groomed. The hike is a walk through an enchanted forest, to a tower that affords exceptional views.

How to Get There

The mountain is far in the north woods of Somerset County on (Bowater) Great Northern Paper Company land northwest of Pittston Farm. Your car should be dependable with an odometer that works. Starting on ME 6/ME 15 at Rockwood (30 miles east of Jackman and 20 miles northwest of Greenville), cross the Moose River bridge and fork right onto the Great Northern dirt road that leads 20 miles north to Pittston Farm at the west end of Seboomook Lake. You must register at a gate shortly before arriving at Pittston Farm. Pass Pittston Farm and stop at the Maine Forest Service (MFS) ranger station just beyond it on your left. Here you can obtain the "Sportsman's Map of the North Maine Woods" and confirm the directions to Green Mountain. Paper company roads are always changing—new roads are built, and old roads are discontinued—sometimes confusing travelers. (See the

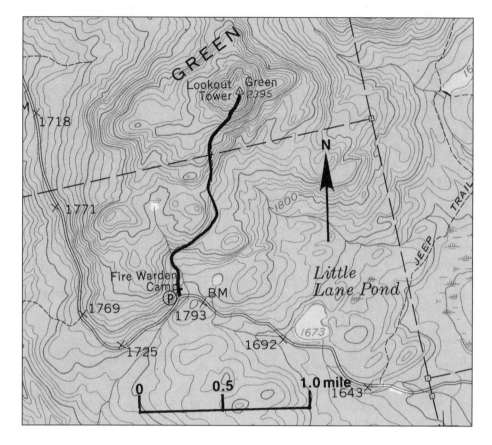

Aroostook County introduction, page 204, for more information on the North Maine Woods.) You should carry water on this hike.

From the MFS station, drive 0.2 mile and bear right at the fork. At 1.6 miles, pass the MFS Lane Brook Campsite on your left; at 1.9 miles fork left; at 4.3 miles fork right; at 5.8 miles fork right; and at 6.4 miles fork left. At 8.7 miles, you will see a sign at the Green Mountain trailhead, which begins by the driveway to the former ranger's cabin site. Park off the road.

The Trail

Walk to the cabin site. In the former cabin dooryard and driveway in May you can see Dutchman's-breeches, a rare wildflower that blooms in abundance here. Yellow, blue, and white violets carpet the ground in June.

The trail turns left behind the cabin site and heads generally north for 1.5 miles to the summit tower. Beginning in a boggy area, the trail takes you through violets, Canada mayflower, rosy twisted-stalk, clintonia lily, hobblebush, bunchberry, starflower, and trillium. Sugar (rock) maples spread their canopy far above you, inspiring reverence. At a small brook crossing, you can walk 50 feet off the trail to your left to a waterfall. The trail ascends at an easy grade through wood sorrel and Indian cucumber, rosy twisted-stalk, patchwork mosses, and bracken fern. Rosy twisted-stalk is a charming member of the lily family. Its zigzag stem supports alternate pointed leaves, each with a tiny pink, bell-shaped flower hanging under it. Now and then on the trail, outcroppings of pure white milky quartz are visible, and occasionally you can see a clump of Indian pipe. The last 0.5 mile is steeper as you mount the wooded summit to the 60-foot steel tower. You will retrace this trail to return to your car.

The summit tower offers views of the northwestern Maine wilderness to Mount Katahdin 58 miles east, and over pastoral Quebec with its farms and villages. Far to the north-northeast looms the conical peak of Allagash Mountain on Allagash Lake. Northeast beyond the North Branch of the Penobscot lie the five St. John ponds. Look east over Lane Pond to Foley Pond and Mount Katahdin on the horizon, and southeast to Seboomook Lake and beyond to Big Spencer Mountain on the left (Hike 31) and Big Moose on the right (Hike 28). To the south-southeast, Ironbound Mountain rises behind Canada Falls Lake and in front of Brassua Lake. Look south over the South Branch of the Penobscot to Long Pond and south-southwest to Boundary Bald Mountain (Hike 22), beyond which Sugarloaf (Hike 48) and Bigelow (Hike 12) can be seen 70 miles away. South is Coburn Mountain. Look west over Long Pond and Penobscot Lake into Canada. To the northwest, it is 26 miles to Canada, where clear-cutting on the Canadian side defines quite visibly the international border. You can see 30 miles to the farmland, villages, and Catholic church spires of Quebec.

While you are in the area, there are some interesting side trips you may want to take. The ranger at the MFS station on the access road can direct you to Little Russell Mountain, a tedious but beautiful drive north up Caucomgomac Road, for a 3-mile hike to and from an old fire tower. This trail is just over 1.2 miles beyond Lost Pond Campsite,

a beautiful place to camp by a fly-fishing-only pond. The walk-in campsite is 0.2 mile off the road.

Directly south of Little Russell Mountain is the town of Seboomook, located between the east end of Seboomook Lake and the Northwest Carry of Moosehead Lake. Today Seboomook amounts to some private camps, a campground, and a store, but at one time it had a large tourist hotel, the Seboomook House. During World War II, from 1944 to 1946, Seboomook also was the site of a prisoner-of-war camp for 250 German soldiers captured in Africa. At the store you can see photographs of the camp, its three sentry towers, barracks, mess hall, cell block, infirmary, icehouse, ration building, staff house, PX, and recreation building. Now only the foundations and the chimney of the mess hall remain. Using horses, the prisoners cut and drove softwood into Seboomook Lake, through the dam, into the West Branch of the Penobscot, past Lobster Lake, and into Chesuncook Lake. They worked hard, were paid, and were treated well. After they were returned to Germany, some of them came back to work for Great Northern, and today many still return with their families to camp at Seboomook.

Pittston Farm, directly on your way back to Rockwood from Green Mountain, is also worth a stop. It is located at the head of Seboomook Lake (west end), where the North and South Forks come together to form the West Branch of the Penobscot River. Its history begins with the clearing of roads through the wilderness in the 1830s for the passage of troops to the Canadian border. Here the "Old Canada Tote Road" crossed the South Branch of the Penobscot at the site of Pittston Farm, but it was never used for military purposes. In the 1850s woodsmen and river drivers used a log cabin built here by a man named Knight.

Former ranger Ray Hearn sharpening a scythe, in the days when he groomed the Green Mountain Trail

In 1900 more land was cleared, and five or six more log buildings were built. In 1906 Great Northern bought this area, known as Pittston Township, from the owners, the Holyoke family of Brewer, Maine, and the 100-acre farm became headquarters for cutting operations on the North and South Branches of the Penobscot.

From 1908 to 1913 the farm took on its appearance of today. Buildings were frame construction on concrete or masonry foundations and housed workers, executives, and guests of Great Northern. There were stables, a blacksmith shop, a wagon shed, a storehouse, a boardinghouse, an icehouse, barns, waterworks, a potato house, an office, a henhouse, a cannery, and a slaughterhouse. In 1913 the construction of Seboomook Dam (rebuilt in the winter of 1926–27) flooded the lower land, destroying the original log buildings. From 1914 to the late 1950s, Pittston Farm also served as the central telephone switchboard in the area, linking remote areas of Maine with the telephone and telegraph system of the rest of the country.

From the early 20th century to the late 1930s, men stayed at the farm, going to and coming from woods operations and river drives. Enough produce was raised to supply all operations in the area. Pittston Farm was no longer an isolated frontier stopover for woodsmen as in the 19th century, but as comfortable as a resort. Running water, electricity, steam heat, telephones, daily mail service, white paint, bedsheets, and a lounge equipped with magazines and newspapers, playing cards, stationery, and a Victrola were among its comforts. Woodsmen and laborers slept in the third-floor "ram's pastures" of the two lodges, while superintendents, paymasters, clerks, and visitors—tourists, hunters, and fishermen—occupied the second-story rooms.

Truck transportation and bulldozed roads brought about the decline of Pittston Farm's importance, and farming was discontinued. When river driving ended in 1976, Pittston Farm was shut down. Today some of the buildings are gone, but most remain, maintained by the (Bowater) Great Northern Paper Company and used occasionally for special purposes. All summer long, the farm bustles with Boy Scouts from all over the United States. Since 1973, it has been the Seboomook Base, center for the Maine National High Adventure Program, Boy Scouts of America. The old potato barn now houses canoes and other equipment, gear and trail food, a trading post, and an exhibit of old tools. Staff and Scouts live in tents in the fields and woods.

Pittston Farm now offers overnight accommodations and delicious home cooking. Visitors are always welcome. A stop can give you an interesting perspective on history and geography in the area of Green Mountain.

31

Big Spencer

Location: Northeast of Moosehead Lake

Total distance: 4 miles (a return hike)

Hiking time: 2 hours

Vertical rise: 2,000 feet

Maps: USGS 7.5' Big Spencer Mountain; USGS 15' Ragged Lake; DeLorme maps 41, 49

Big Spencer and its close neighbor Little Spencer rise high over wild lake country in western Piscataquis County. The tower offers the best views of Maine's big lakes west of Katahdin and south of the Allagash. You can see the whole 40-mile length of Moosehead and the 30-mile length of Chesuncook Lake. Many of Maine's highest mountains ring the horizon.

How to Get There

From the blinking light in downtown Greenville, at the southern tip of Moosehead, leave ME 6/ME 15 and drive north on Lily Bay Road (also known as Ripogenus Road) 19 miles to Kokadjo. Bear left at the fork 0.2 mile beyond Kokadjo, and 5 miles beyond Kokadjo check in at the Siras Gate of the Great Northern Company. In another 3.2 miles (2 miles southwest of Grant Farm), turn left (northwest) on a side road just after the Maine Forest Service (MFS) Bear Brook Campsite. Driving from Kokadjo, you can see the 2-mile ridge of Big Spencer on your left, stretching northeast to southwest. After the turn at the Bear Brook Campsite, drive 6 miles, forking right at 1.4 miles and left at 2.5 miles. At 6.1 miles, the trail (a woods road) takes off left (south). Park at the trailhead.

The Trail

The first 0.5 mile rises gently through spruce, birch, beech, and maple. The unused road offers sign of moose and deer. (At 0.4 mile, a trail comes in from your left and joins the trail to Big Spencer.) Keep walking uphill, more steeply now, through

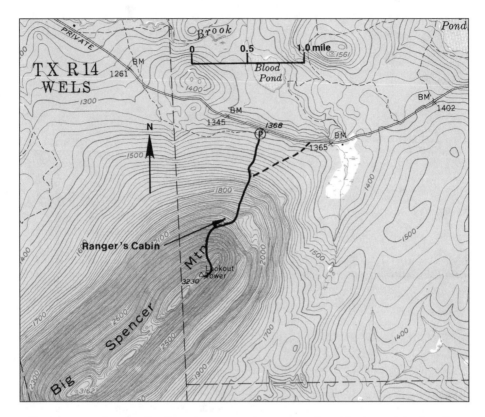

trillium, rosy twisted-stalk, Canada may-flower, and wood sorrel. The trail abounds with Indian cucumber, a single-stemmed plant 1 to 3 feet tall with a small circlet of three to four leaves at the top and a larger rosette of six to ten pointed oval leaves mid-way down the stem. At the top, tiny green-ish yellow flowers dangle in spring, maturing to dark blue berries in fall when the upper leaves are tinged with red. The root of Indian cucumber is an edible tuber with a sweet, succulent, earthy taste resem-bling that of a cucumber. The root cannot be pulled up by the stem; it must be dug with fingers.

The trail rises through mixed hardwoods with many striped maples, passes the fire warden's cabin, levels out in open spruce-birch woods, and crosses a brook into the forest ranger's cabin site at 1.3 miles. From the cabin, views north and east are splen-did. Look north over Blood Pond to Blackcap Mountain, east to Ragged Lake, and beyond to Caribou Lake, which opens into Chesuncook Lake. East behind the lake stands Katahdin (Hike 35), showing you its Hunt Spur where the Appalachian Trail as-cends to the Tableland and Baxter Peak. You can also see the many slides on Mount O–J–I (Hike 39) left of Katahdin with the cap of Mount Coe behind it. The tallest mountain behind O–J–I is North Brother (Hike 40), and the low mountain in the midground is Sentinel (Hike 38). The left-most of the big Baxter Park mountains are Doubletop (Hike 41) in front and The Traveler (Hike 44) behind. To the northwest is Lobster Lake.

The view to Big Spencer from Lazy Tom Bog

South behind the cabin, the summit looks like the volcano it was 400 million years ago, now eroded down to the mere roots of its former hulk. The trail is unblazed but easy to follow. Leave from behind the cabin, crossing an icy spring-fed brook, and begin the steep and rocky 0.7-mile ascent. The trail curves southwest and south, rising through some large red spruce, balsam fir, mountain ash, blueberries, mountain cranberries, and lots of large boulders. Ladders are placed helpfully at various spots. Near the top, you ascend several ladders through dwarfed red spruce, Labrador tea, and sheep laurel to the rocky open northeast summit, 3,230 feet in elevation and composed of volcanic rhyolite. (From cabin to tower you gain 1,000 vertical feet in 0.7 mile.)

The tower, erected in 1917, was last operated by MFS watchman John Boydston, who served for many years. Views sweep over vast lake country, northeast over Ragged Lake, past Sentinel Mountain to Katahdin, and east-southeast over Farrar Mountain to Jo-Mary Mountain. Southeast behind Shaw Mountain is White Cap (Hike 27) and to its right are Hay, West Peak, and Gulf Hagas Mountains. South beyond First Roach Pond is Number Four Mountain, and beyond, Lily Bay Mountain and Baker Mountain. To the south is Greenville on Moosehead Lake, where you can see ski slopes on Big Moose (Hike 28). Southwest rises Little Spencer Mountain (Hike 32) close by, and Mount Kineo (Hike 29) beyond. Past Kineo you can see the thin line of Brassua Lake. West-southwest beyond Kidney Pond lies Moosehead Lake, and behind it rises Boundary Bald Mountain (Hike 22) on the Canadian border. Northwest is Lobster Lake, and north are Blood Pond, Blackcap Mountain, and Ragged, Caribou, and Chesuncook Lakes.

Take the same trail back to the cabin and trailhead. It is much easier going down!

32

Little Spencer

Location: Northeast of Moosehead Lake

Total distance: 2.5 miles (a return hike)

Hiking time: 4 hours

Vertical rise: 1,760 feet

Maps: USGS 7.5' Lobster Mountain; DeLorme maps 41, 49

Little Spencer is almost as tall as its big sister, Big Spencer, and the hike is much more challenging and strenuous. It becomes very exciting when you have to pull on ropes someone has provided in order to climb through a formation that resembles a chimney.

How to Get There

Drive to the town of Greenville at the south end of Moosehead Lake, and take Lily Bay Road (also known as Ripogenus Road) north along the east shore of Moosehead for 19 miles to Kokadjo, a small sporting village at the west end of First Roach Pond. From Kokadjo, drive north, bearing left outside of town where the road turns to dirt. At 1.5 miles from the store in Kokadjo, bear left at an intersection (the right takes you to Baxter State Park). Stay straight after that, crossing a bridge over Lazy Tom Stream at 1.9 miles. Both the stream to your left and Lazy Tom Bog to your right are excellent places to sight moose. As you look to your right over Lazy Tom Bog, you will see Big Spencer (Hike 31), long and rectangular, and Little Spencer to its left.

At 3.4 miles stay straight, and at 8.8 miles you will come to a big intersection with a sign to your right to the Spencer Pond Camps. Turn right here, and you will see Little Spencer ahead of you as you drive. At 10.2 miles, bear left at a fork and begin looking for a trail sign on your right. At 10.9 miles, a sign on a tree in the woods to your right shows the trailhead. Park off the road just beyond the trail sign.

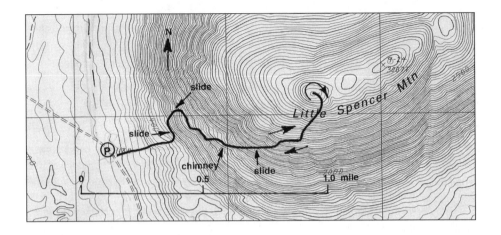

The Trail

Your pathway follows orange flagging through mixed hardwoods—maple, beech, viburnum shrubs—with occasional views of the sheer ledges above you. A few blowdowns add to the exertion of the trail, but "you ain't seen nothin' yet." The trail steepens into tall white pines and trends to the left (north) before swinging back south and east. You climb past boulders covered with rock fern (polypody) and moss with wood fern at the base.

The first views, behind you to the west, are of Spencer Pond. An occasional vole in the blowdowns or a hawk in a pine makes the trail interesting. The trail rises through a stand of white (paper) birch to the first of three rockslides, in this case a stationary slide of boulders. Follow red paint blazes and ribbons as the trail levels off momentarily, skirting the west shoulder of the mountain. Bird sightings in this area include broad-winged hawk, spruce grouse, chickadee, and hairy woodpecker.

After a steeper climb with occasional scrambling, you will reach the second slide—loose scree. Stay to the left of the slide through raspberries and cedar—the scrub variety and beautiful big cedars, as well.

Halfway up the trail you reach the chimney, a narrow vertical crack in the rock that is a strenuous pull-through. Nylon ropes have been attached to help the climber. This is no place for small children or dogs. From the top of the chimney, the view south shows the massive flanks of Big Moose Mountain (Hike 28) across Spencer Bay of Moosehead, behind nearby Spencer Pond.

At the third slide, stay left again, as the trail steepens and handholds are necessary. The next ledges offer views to the south. The trail ascends at a more moderate grade from here, but still with a few handholds necessary. You enter a forest of dead spruce and fir with a young spruce-fir forest growing up at its feet. Perhaps these dead trees are casualties of spruce budworm disease, which cycles every 30 years; its last peak was in the late 1970s.

Continue at an easy grade through blueberry, bunchberry, and moose droppings to the 3,040-foot summit, which is wooded and marked with a cairn of rocks. Better views are a few yards before or after the summit. From the outlook before the summit, the view southwest is the wide expanse of Moosehead with Sugar Island and Big Moose (Hike 28). Behind Moose to the left

Climbing the Chimney on Little Spencer

is Moxie Bald Mountain (Hike 19). Moving toward the west down the right flank of Moose, you can see the east outlet of the Kennebec River open into long Indian Pond directly in line from where you stand. To the west is Little Kineo Mountain. To the southeast behind First Roach Pond stands the perfectly shaped Number Four Mountain (Hike 33).

From the outlook a few yards past the summit, you can see Big Spencer (Hike 31) close by to the east. Past it to the left is Black Cap Mountain, and to the north through the trees is Lobster Mountain.

The return is by retracing the same trail down. Take extra care on your descent. Ledges, chimney, and slides are all more dangerous going down. The descent will probably take as long as the ascent. A friend of mine has given this hike a 5-star rating based on its challenge, excitement, and beauty.

33

Number Four Mountain

Location: Near First Roach Pond in Kokadjo, east of Moosehead Lake

Total distance (round trip): 3.5 miles

Hiking time: 3 hours

Vertical rise: 1,430 feet

Maps: USGS 7.5' Number Four Mountain, Kokadjo; DeLorme map 41

Number Four Mountain, named for its location in Township Number Four (now Frenchtown Township), is a picturesque gumdrop behind First Roach Pond when viewed from the town of Kokadjo. It is now in the midst of massive clear-cuts, but with time these will regenerate, making the hike wild again. Even though you are surrounded by cuts, you can see moose while driving to this hike, and there are many broad-winged hawks who appear on call when alerted of your presence on the trail. Views from the tower are the best in the state.

How to Get There

To find the trailhead, start from Kokadjo, 19 miles north of Greenville on the Ripogenous Road, also known as Lily Bay Road. From the store in Kokadjo, backtrack south less than 1 mile to Roach Pond Road on your left. Mileage starts here. At 2.1 miles on the Roach Pond Road, turn right onto a road numbered 9279E, where there is a small sign to Number Four Mountain. The road curves left through a clear-cut (look for moose). At 3.5 miles, turn left onto a smaller road that passes alternating clear-cuts and stands of trees. At 4.3 miles, while in a stand of trees, the road crosses tiny Lagoon Brook on a small bridge. This is the signal that the trail is 0.1 mile ahead on the left. At 4.4 miles, in the woods on your left, look hard for a small red wooden sign and a white metal sign. You can park 50 yards past the trail at a pullout on the right. You are a guest on Plum Creek timberlands.

The Trail

A stone cairn also marks the trailhead. The trail starts level as it parallels a clear-cut to its right. It passes through striped and rock (sugar) maple, ash, and birch, and typical hardwood ground cover of wood fern, oak fern, long beech fern, wild strawberry, and wild geranium. After 0.25 mile, a sign on a tree tells you that Number Four is 2 miles away, but it is really only 1.5 miles from here.

The trail rises gently through bracken fern and mushrooms with toads under them. At 0.5 mile the trail begins a steeper rise. The treetops and trunks are magical in early morning sunlight; it is hard to believe that a forest so enchanting can lie next to a clear-cut. The grade soon becomes very steep and continues so the rest of the way to the top. You are now in a lovely white birch forest with wild sarsaparilla, rosy twisted-stalk, Indian cucumber, clintonia lily, wood sorrel, and white trillium on the forest floor.

At 0.75 mile, the white birch are diluted by yellow (silver) birch, and softwoods which show evidence of spruce budworm infestation. On the forest floor are star flower, bunchberry, lots of wood sorrel *(Oxalis),* wood fern, violets, asters, sphagnum moss, and hobblebush.

At a rest stop we were buzzed by two broad-winged hawks circling in figure eights around each other in a pas-de-deux. At one mile, moose droppings decorate the trail and the spruce-fir forest opens into less dense forest. It soon begins to level out toward the summit, and an open ledge offers a view of First Roach Pond with the tiny village of Kokadjo at its north end. Behind it on the right stands Big Spencer (Hike 31), and on the left is Little Spencer (Hike 32).

From the ledges, the now easy trail takes you past remnants of telephone wire from fire warden days to the tower on the 2,894-foot summit. The tower is in good condition, but the platform on top is very small, has no sides, and is unmaintained. Be careful.

This is my favorite tower in Maine for views. It is also a heartbreaker to see that nearly 100 percent of the surrounding land has been clear-cut in the recent past. Some of it is already in regrowth, however, and with time the area will once again be beautiful.

To the southwest, look across Moosehead and Sugar Island to Big Moose (Hike 28) and Coburn Mountains behind it to the right. To the west, the east outlet of the Kennebec River leaves Moosehead and opens into long Indian Pond. To the northwest, Boundary Bald (Hike 22) lies behind Mount Kineo (Hike 29). To the north, Big and Little Spencer (Hikes 31 and 32) stand behind Kokadjo at the north end of First Roach Pond. To the northeast, the biggest mountain is Mount Katahdin and its companion peaks are other mountains at Baxter State Park (Hikes 34–41). South of Katahdin is the lake country, including Pemadumcook and Jo-Mary Lakes. Look east to big, round Jo-Mary Mountain, and to its right (southeast) to White Cap, Hay, West, and Gulf Hagas Mountains. Southeast the ridge of Number Four runs to its lower summit, and behind is Baker Mountain. To the right (south) of Baker is Lily Bay Mountain. On a clear day, between Lily Bay and Moose mountains, way off in the distance, the four peaks of Bigelow resemble a capital *M* and a small *m.*

From the tower, the trail continues a few more yards south to an overlook of Baker and Lily Bay Mountains, with White Cap on the left. Someone has built a bench for enjoying the view. Your return is by the same trail you came up. It is much faster going down, but as always, take care when hiking downhill.

Sitting on Number Four tower one morning, we had an incredible experience. A few broad-winged hawks began circling us and

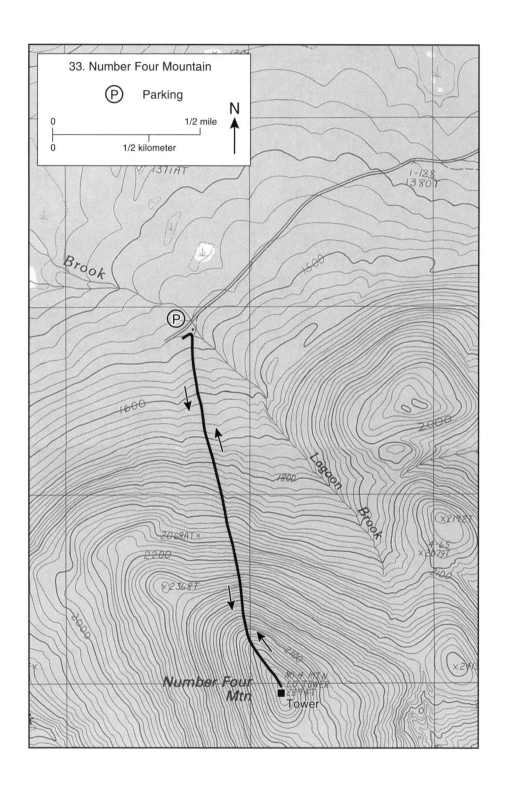

33. Number Four Mountain

Ⓟ Parking

N

0   1/2 mile
0   1/2 kilometer

Brook

Lagoon Brook

Number Four Mtn

Tower

Moose scat, and bunchberry in bloom

one was crying an alarm call. In minutes, nine of the hawks were diving at us, swooping close to our faces. We got the message and obediently climbed down the tower stairs to watch from a lower level. We figured they had been so squeezed for habitat that they were fighting to preserve what little remained. They were certainly organized!

Monson to Moosehead

Baxter State Park—Southern Section

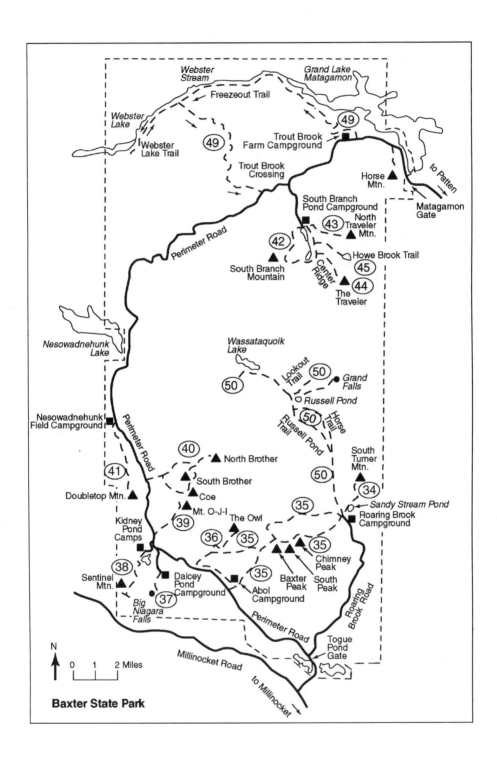

Baxter State Park

Introduction to Baxter State Park

Officially established in 1933, Baxter State Park covers 204,732 acres in north-central Maine. From 1930 to 1962, Percival Baxter, governor of Maine from 1920 to 1925, made gifts of land to the state with the stipulation that the area remain "forever wild." Mile-high Mount Katahdin, a granite monolith and Maine's highest mountain, rises in the southern half of the park, surrounded by the Cross Range and other peaks at the northern end of the 500-million-year-old Appalachian Mountain range. Numerous streams and ponds are scattered at its base. The northern half of Baxter Park features South Branch Pond and The Traveler, a large volcanic mountain with radiating arms like a starfish. Central in the park's interior are Russell Pond and Wassataquoik Lake. Numerous trails crisscross Katahdin, and several longer trails course through the entire park, disclosing many wonders: waterfalls, mountain peaks, trout ponds, wildflowers, and historical sites.

In this guide, Baxter State Park is the location for several day hikes (Hikes 34–45) and two backpacking trips (Hike 49, Webster Brook Trail, and Hike 50, Russell Pond).

Campsites and lean-tos in Baxter State Park are limited in number to control the number of people using the park at one time. Reservations should be made in writing and paid for in advance. It is risky to plan on arriving and finding a vacancy. Write and send fees to Reservation Clerk, Baxter State Park Office, 64 Balsam Drive, Millinocket, ME 04462. Familiarity with park regulations is very important. Among other rules, no pets are admitted, and there is a size limit on vehicles, because of narrow park roads. There is no need for a reservation if you enter the park for day use only. From the Millinocket office you can also purchase an excellent guidebook and a map of the entire park, Stephen Clark's map and his *Guide to Baxter State Park and Katahdin.* Smaller, less detailed maps issued at the park gates are adequate for trails, and USGS maps are especially good for identifications.

Most often used is the southeastern Togue Pond Gate, the access for Hikes 34–41 and 50. The gate is approached from Millinocket, which is reached from the Medway exit of I-95, about 80 miles north of Bangor. The (Bowater) Great Northern Paper Company has a large mill west of the town and another in East Millinocket. Daily tours of the mill are open to the public. Gasoline and groceries should be obtained in Millinocket.

From Millinocket, follow signs north 9 miles to Millinocket Lake, where you will find a small store with a gas pump and telephone, a campground, floatplane service, and a public beach on the lake. From Millinocket Lake it is 6.5 miles to an important fork. The gravel Baxter State Park Road forks right, while the tarred road to your left is a snowmobile trail of ripped tar sure to puncture tires. Take the right fork and drive 1.5 miles to the Baxter State Park Visitor Center and, just beyond it, the Togue Pond Gate into Baxter Park.

The Matagamon Gate is the northeast entrance of the park (access to Hikes 42–45 and 49), approached from the town of Patten. Drive I-95 about 90 miles north of Bangor to the Sherman exit. Follow ME 159/ME 11 through Sherman to Patten, a farming community in the potato belt of northern Penobscot County. Gasoline and groceries should be obtained here and, if time permits, a visit to the Lumberman's Museum north of town is exciting and educational. It has interesting displays of equipment, including an old Lombard Steam Tractor, models of old lumber camps showing how lumbermen and log drivers lived, and a complete sawmill.

From Patten, drive ME 159 northwest 10 miles to Shin Pond, where you will see a small store and floatplane service. Beyond, follow Grand Lake Road, named for Grand Lake Matagamon. You cross the Seboeis River 16 miles from Patten and the East Branch of the Penobscot in 26 miles, where you'll see a small store with a gas pump and campground. The Matagamon Gate to Baxter State Park is 1 mile farther.

Once in the park, you will follow Baxter State Park Road (also called Park Tote Road), which makes a three-quarter circle through the park. A section of Baxter State Park Road still bears its original name, Nesowadnehunk Tote Road. It is a narrow gravel woods road offering few views.

Baxter is open for general use from May 15 to October 15 each year, and from October 15 to December 1 and April 1 to May 15 for day use only. Permits may be necessary to hike in Baxter at times other than during the main May-to-October season. Contact Baxter State Park authorities before planning an off-season trip.

Winter use of the park for cross-country skiing and backpacking is becoming increasingly popular. Maintaining close contact with authorities and following the stringent winter regulations are necessary to ensure a safe adventure. Budget plenty of time, and be sure to include someone with winter camping experience on a trip of this nature.

34

South Turner Mountain

Location: In the shadow of Katahdin

Total distance: 4 miles (a return hike)

Hiking time: 3½ hours

Vertical rise: 1,630 feet

Maps: USGS 7.5' Katahdin Lake; USGS 15' Katahdin; Baxter Park Map; DeLorme map 51

The writers of the *Guide to the Appalachian Trail in Maine* suggest that the panoramic view from the top of South Turner ranks second only to that of Katahdin, and I am hard put to argue with them. Turner is an unusual gem of a mountain, affording a nearly perfect vista of the eastern portion of Baxter State Park. South Turner will also treat you to splendid views to the South, Great, North, and Little North Basins of Katahdin.

How to Get There

Head west from Millinocket on the Millinocket-Greenville Road and enter the park via Togue Pond Gate. Just beyond the Togue Pond Gatehouse, turn right and follow a gravel road 7.3 miles north to Roaring Brook Campground. The South Turner trail begins at the camping area. You'll usually find plenty of room for overnighting here, but reservations are necessary, particularly at the height of the summer season. (See the Baxter State Park introduction.)

The Trail

Your pathway heads due north from the parking lot at the ranger station and follows the Russell Pond Trail for a short distance. Cross Roaring Brook and continue straight on the Sandy Stream Pond Trail when the Russell Pond Trail turns left. You will walk on the level to the left of an outlet stream of Sandy Stream Pond, cross an outlet brook, and then begin to skirt the southeast shore of the pond at just over 0.3 mile. This is moose country, and sightings are frequent. You will be more likely to see one of the

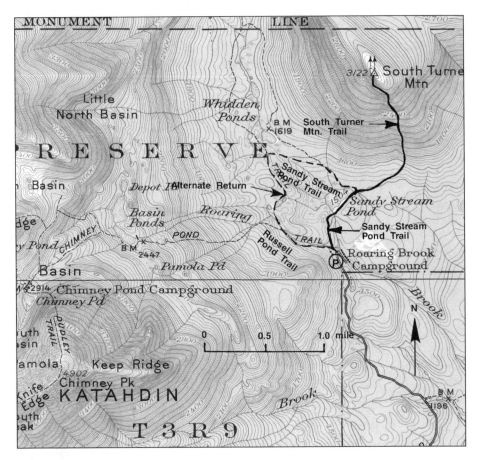

large creatures on your descent, around sundown.

At approximately 0.7 mile from the trailhead, you'll reach a junction where Sandy Stream Pond Trail curves to the left around the pond. Turn right here on South Turner Mountain Trail on a level stretch through a field of boulders and stands of mixed hardwoods. At slightly over a mile, the grade steepens as you continue generally northeastward. A short trail on your right to a brook is passed at just over 1.5 miles.

Not long after passing the brook side trail, you emerge from the scrub and get a taste of the fine views that prevail on the upper limits of the mountain. The trail runs over ledges on a ridge from here to the summit. Especially when visibility is poor, keep your eyes open for blue blazes on the rocks. The scramble up the ledges ends on the summit at 2 miles from Roaring Brook.

From South Turner's open, rocky apex you can look northeast over the high tableland that connects this elevation with North and East Turner Mountains. Katahdin Lake stretches out to the southeast, while the Whidden Ponds are immediately below to the west. Fine views take in the Russell Pond area to the northwest. The full spectacular expanse of Katahdin (Hike 35) is to the west, between Abol and Rum Mountains in the south and Russell Mountain in the

Barren Mountain and The Owl viewed from Daicey Pond in Baxter State Park

north. A copy of the 15' USGS Katahdin quadrangle makes a good addition to your pack on this trip to help you identify the many peaks visible from South Turner.

South Turner Mountain was born as a part of Mount Katahdin 360 million years ago when a vast dome of molten magma intruded from underground, pushing up the land above it like a blister. As the melted rock cooled, crystals solidified, producing the Katahdin granite unit, a mixture of quartz, feldspar, and mica.

The granite exposed near South Turner's summit looks different from the rock on Mount Katahdin, even though they came from one mass. The individual mineral grains in the rock on South Turner are much smaller and more difficult to single out, giving the granite a sugary appearance. Mount Katahdin's granite, with its large, obvious mineral grains, probably cooled more

slowly, at greater depths in the earth, whereas the finer-grained South Turner outcrops must have experienced more rapid cooling.

Since the creation of this huge mass of granite, erosion has carved it into the various granite mountains here today, such as Katahdin, Turner, Doubletop (Hike 41), O–J–I (Hike 39), and the Brothers. Mount Katahdin is perhaps only one-third the original height of this granite body.

The descent from the mountain retraces your route in, keeping left at the east end of Sandy Stream Pond. You may vary the return if you wish by turning right at Sandy Stream Pond and following the trail north and west to its junction with the Russell Pond Trail. Bear left on Russell Pond Trail and head south to Roaring Brook. This variation is somewhat longer than heading back directly along the pond's southeast shore.

South Turner Mountain

35

Katahdin

Katahdin is Maine's most famous hike, its most challenging (tied with Bigelow, from my point of view), and one of its most beautiful. Its name means "Sacred Mountain," as indeed it is to the Native American people. The supreme effort required by this climb is well worth the experience.

There are four major approaches to Mount Katahdin. This description will show you all four, two in one round-trip—I. the Helon Taylor Trail and Roaring Brook Trail, which take you across the Knife Edge and up Chimney and Baxter Peaks—and two in a second round-trip—II. the Abol Trail and the Hunt (Appalachian) Trail.

This is a hike that should be attempted only in good weather. Even then, the climber should be completely prepared for emergencies, both of weather and physical limits. Plenty of food, water, extra-warm clothing, and foul-weather gear should be carried.

I. KATAHDIN: PAMOLA, THE KNIFE EDGE, CHIMNEY, SOUTH, AND BAXTER PEAKS

Location: Southern end of Baxter State Park

Total distance: 9.8 miles (a circuit hike)

Hiking time: 8 hours

Vertical rise: 3,700 feet

Maps: USGS 7.5' Mount Katahdin; USGS 15' Katahdin; Baxter Park Map; MATC map 1 (1993); DeLorme maps 50, 51

The Helon Taylor Trail, named after H. N. Taylor, who was for many years Baxter State Park's superintendent, provides a 3,400-foot ascent up Keep Ridge to Pamola, the Knife Edge, and the rest of Katahdin's highest peaks. There are outstanding views along the route's entire length, and the hiker has opportunities to experience stretches of mountain terrain (on the Knife Edge) found nowhere else in the East. This hike, as could be expected on an ascent of Maine's highest mountain, will test your endurance a little. The trail demands steady work on the ascent and will test your brakes on the way down.

Register with the ranger at the Roaring Brook Campground, where the hike begins, before starting out on the trail and *again* on your return. This hikers' log helps keep tabs on foot traffic on the great expanse of Katahdin in case a rescue is needed.

Keep Ridge and the peaks of Katahdin are exposed to high winds, so carry extra clothing with you even if the weather seems mild. Wind shells, sweaters, rainwear, a hat, and gloves belong in your rucksack. You should also take along ample food. Roaring Brook is the only sure place to fill canteens for 6 hot, strenuous miles of climbing, so be sure to carry plenty of water.

How to Get There
Reach the Roaring Brook Campground on a gravel road about 8 miles north of the Togue Pond Gatehouse. Because parking is limited, you should arrive before 8 AM during the peak summer and fall seasons. When the parking lot is full, the trail is closed to hiking. You can also camp at Roaring Brook by reservation.

The Trail
The Taylor Trail departs from the Chimney Pond Trail 0.1 mile from the Roaring Brook Campground, following Keep Ridge, named for the Reverend Marcus Keep, who first opened the trail on this ridge in the 1840s. You hike to the west, climbing rapidly to a bare spot (Ed's Lookout) in 0.3 mile. The trail levels off momentarily here, and there are good views to the ridges higher up. Passing through scrub growth and boulders, you continue on nearly level ground to the southwest and west.

One mile above Roaring Brook, you begin to climb more steeply again, moving out of birch growth, and then descend briefly to the bed of Bear Brook at 1.3 miles. After passing groves of spruce and balsam, you move out more into the open, climbing on a pronounced grade. Views of the mountains and ponds in the southeast corner of Baxter State Park are frequent from this section of Keep Ridge.

Continuing upward, you hike through more boulders above the 2-mile point and along the bare ridge. The route levels off again for a moment 2.5 miles from the road by a large boulder, where excellent views of Pamola, Chimney Peak, and the Knife Edge are ahead to the west. The route ahead lies in the open but can be lost in cloud and wind; thus, caution should be used if the weather turns inclement. The summit of Pamola is reached 3.2 miles from your starting point.

Pamola looks down on deep, rocky South Basin and tiny Chimney Pond. It also provides an excellent lookout over the north ridge of the mountain, along which the Dudley Trail descends to the pond. To the southwest, you'll see the Knife Edge, probably the most exciting nontechnical traverse in the East. Hikers are advised to terminate their climb at this spot if the weather turns bad and either retrace the Taylor Trail back to Roaring Brook or descend the Dudley Trail from Pamola Peak to Chimney Pond and from there descend the Chimney Pond Trail back to Roaring Brook.

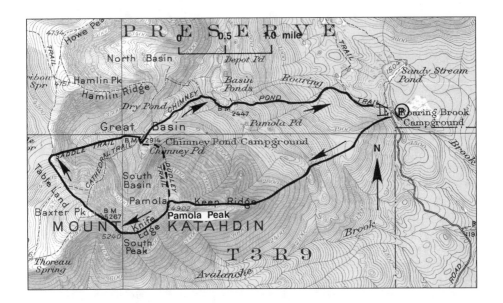

To head over to Baxter Peak, bear left or southwest on the Knife Edge Trail and descend into a gully between Pamola and nearby Chimney Peak. Cairns and paint blazes mark the route. On your right you'll pass the Chimney, a steep cleft suitable only for technical climbers. The trail rises steeply to the summit of Chimney Peak. Beyond it, you are entirely in the open on the Knife Edge as you move southwestward to the two highest summits on Katahdin.

The Knife Edge is a 2- or 3-foot-wide path that drops off precipitously on both sides. On the east side, the ridge plunges quickly down to the Avalanche Brook drainage area and on the other toward the South Basin. High winds and clouds can make this a dangerous section of trail. You proceed over a series of knobs and arrive at the lowest point on the Knife Edge in 0.5 mile. The trail then ascends the South Peak of Katahdin on steep grades, crossing the summit 0.8 mile from Pamola. In another 0.3 mile you'll arrive on Baxter Peak, Maine's highest summit and the northern terminus of the Appalachian Trail.

The views from Baxter Peak are described in detail in the second part of this hike, which approaches Katahdin from the south side of the park. You may have noticed that, although the Knife Edge looks greenish gray overall, where foot traffic has worn a path the rocks are pink. A brief geological explanation of the rocks on Baxter Peak and on the Tableland is provided in part II. You may also be interested in the differences between the granite of Katahdin and that of its closest neighbor, described in Hike 34, South Turner Mountain.

From Baxter Peak, you could retrace your steps back over the Knife Edge and down; however, in less time you can complete a circuit and see new trails. The distance is a bit farther, but easier traveling will make up the time.

From the peak, descend gradually northwest on the Tableland, away from the Knife Edge and toward the Saddle, passing the Cathedral Trail, Baxter Peak Cutoff, and Cathedral Cutoff Trails. (You can also take the Cathedral Trail down to Chimney Pond if there are no children or inexperienced hikers in your group. This book recommends the Saddle Trail down to Chimney Pond because it is easier and safer for someone who is already half worn out from the Knife Edge.) From Baxter Peak, the Saddle Trail leads in 2.2 miles to Chimney Pond.

After you have walked 1 mile down into the Saddle, you will be standing between Baxter and Hamlin Peaks. The Saddle Trail turns right and drops off the Tableland down a fairly stationary rock slide for 0.2 mile. Be careful not to dislodge rocks onto people below; likewise, keep a defensive eye on people above. The slide came down in 1893, and in 1927 LeRoy Dudley opened the trail from Chimney Pond to the bottom of the slide.

Below the slide, the trail enters scrub growth, crosses a small brook, and descends more gradually through birch and spruce-fir woods, flattening out at the bottom of the Great Basin. The trail ends at the center of the Chimney Pond Campground, where there are lean-tos and a bunkhouse available by prior reservation.

Chimney Pond is the campground's drinking water supply, and no washing or swimming is allowed here. In another 20 minutes, however, 1.3 miles down the trail to Roaring Brook, you'll be able to enjoy the cold glory of the Basin Ponds. Meanwhile, feast your eyes on picturesque Chimney Pond, with its large boulders fallen from the Knife Edge. The Great Basin is a cirque carved by a glacier that ground downward from the top of Katahdin. The Knife Edge was carved when glaciers grated down both its sides, leaving the slender arête, or backbone, standing. The glaciers pushed rock debris down the mountainside and left the bulldozed piles and walls, called moraines, when they melted. The Basin Ponds are dammed by such moraines. Chimney Pond is only 6 to 8 feet deep and freezes to the bottom in winter, rendering it uninhabitable for fish.

You will descend the Chimney Pond Trail, which exits from behind the bunkhouse, for 3.3 miles to Roaring Brook. At 0.6 mile, you'll pass on your left a depression called Dry Pond that holds water in spring or after a heavy rain and is rimmed by a glacial moraine. Once, after a hurricane, Dry Pond flooded the trail waist deep in white water! You'll cross several brooks, and at 1 mile you will pass the North Basin Cutoff, which leads in 0.7 mile to the North Basin Trail. At 1.3 miles you reach an open area near the shore of Basin Pond, an excellent place for swimming. To your left along the shore is an old lumberman's dam at the outlet. The Basin Ponds are a string of three ponds along a glacial moraine; this one is the lowest of the three.

Beyond Basin Ponds the descent is more moderate, following an old lumbering road through a hardwood forest. At 2.2 miles from Chimney Pond, you cross a bridge over the outlet brook from Pamola Pond and then cross several smaller brooks. At 2.7 miles, you begin paralleling Roaring Brook, occasionally seeing pieces of old telephone wire that used to connect to the Chimney Pond ranger station. Finally, at 3.3 miles, you pass the Helon Taylor Trail (your earlier ascent) and the Russell Pond Trail and return to the Roaring Brook Campground, where you sign in, having completed your 10-mile circuit of Katahdin.

Lunch at Thoreau Spring on Katahdin's Tableland

II. KATAHDIN: ABOL SLIDE AND HUNT TRAIL

Location: Southern end of Baxter Park

Total distance: 11 miles (a circuit hike)

Hiking time: 9 hours

Vertical rise: 3,980 feet

Maps: USGS 7.5' Mount Katahdin; USGS 7.5' Doubletop Mountain; USGS 15' Katahdin; USGS 15' Harrington Lake; Baxter Park Map; MATC map 1 (1993); DeLorme maps 50, 51

The Abol Trail on Mount Katahdin provides a steep, direct ascent to Thoreau Spring on the Tableland and to Baxter Peak, Maine's highest summit. The spring, at 4,636 feet, is located at the junction of the Abol, Hunt (Appalachian), and Baxter Peak Cutoff Trails. This route ascends the old Abol Slide, formed in 1816, and its outwash. The Abol Trail, probably the oldest regular route to the summit, is the second of two approaches to Katahdin's major peaks suggested in this book. The 11-mile circuit can be shortened by 2 miles (45 minutes) if you

spot a bicycle or car at the Katahdin Stream Campground, 2 miles west of the Abol Campground (the trailhead). The only water available on the trail besides surface water is Thoreau Spring, which can almost dry up in summer. It is best to carry plenty of water with you.

How to Get There

Begin your climb from the Abol Campground, 6 miles northwest of the Togue Pond Gate on Nesowadnehunk Tote Road.

The Trail

From the trail signs at the northeast corner of the Abol Campground, you depart northward as the trail ascends, following blue blazes to the south side of a feeder brook at about 0.2 mile. Evidence of moose is frequently seen in the hardwood forest and later in the spruce-fir forest. As the walk grows more steep, you proceed through tall, dense spruce forest, bearing northeast away from the brook at 0.8 mile from the campground. At just over 1 mile you cross a small brook where old logging roads intersect the trail.

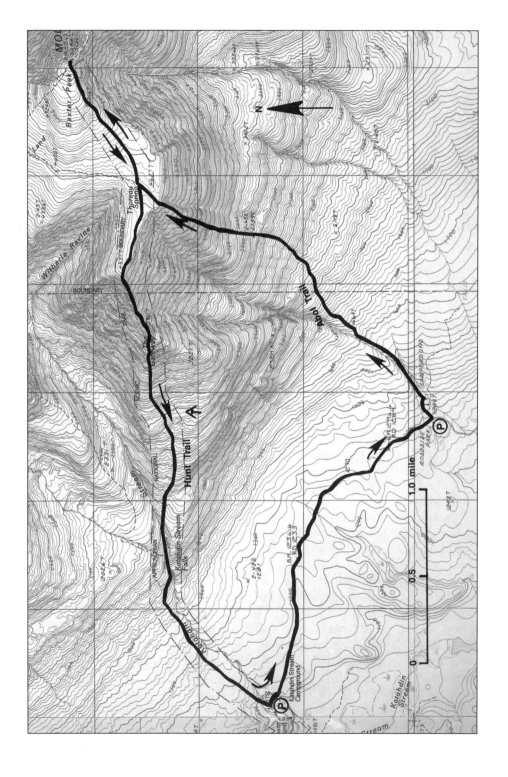

Continuing northeast, you arrive on the gravelly terrain that marks the beginning of the slide outwash area at 1.3 miles. The outwash, once barren, is now covered with mixed growth, which gradually thins out as you ascend. The grade becomes increasingly steep in this section and ascends on gravel and loose scree. Use caution, as the footing is poor. Be careful, too, not to dislodge stones onto hikers below.

The slide is made up of many different rock types. Katahdin granite at this level is gray or white, but pink rocks from the top have been carried down here by water and ice. You may see some sedimentary rocks containing fossils, rocks much older than Katahdin itself. These are glacial "erratics," which were carried from the northwest by glaciers, bulldozed up and over Katahdin, and deposited on the south side. For a more thorough explanation of erratics, see Hike 41, Doubletop.

At just under 2 miles, the trail levels off briefly and then climbs up a more recent slide. Excellent views begin to open up to the south, but given the stiff angle of ascent, you'll need to focus your attention on your footing. Still climbing steeply, you'll crest the slide at 2.3 miles, moving onto the Tableland through a field of sharply angled boulders. The trail takes a more comfortable route across the plateau above the boulders, following blue blazes and arriving shortly at Thoreau Spring. In fair weather, this spot makes a good rest stop, given its excellent perspectives on the south and west.

If the weather is bad, head left on the Hunt Trail (also the Appalachian Trail) to descend. Otherwise, turn right or east for the 1-mile trek to Baxter Peak. Follow the signs and white blazes for the Hunt (Appalachian) Trail to the summit. The climb is gradual here, nothing like the slide, and, in 0.3 mile,

you move up over a ledgy section along the lip of the plateau. In this link between Thoreau Spring and Baxter Peak you are traversing the final portion of the Appalachian Trail (AT), which ends on the summit. (Beginning on Springer Mountain in Georgia, the trail wends its way the full length of the Atlantic Coast states over 2,100 miles to Katahdin. Nearly 280 miles of the AT lie in Maine.) A brief sprint above the Tableland brings you onto 5,267-foot Baxter Peak.

The actual climb in this last part of the hike is moderate, but the trail is extremely exposed. Don't get caught here in inclement weather. Climatic conditions on Katahdin rival those of Mount Washington in severity. Storm systems can move in without warning in just minutes. Be prepared to head down.

The views from Baxter Peak are enough to shake up even the most jaded (if the scramble up the slides didn't do that for you already). Due north, across the majestic South and Great Basins, are Katahdin's three northern peaks. To the southeast is South Peak, connected, on its left, by the Knife Edge to Chimney Peak and Pamola. From here, you begin to get an idea of the mountain's massive size. Pack along a USGS 15' Katahdin map. It will help you to identify the dozens of peaks that surround the Katahdin massif, trailing west and north toward Canada.

To the south, the many ponds in and outside the park lie like glass fragments, and behind them lies Nesowadnehunk Deadwater on the West Branch of the Penobscot. Southwest, Big and Little Spencer Mountains (Hikes 31 and 32) lie together behind Chesuncook Lake, with Big Moose (Hike 28) in the distance.

At Baxter Peak and on the Tableland, you may have noticed that the rocks are a different color from those on the Abol Slide. All these rocks are Katahdin granite, but at higher elevations the granite is pink instead of white due to a higher potassium content in the granite's feldspar. Higher potassium levels were the "melt" of the molten magma that welled up underground from deep inside the earth and formed the Katahdin granite pluton. More of the story can be read in Hike 41, Doubletop, and Hike 34, South Turner Mountain. Of course, the whole Tableland and Knife Edge look greenish gray because the rock surfaces are covered with lichen, but if you look at recently overturned rocks in the trails and where foot traffic has worn off the lichen, you will see that the actual granite is pink.

It is also curious that so many of the rocks here are broken to nearly the same size and shape. This is because granite has its own pattern of jointing, or breaking, at certain intervals and at specific angles. Although jointing size varies from location to location (compare with South Turner and other granite mountains), the jointing is locally uniform, and the angles are always consistent. Katahdin's Tableland thus looks like a field of uniform boulders.

To descend the mountain, retrace your steps 1 mile from Baxter Peak to Thoreau Spring. From here you can climb back down the Abol Slide; or, for a more scenic and exciting trip down, take the Hunt Spur (AT), a longer trail that leads to the Katahdin Stream Campground, 2 miles from where you started at the Abol Campground.

To descend via the Hunt Spur to the Hunt Trail, cut by Irving Hunt in the 1890s, follow the white AT blazes west from Thoreau Spring across the Tableland. When you reach the "Gateway" at the edge of the Tableland, the trail literally drops off over the side, down a knife-edge of the Hunt Spur for the first 0.2 mile. Views here are

breathtaking, but stop walking when you want to gaze—the pathway here is narrow and dangerous, unforgiving if you should take a wrong step.

Witherle Ravine is the deep pit on your right, walled by The Owl (Hike 36). Beyond it are Klondike and Fort Mountains, with their "fir waves," peculiar stripes of downed trees, which have numerous hypothetical explanations of origin. You scramble steeply down huge boulders until the trail becomes less steep and dangerous at the 3,849-foot elevation point, 0.5 mile below the Gateway. Here is the end of the Hunt Spur, and the Hunt Trail continues down through enormous boulders, some the size of a house. One year I climbed Katahdin on this trail with a full backpack on a 5-day trip. Luckily, I met a minister and his two sons who helped me pass my pack up over some of these ledges and through the "lemon squeezes" along the way.

You enter woods 1.5 miles from the Gateway and shortly pass the Cave, a small slab cave that is the first possible shelter on your trip down. Nearly 1 mile into the trees you reach O-Joy Brook, so named by thirsty hikers who had found Thoreau Spring dry. The woods get prettier as you descend a ravine and begin to hear Katahdin Stream as it approaches the falls. About 2.5 miles from the Gateway, several side trails to your right take you to viewpoints of Katahdin Falls. Soon the trail passes close by the falls.

Katahdin Stream is usually spanned by a footbridge. If the bridge here is out of commission, though, keep walking to a crossing farther downstream. Pick your way across the stream, using a stick if necessary. As in all stream crossings, unbuckle your backpack before crossing so that, should you fall, you can extricate yourself quickly to avoid drowning.

You pass the trail to The Owl and then walk for 1 more mile through wonderfully level terrain and hardwoods to the Katahdin Stream Campground. Your trip now ends if you have left a car or bicycle here. If this isn't the case, head east (left) on the park road for 2 miles to the Abol Campground and your car.

36

The Owl

Location: In the shadow of Katahdin

Total distance: 6.6 miles (a return hike)

Hiking time: 5 hours

Vertical rise: 2,630 feet

Maps: USGS 7.5' Mount Katahdin; USGS 7.5' Doubletop Mountain; USGS 15' Katahdin; USGS 15' Harrington Lake; Baxter Park Map; DeLorme map 50

The Owl rises, rather like an observation post, in the midst of Baxter and close to Katahdin just west of Baxter Peak. The structure is actually a granite knob severed from Katahdin by Katahdin Stream. From The Owl, you can look north to North Brother, Fort, and Mullen Mountains. These peaks lie beyond Klondike Pond and the great boggy area known as the Klondike. The Klondike, itself, forms a kind of catch basin for all water runoff from Coe, O–J–I, and Barren Mountains, The Owl, and the western arms of Katahdin. It's ideal moose territory. To the east lies Witherle Ravine. Baxter and Hamlin Peaks tower more than a thousand feet above. The Owl also affords a fine outlook onto the ponds to the southwest.

Water should be carried on this hike.

How to Get There

The route to The Owl begins on the Hunt Trail (Appalachian Trail) at the Katahdin Stream Campground, on Park Perimeter Road, midway between the Nesowadnehunk Campground and Togue Pond Gatehouses.

The Trail

Although the Hunt Trail had once been relocated to the south side of Katahdin Stream to decrease wear on an eroded section, the trail has been relocated yet again and follows the stream's north side once more. You will travel north and northeast along the stream, following white (AT) blazes.

Continue northeast on easy grades to just over 1 mile, where The Owl Trail bears

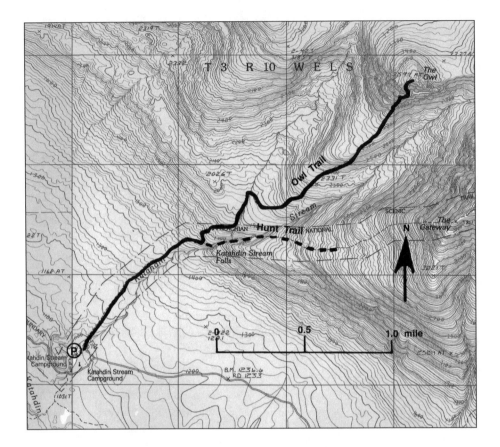

left onto a blue-blazed trail, as the Hunt Trail runs nearly due east. You ascend more rapidly, and cross a stream 0.5 mile above the trail junction, 1.6 miles from the trailhead.

After a relatively easy half mile, you begin a steep ascent into a shallow ravine and out onto an old slide. At 3.1 miles, a side trail will take you a few feet away to a cliff overlooking Katahdin, with the Hunt Spur—the upper part of the Hunt Trail (AT)—rising on its southwest flank. The main trail then climbs more steeply through dense scrub spruce to the upper ledges, past a balancing rock. You see views of The Owl's cone-like summit at 3.2 miles. A short walk on less steep, grassy terrain brings you to the top at 3.3 miles.

Standing on The Owl's summit, you are on the lower right section of an L-shaped formation of mountains called the *Katahdinauogh* by Native Americans. Stretching northwest and then northeast, other peaks in the L include: Barren (Hike 25), Mount O–J–I (Hike 39), Mount Coe, South and North Brother (Hike 40), and Fort and Mullen Mountains.

Two waterfalls in Witherle Ravine may be seen if you walk 50 yards through scrub growth along the ridge. Above, to the east, rise Katahdin's highest peaks. Henry David Thoreau climbed to the summits near here on his first trip up the Penobscot in September 1846. His words, even now, capture the wild, lonely spirit of the great expanse of Katahdin and its surrounding mountains:

The Owl and Mount Katahdin

I climbed alone over huge rocks, loosely poised, a mile or more, still edging toward the clouds; for though the day was clear elsewhere, the summit was concealed by mist. The mountain seemed a vast aggregation of loose rocks, as if some time it had rained rocks, and they lay as they fell on the mountainsides, no where fairly at rest, but leaning on each other, all rocking stones, with cavities between, but scarcely any soil or smoother shelf. They were the raw materials of a planet dropped from an unseen quarry, which the vast chemistry of nature would anon work up, or work down, into the smiling and verdant plants and valleys of earth. This was an undone extremity of the globe.

Like the other mountains surrounding Katahdin, The Owl was once part of the same granite mass as Katahdin, long before the mass was cracked, weathered, and carved down into separate smaller mountains. More detailed descriptions of this process can be found in Hike 34, South Turner Mountain; Hike 35, Katahdin; and Hike 41, Doubletop.

Use the same trail on the trek down.

37

Niagara Falls

Location: Near Daicey Pond in southern Baxter State Park

Total distance: 2.5 miles (a return hike)

Hiking time: 1½ hours

Vertical rise: None

Maps: USGS 7.5' Doubletop Mountain; USGS 7.5' Rainbow Lake East; USGS 15' Harrington Lake; Baxter Park Map; MATC map 1 (1993); DeLorme map 50

Big Niagara and Little Niagara Falls are within minutes of each other on Nesowadnehunk Stream at the south end of Baxter State Park. Both sets of falls are dramatic and, along with Toll Dam, offer some interesting stops on your hike.

How to Get There

The hike to Niagara Falls begins at Daicey Pond. Follow the Nesowadnehunk Tote Road 10.7 miles from the Togue Pond entry gate to the turnoff (sign) for Daicey Pond Camps, and drive 1.4 miles to the camps, where you park. (If you are staying in a cabin, you may park in the cabin parking area; otherwise park in the field to the right of the road, just before you get to the pond.)

The Trail

Look for the Appalachian Trail (AT) sign and follow the trail's white blazes south away from the pond and camps, toward Nesowadnehunk Stream. The path is often wet and muddy.

When the trail curves west (right), you can see Nesowadnehunk Stream to your right through the raspberries and alders. Continue through dense spruce and long beech fern. In early spring you can also see Canada mayflower, chickweed, trailing arbutus, and wild oats. You pass near an alder-choked deadwater beside the stream into an opening. To your right lie the ruins of a cabin; and Moose Mountain and Doubletop (Hike 41) outline the background. In a few more yards, on your left, another cabin stands in ruins.

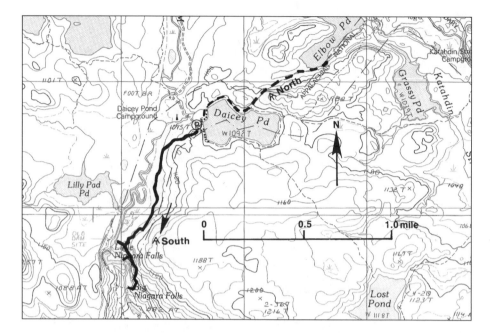

Shortly, a side trail on your right takes you 100 feet through raspberries and alders to Toll Dam, which has had three lives in the lumbering history of the Nesowadnehunk. The high wooden supports still standing are part of the original dam, built in the 1850s without a spike—it was put together entirely with hardwood pegs, which are still visible. This was also one of the first sites in the country to be dynamited. The stagecoach company refused to haul the dynamite, and it was finally carried to the dam site by horse and bateau. The dam was abandoned when its operators went out of business for charging exorbitant rates for log driving.

The dam was rebuilt twice more, the last time by the Great Northern Paper Company in 1929. The two ruined camps you passed earlier were part of this operation—the one on your right was once the kitchen and main quarters of the crew who built the dam and later of the crew who drove the logs. The cabin on your left was an office and later a tractor shed.

Just after you return to the main trail from Toll Dam, another short side trail leads you to the right to Little Niagara Falls, where you can stand on a giant boulder and watch the stream froth and pitch below you. Upstream is Toll Dam, with Mount O–J–I (Hike 39) and the cap of Mount Coe (Hike 40) in the background.

Return to the AT and walk another 0.3 mile (passing a spring 60 feet off the trail on your left) to a side trail on your right that takes off steeply downhill to Big Niagara Falls. Here you can pick your way out onto rocks in the stream for a trout's-eye view of the falls.

The rock of Big and Little Niagara Falls is Katahdin granite, part of the vast mass of rock that included Katahdin, Turner, Doubletop, and surrounding mountains in one huge pluton (an underground mass of rock that was intruded as molten magma).

Nesowadnehunk Stream has cut down through the granite at the falls, exposing impressive sections of granite with its flashy flecks of mica, white chunks of feldspar, and transparent jewels of quartz.

Here and there you can see where the granite, which is easily cracked or "jointed" by weathering conditions, was cleaved and the cracks later filled with different rock in-truding up from the earth's mantle. Katahdin granite, the youngest rock unit in Baxter Park, is approximately 360 million years old, and the crack fillings, or dikes, have formed since that time.

When you've had your fill of falls, scramble back up the steep bank, turn left onto the AT, and follow the white blazes back to Daicey Pond.

38

Sentinel Mountain

Location: The southern boundary of Baxter State Park, near the West Branch of the Penobscot River

Total distance: 5.8 miles (a return hike)

Hiking time: 4 hours

Vertical rise: 1,100 feet

Maps: USGS 7.5' Doubletop Mountain; USGS 7.5' Rainbow Lake East; USGS 15' Harrington Lake; Baxter Park Map; DeLorme map 50

Sentinel Mountain is truly the sentinel of the southwestern corner of Baxter State Park. Its summit affords dramatic views north to Mount Katahdin, Doubletop, and the Cross Range, and south outside the park to Rainbow Lake, distant mountains on the Appalachian Trail, Chesuncook Lake, and the West Branch of the Penobscot River.

How to Get There

Drive Baxter State Park's Nesowadnehunk Tote Road (Park Perimeter Road) from the Togue Pond Gate west to Foster Field and turn south at the sign to the Kidney Pond Camps, where you will park.

The Trail

Your pathway runs west from the library and goes behind the cabins. Beyond the last cabin a trail sign indicates where the blue blazes for both Sentinel Mountain and Doubletop Mountain (Hike 41) trails begin. Skirt the shore 0.2 mile to Jackson Landing. Canada mayflower is abundant along the trail, as is clintonia lily, named for Governor De Witt Clinton of New York. It is also called yellow bead lily. Its two to three distinct lily leaves encircle one stem bearing yellow blossoms in spring and inedible blue beads in late summer and fall. Also noticeable around Kidney Pond are numerous grackles and the sweet song of the white-throated sparrow.

At Jackson Landing, a trail leads right to Jackson and Celia Ponds, but you continue skirting the pond another 0.2 mile to the next junction. Here you leave the Kidney Pond

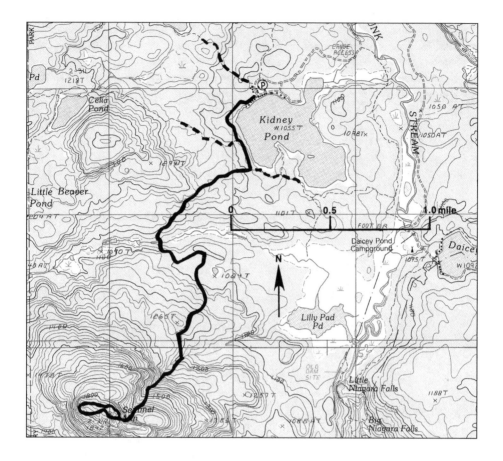

Trail and turn right (west) on the trail to Sentinel Mountain, the summit of which is 2.2 miles from this turn. The trail ascends, gradually at first, through birch and spruce, blackberries, painted trillium, and purple wake-robin in early spring. In summer the wood sorrel and spinulose wood fern are more evident. As the trail rises, the spruce get taller. The trail clears a ridge, where I once came face-to-face with a bull moose, and then descends the ridge through violets, chickweed, and trillium to a log bridge over Sentinel Mountain Brook. Across the brook the trail rises gradually southwest through spruce and birch, crosses a bog of cedar and sphagnum moss, and then opens into

sheep laurel, bunchberry, and wintergreen. You cross a log into a green setting of fallen trees and rocks carpeted with moss.

Keep walking southwest through mixed woods, more open because the trees are larger and therefore less numerous. The trail crosses Sentinel Brook again and follows it a short way before crossing it yet again near a huge boulder cave. Here the trail becomes steep, still following the streambed through clintonia lily, trillium, and rosy twisted-stalk. Long beech fern grows on the rocks in the dry streambed.

You cross and recross the stream bed, and then leave it and rise into a notch between the east and west summits of

Sentinel Mountain. The west peak to the right is the more interesting, with its loop trail around the summit. Climb boulders to the top and begin the summit loop clockwise, looking south across the West Branch of the Penobscot and Rainbow Lake to distant mountains on the Appalachian Trail. As you circle through blueberries and reindeer lichen you may see a red-eyed spruce grouse. At the far end of the loop, Parson's Pulpit offers a dramatic view north to Moose Mountain, Doubletop (Hike 41), O–J–I (Hike 39), with the cap of Mount Coe behind, Barren, and Katahdin (Hike 35). Completing the loop, you have a good view down between Sentinel and Katahdin of Lily Pad Pond, shaped startlingly like a lily pad, complete with stem.

At the end of the summit loop, retrace the trail back to Kidney Pond.

39

Mount O–J–I

Location: 5 miles west of Katahdin

Total distance: 6.4 miles (a circuit hike)

Hiking time: 5½ hours

Vertical rise: 2,340 feet

Maps: USGS 7.5' Doubletop Mountain; USGS 15' Harrington Lake; Baxter Park Map; DeLorme map 50

Rising north of the Nesowadnehunk Valley in the southwestern area of Baxter State Park is Mount O–J–I, named for the three slides on its southwest face that at one time resembled these letters. A storm in September 1932 caused more slides, changing the letter configuration. Today, the J resembles an ostrich. A new slide in 1954, southeast of the I slide, forms the South Slide Trail and provides a circuit route from the North Slide Trail, which is part of the former letter O. The loop trail ascends the North Slide Trail, runs the ridge, and descends the South Slide Trail.

How to Get There

The O–J–I hike begins at Nesowadnehunk Tote Road (Park Perimeter Road) at a point 10.9 miles west of the Togue Pond Gate (the southeastern entrance to Baxter State Park), across the road from Foster Field (sign) and the turn for the Kidney Pond Camps. Park in Foster Field.

The Trail

Follow the blue-blazed trail north into the woods, passing first a small brook on your left and then cutting through a cedar swamp. At 0.4 mile, the left fork to the North Slide Trail has been closed. There have been some nasty accidents on the treacherous North Slide, so now the trail goes up and returns by way of the South Slide Trail only.

From here, it is 1.6 miles to the summit. The trail ascends gradually through the 1974 blowdown and a mature beech forest to the base of the South Slide. At this point

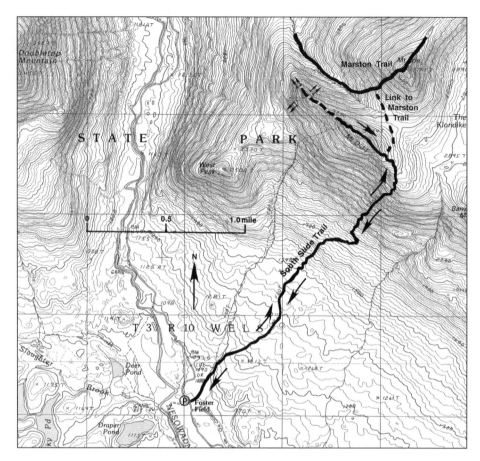

the trail ascends very steeply for 0.5 mile, to the head of the slide. Take caution on the bare rock, especially if it is damp. It if is raining, choose a different hike.

In another 0.2 mile, you reach the junction of the O–J–I Link Trail (which heads right 0.5 mile to the Marston–Mt. Coe Loop). In another 0.1 mile, you'll pass on your left a short side trail to Kidney Pond Lookout, with open views to the southwest and a topside to the view of the J slide below. The 3431' summit is one more tenth of a mile up, and get ready for amazing views.

To the southeast, you have a close-up of Barren Mountain, an inadvisable bushwhack away. Farther east is an impressive view of the west side of Katahdin. Just below you, look east into the Klondike Bowl, which holds Klondike Pond, one of the highest ponds in Maine at 3,400 feet. The Klondike is one of two spots in Baxter State Park too impractical ever to be logged. (The other is up the side of The Traveler from Howe Brook; see Hikes 44 and 45.) Few people have entered the dark, dense, swampy Klondike, and I understand that even fewer have returned to tell about it.

In 1963 a herd of Newfoundland caribou was transported by helicopter to the northwest plateau of Katahdin with the hope of establishing a permanent herd. The adults,

Mount O–J–I behind Little Niagara Falls and Toll Dam

however, with migration patterns imprinted in Newfoundland, left the mountain never to return. Since then there have been two possible sightings of individual caribou, in 1975 and 1979. Twenty-six years later, in 1989, another herd of caribou was set free in Baxter State Park; there were 12 adults initially, with plans to add to the herd periodically to build it to 100 animals. None of the 12 survived in the area.

Fifty yards ahead is O–J–I's second peak looking north to Mt. Coe and northwest up the Nesowadnehunk Valley.

And 0.4 mile past that is Old Jay Eye Rock, an intriguing sculpture by Mother Nature, and a choice lookout over the Nesowadnehunk Valley.

From here, retrace your steps to the beginning, using extra caution descending the South Slide.

40

Marston Trail—Mount Coe Loop

Location: 5 miles northwest of Katahdin

Total distance: 8.8 miles (a circuit hike)

Hiking time: 7 hours

Vertical rise: 2,935 feet

Maps: USGS 7.5' Doubletop Mountain; USGS 7.5' Mount Katahdin; USGS 15' Harrington Lake; USGS 15' Katahdin; Baxter Park Map; DeLorme map 50

The Brothers, rising southeast of the Cross Range, provide a strenuous hike from Nesowadnehunk Tote Road that culminates in excellent outlooks over the Klondike, the Northwest Basin and Plateau, and the Howe Peaks of Katahdin. The trail runs from Slide Dam to North Brother Mountain over the northwest shoulder of South Brother to the summit. The trail then traverses Mount Coe before circling back on the former Mount Coe Trail to where it began. This is one of my favorite hikes in Baxter Park—a wild and beautiful trail.

How to Get There

The Marston Trail, constructed in the mid-1950s by Philip and James Marston, begins at Slide Dam on the park service road about 6 miles north of Katahdin Stream Ranger Station and about 2.8 miles south of the Nesowadnehunk (Sourdnahunk) Field Campground. Park off the road here.

The Trail

Leaving the east side of the road opposite the Slide Dam picnicking area, you head eastward along the blue-blazed Marston Trail on the north side of Slide Brook. In a short while you bear left, climbing through a forested area to the south of another brook. Ascending briskly, the path stays with this brook, crossing and recrossing the waterway several times.

At 1.2 miles, passing through stands of mixed hardwoods and conifers, you cross the brook once again and arrive at a signpost. The former Mount Coe Trail departs to your right here. It is now your return loop;

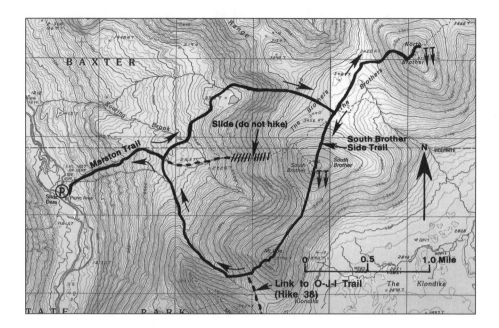

remember this junction. Continue along the Marston Trail, cross Roaring Brook at 1.4 miles, and ascend steadily into a bowl between South Brother and the Cross Range. The trail begins an increasingly steep march, up the south slope of the Cross Range, with occasional views to Doubletop Mountain to the west.

The top of the climb is crested at 2.5 miles, where you plunge back into spruce and fir woods and into a sag between North and South Brother. At 3.1 miles, the trail divides, left to North Brother or right to the rest of the loop over South Brother and Mount Coe. Go left first, toward North Brother. The steep climb resumes. At 3.7 miles, you emerge from scrub woodland and begin the final ascent above timberline through a boulder-strewn area, arriving on the North Brother summit after a few minutes' climb, 3.8 miles above your starting point.

The summit of North Brother (4,143 feet) makes a first-class observation point for the western area of Baxter. Hamlin Peak and the Howe Peaks of Katahdin are just to

the southeast. Russell Mountain is to the northeast; Mullen Mountain is to the north. The Cross Range strikes out to the northwest and, of course, Doubletop (Hike 41) makes an imposing sight to the west. One of the virtues of the long hike to the top of North Brother is the feeling of wildness, of isolation that comes only in country where so little human evidence is visible.

Retrace your steps back to the loop trail, turn left, and continue on the loop toward South Brother. Views from its 3,942-foot summit of miniature trees are as wild and beautiful as those from North Brother.

The loop then continues, using the Mount Coe Trail, a mile to the summit of Mount Coe (3,764 feet), with open views of the Nesowadnehunk Valley, Doubletop, the Brothers, O–J–I, and the Klondike, a flat bowl to the southeast. The trail then descends the southwest side of Mount Coe on a long, steep rock slide. It is nontechnical climbing, but extreme caution should be exercised on the walk down. This section is even more dangerous when wet.

Half a mile down from the summit, you pass the O–J–I Link Trail to your left, which connects to the O–J–I Trail in 0.5 mile. (From there the trail climbs 0.7 mile to the summit of O–J–I, Hike 39.)

After negotiating the nearly 2-mile slide of Mount Coe to lower elevations, the trail loops back and intersects the Marston Trail at the signpost. From here turn left and walk 1.2 miles back to the road.

41

Doubletop Mountain

Location: 6 miles northwest of Katahdin

Total distance: 6.6 miles (a return hike)

Hiking time: 5 hours

Vertical rise: 2,450 feet

Maps: USGS 7.5' Doubletop Mountain; USGS 15' Harrington Lake; Baxter Park Map; DeLorme map 50

The trek up this mountain leads to excellent views of many of the western peaks in Baxter State Park, particularly to the west flanks of Katahdin and southwest to the low, wild hills along the West Branch of the Penobscot. Doubletop's east side plunges sharply down to the Nesowadnehunk Valley in ripples of bright, weathered rock, making a striking sight from the road. With the opening of a new trail from the north in 1969 and 1970, the trail from the south (not described here) became less traveled. It is now possible to make a complete traverse of the mountain, though, from Nesowadnehunk Field in the north to Kidney Pond in the south. The trail described here takes you from the north side to the two peaks, returning round-trip to the north where you parked at the Nesowadnehunk Field and Campground.

Many hundreds of acres in southwest Baxter Park were damaged by high winds in 1974. This blowdown was especially destructive on the slopes of Doubletop. You will see the young forest recovering from the devastation.

How to Get There

The path in to Doubletop begins at the Nesowadnehunk Campground, 16.8 miles from the Togue Pond Gate. You can park at the campground parking lot.

The Trail

Walk to the last tent site on Nesowadnehunk Stream, where a sign marks the trail to Doubletop. It is 3.1 miles to the

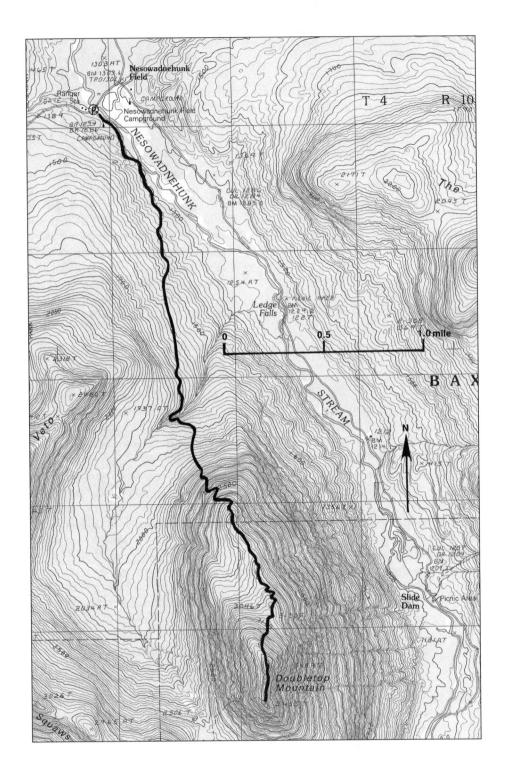

3,488-foot north peak and 3.3 miles to the slightly lower south peak.

You are hiking the favorite trail, in all of Baxter Park, of the late Gerald Merry, former park naturalist. He loved this trail for its woodland splendor—its many species of ferns and wildflowers and its tremendous yellow (silver) birches and maples.

The trail lies near Nesowadnehunk Stream, which you can often hear, and crosses its tributaries from time to time, staying fairly level for the first 1.2 miles to Doubletop Brook. The woods are spruce-fir mixed with abundant mature hardwoods. The forest floor, rich in leaf litter, is typical of a hardwood forest, festooned with fern species (interrupted, oak, long beech, and spinulose wood fern) and dainty wildflowers such as rosy twisted-stalk, clintonia lily, violets, Canada mayflower, painted trillium, hobblebush, oxalis (wood sorrel), and lady's slipper. From time to time, Indian cucumber root is abundant along the trail.

At 1.2 miles, the trail crosses Doubletop Brook on a footbridge and shoots steeply up a raw, eroded slope denuded by the 1974 blowdown. The woods will be recovering from this storm for a long time. Rotting trunks and exposed roots bear witness to the damage this windstorm caused. One consolation is the views to your right (west) of Mount Veto, not visible before the blowdown. The trail shows frequent sign of moose, and for about a mile it is excruciatingly steep.

An unusual rock lies in the trail here—a 2-foot rounded hunk of white limestone covered with fossil imprints of brachiopods.

Just when you can take the steep grade no longer, the trail eases and nearly levels out on a comfortable plateau forested with a wonderland of wildflowers, sphagnum moss, and dwarfed trees. The haunting pull of this glen might have made this the naturalist's favorite section, and it is a lovely flat walk that allows you to rest before the final

steep, but short, ascent of the 3,488-foot north peak. From the peak, excellent views spread in all directions, although the fire tower has been toppled to avoid liability. Below you lie Ledge Falls, Nesowadnehunk Field, and Nesowadnehunk Lake, "Sowdyhunk" in local parlance. To your right (east), Mount O–J–I (Hike 39) rises with its three slides, Mount Coe (Hike 40) lies close beside it, and South Brother rests in front of North Brother. The Cross Range is slightly to the left. Over O–J–I is the regal outline of Katahdin, from Hamlin Peak in the north to Baxter Peak in the south behind The Owl (Hike 36). To the west, Mount Veto is bisected by the park's western boundary, which continues south to Moose Mountain. A short side trail to the east takes you to a plaque mounted in a granite slab, a monument to Keppele Hall, whose ashes were given to the winds on Doubletop in 1926.

From the north peak, it is a 0.2-mile walk to the south peak, where the view of lakes and ponds is spectacular. To the west, the big lakes are first Harrington, then Ripogenus and Chesuncook, with Rainbow Lake in the distance beyond the West Branch of the Penobscot and Nesowadnehunk Deadwater. South of you, like a shattered mirror, lie more than a dozen ponds, including Slaughter, Rocky, Kidney, Jackson, Lily Pad, Daicey, Elbow, Grassy, and Lost Ponds.

From here it is 4 miles south to Kidney Pond, on an even steeper and less scenic trail down. I suggest retracing your steps the 3.3 miles over the north peak and down the naturalist's favorite trail to Nesowadnehunk Field Campground.

As you descend and again pass the limestone rock with brachiopod fossils, you might wonder where it came from and how it got there. The answer is a long story. A shallow ocean covered eastern North

America, including all of Maine, for 200 million years in the early Paleozoic era, during which time layers of sediment eroded from the continent, washed into the ocean, and accumulated in layers. Ancient marine organisms, like these brachiopods, lived and died in the layers of sediment, which gradually hardened and turned to sandstone, shale, and limestone. Since that time, volcanoes erupted about 400 million years ago from the ancient sea, creating The Traveler rhyolite seen in Hikes 42–45. Then, 360 million years ago, the Katahdin granite was formed as a huge underground "blister" of molten rock that welled up, cooled, and hardened over millions of years. Doubletop is a fragment of the huge buried Katahdin granite mass, which was gradually exposed by erosion and shattered by weathering into the many fragmentary pieces visible today—the Cross Range, the Brothers, Mount Coe, Doubletop, The Owl, South Turner, Katahdin, and others.

In the last million years, glaciers have periodically covered Maine and much of North America, moving loads of rock, gravel, sand, and clay from northwest to southeast. Pieces of many different kinds of rock were broken off, "entrained" by the glaciers, and carried south. The fossil limestone on Doubletop is an "erratic," a rock from another location transported here probably 25,000 years ago by a glacier. It came an unknown distance from sedimentary rock that formed under the ocean long before the Katahdin granite welled up from inside the earth. If you look carefully, you can find other fossiliferous rocks under uprooted trees and along streams. Note, however, that rocks are protected, just as plants and animals, in Baxter State Park. They may not be collected or taken from the park.

Baxter State Park—Northern Section

42

South Branch Mountain

Location: Near South Branch Pond in Baxter Park, northern end

Total distance: 6 miles (a circuit hike)

Hiking time: 4½ hours

Vertical rise: 1,600 feet

Maps: USGS 7.5' Wassataquoik Lake; USGS 15' Traveler Mountain*; Baxter Park Map; DeLorme map 51

Note: *On the 15' USGS map for this area, South Branch Mountain is referred to as Black Cat Mountain. The latter name is now associated with the east peak of Black Brook Mountain.*

The best views of The Traveler (Hikes 43 and 44) and Pogy Notch are seen from the ledges of South Branch Mountain. First blazed in 1964, the South Branch Mountain Trail provides a fine circuit over the mountain, around the ponds, and back to the South Branch Campground. This route makes an excellent climb in conjunction with the hikes up The Traveler and Howe Brook. Good camping facilities, some interesting fishing possibilities, and a place to leave your car are all to be found along the shore of the ponds, and don't be surprised if you wake up to the sound of moose wading in the shallows at dawn.

Water should be carried on this hike.

How to Get There

The trail commences at the west side of the campground near the northwest shore of Lower South Branch Pond.

The Trail

To begin, you must ford the pond outlet stream; it is shallow. The trail runs southwest from the stream, shortly paralleling another brook for about 0.2 mile. Climbing on comfortable grades, you ascend a ridgeline, bearing hard to the left (south) at 0.8 mile above the trailhead.

Continuing southward, you shortly reach bare ledges that overlook the ponds and across to North Traveler. The trail runs along the side of the ridge, over a knob, and across more ledge, allowing good views back toward the north end of the lower pond. The north summit of the mountain comes into sight in minutes as the trail pulls

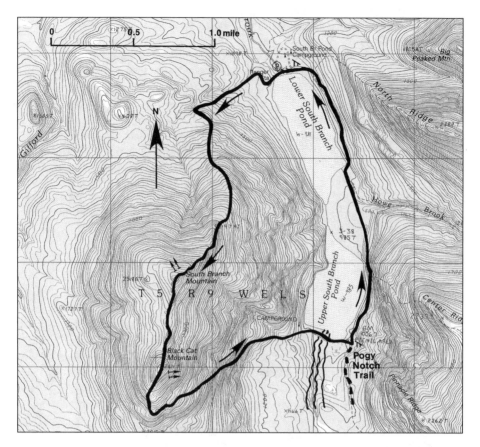

more to your right on steady grades. You top North Peak at 2 miles; here views to the south begin to open up. The elevation of North Peak is 2,599 feet.

Continuing southward, you drop into a slump briefly, then climb again to a trail junction where, at 2.5 miles from the campground, a short side trail leads right to the grassy, open south peak of South Branch Mountain, elevation 2,585 feet. You can see in all directions here, especially over the Deadwater Range, which runs toward your right to Nesowadnehunk Lake. Black Cat and Black Brook (see Note, p. 190), Squirt Dam, Burnt, McCarty, Morse, and (more to the south) Strickland Mountains form a staggered line southwest.

To the east, the ponds are below, and behind them rests the great hulk of The Traveler. To the southeast you can pick out North Turner Mountain and, farther down to the right, Katahdin. Due northwest lies the wild, remote country Thoreau traversed by canoe more than one hundred years ago and then wrote about in *The Maine Woods*.

From South Peak the trail continues down the south ridge through open meadows on easy grades. At the end of the meadows, at some rock outcrops, the trail turns left into a hardwood forest, descending steadily. There are some short, steep sections here. The angle of descent becomes more comfortable 1 mile below the

---

summit as you follow a brook, continuing eastward. At 4.3 miles, a side trail leads 200 feet to Upper South Branch Pond Lean-to, a quiet place to stay if you have made reservations with the Baxter State Park office (see the introduction to this section). A network of brooks that feed Upper South Branch Pond is crossed soon in a boggy area grown up with alder scrub and marsh grass.

There are several attractive spots along the upper pond to stop and rest. On your way again, continue walking east to a junction with the Pogy Notch Trail at a wilderness campsite. Here you swing left (north) along the east shore of the pond. The walk here is nearly level for about 2 miles back to the campground, with pleasant views over the water most of the way. Chances of spotting wildlife as you walk this section are very good.

43

North Traveler Mountain

Location: Near South Branch Pond in Baxter Park, northern end

Total distance: 5.25 miles (a return hike)

Hiking time: 5 hours

Vertical rise: 2,150 feet

Maps: USGS 7.5' Wassataquoik Lake; USGS 7.5' The Traveler; USGS 15' Traveler Mountain; Baxter Park Map; DeLorme map 51

The Traveler is a rangy mountain mass running roughly north and south at the northern limits of Baxter State Park. This great mountain rises below First Grand Lake and close by the South Branch Ponds. The mountain, with its five prominent summits, forms the eastern border of Pogy Notch. Burned over in 1903, the mountain is characterized by bald, open summits and high meadows, while the lower slopes show resurgent hardwood growth.

North Traveler is the only peak of The Traveler range, with the exception of the Peak of the Ridges (Hike 44), with a regular, clear trail. The route was originally cut by Myrle Scott, a Baxter ranger, and is probably the most used of the trails on the mountain.

How to Get There

The trail is approached on the park access road either from the south (if you're already in Baxter) or from the northeast via Patten. From Patten, take ME 159 west to Shin Pond, then follow a service road to the park. You turn left at "the Crossing," 33.5 miles west of Patten, and bear south to the South Branch Ponds Campground. The campground is 1.8 miles in from the Crossing and provides camping in a very attractive setting plus adequate parking for hikers' cars. This area makes a convenient base for all four of the day hikes in the north end of the park covered in this book.

The Trail

To head up North Traveler, you follow the Pogy Notch Trail from the east side of the campground. This first section of the trail

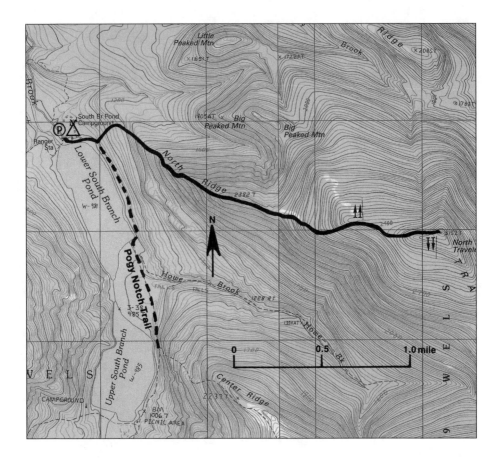

arches around the north end of the northernmost of the two South Branch Ponds. You shortly arrive at a trail junction and bear left onto the North Traveler Trail, commencing a brisk climb. At 0.5 mile from the campground, you move gradually out of deciduous forest, walking in a southeasterly direction along open ledges up the mountain's north ridge.

At just under 1 mile, you will pass a series of cliffs and walk under a knob, the trail leveling off slightly. The crest of the North Ridge is reached in a few minutes at another knob, and for nearly 0.5 mile you have level walking in the open. At 1.8 miles from the campground, you walk through more

scrub growth, climbing again to the southeast. Watch for a short side trail on your left to a spring, which is the last reliable water on this route.

You see frequent sign of moose as the trail runs through a cluster of grassy uplands, dotted with ledges, for the next 0.5 mile. At 2.3 miles you reenter the woods, climbing again through balsam and red spruce. You arrive on the open, ledgy summit of North Traveler in a few more minutes. The trail ends here.

The views from this spot are fine, covering as they do much of the wild lands to the north, west, and east of the park. To the east lie the headwaters of the East Branch of the

Penobscot, while to the northeast you'll see Bald and Billfish Mountains. Barrell Ridge is the low summit immediately to your north. Over the ridge, about 6 miles to the north-northeast, is Trout Brook Mountain and, behind it, First Grand Lake.

You may have noticed the uniform color and consistency of the rock on North Traveler. This rock is Traveler rhyolite, left from 400 million years ago when a volcano erupted here in a shallow sea. The ancient volcano was much higher in elevation, and The Traveler with its starfish-shaped arms is merely its roots, exposed after millions of years of erosion.

You may see signs of a rough path leading to the south toward the other peaks on The Traveler range. This trip is trailless and is not recommended for any but the most experienced, fully equipped hiking party. The distance to the main summit of The Traveler and the return is 4 miles, and the route consists of a difficult bushwhack its entire length.

To regain the ponds, retrace your steps on the North Traveler Trail.

44

The Traveler—
Peak of the Ridges

*Location: Near South Branch Pond in
Baxter Park, northern end*

Total distance: 7.2 miles (a return hike)

Hiking time: 7 hours

Vertical rise: 2,240 feet

*Maps: USGS 7.5' Wassataquoik Lake;
USGS 7.5' The Traveler; USGS 15'
Traveler Mountain; Baxter Park Map;
DeLorme map 51*

The Traveler, once believed to be the second
highest mountain in the state, presides over
the northern end of Baxter State Park. The
main summit is trailless, but approaches may
be made to two lower peaks on the mountain. The higher of the two is Peak of the
Ridges, where this hike will take you.

The Traveler was named by voyageurs who
traveled the waterways of Maine and Canada
trapping and logging. The large bulk and
many radiating ridges of the mountain created
the impression that the mountain moved or
traveled along beside them.

How to Get There

The hike begins at the South Branch Pond
Campground, 2.3 miles down South Branch
Pond Road, which leaves Park Perimeter
Road at a point 7 miles west of Mata-
gamon Gate and 36 miles north of Togue
Pond Gate.

The Trail

From the campground you take off southeast
on the Pogy Notch Trail, skirting Lower South
Branch Pond. At 0.1 mile you pass the North
Traveler Peak Trail on your left. The trail
passes under the sheer North Ridge and
brings you onto the delta of Howe Brook that
separates Upper and Lower South Branch
Ponds. The two ponds used to be one until
they were divided by this delta.

The trail turns left and parallels the left bank
of Howe Brook. At the trail junction 1 mile from
the campground, take the right-hand path,
staying on the Pogy Notch Trail. (The way left
is the Howe Brook Trail, Hike 45.) The Pogy

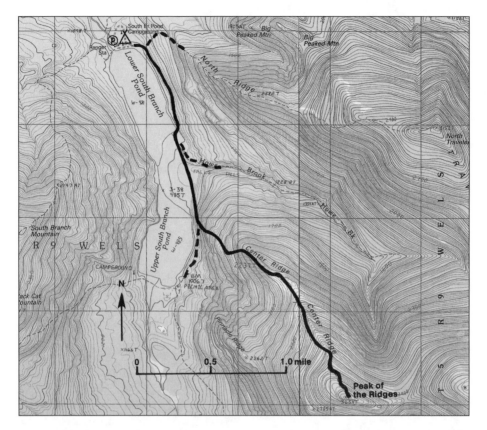

Notch Trail crosses and then leaves the brook to continue 0.3 mile across the flat delta through maturing white birches. You then scramble up a steep slope to the top of sheer cliffs, which drop into Upper South Branch Pond. At 1.5 miles, at the high point on the cliffs, is a trail junction. Ahead to the south, the Pogy Notch Trail continues around Upper South Branch Pond and eventually reaches Russell Pond. Turn left instead onto the Center Ridge Trail, which climbs steeply the next 2.1 miles to The Traveler's Peak of the Ridges.

You begin your ascent up a boulder pile with views opening up over Upper South Branch Pond. Meadowsweet, fireweed, and other dry-soil wildflowers grow among the boulders, softening the mountain's appear-

ance but not the rugged climb. Unlike Katahdin and the other granite mountains in the south end of the park, The Traveler was created by a volcano that erupted 400 million years ago. The rock of The Traveler—and the Deadwater Mountains—is composed of rhyolite, which has a finer-grained, darker tan appearance than granite. Traces of iron in the rhyolite here have stained the rocks red. At 2.2 miles from Upper South Branch Pond, you top a cliff with a dramatic view of Pogy Notch and the South Branch Ponds. Pinnacle Ridge is the sheer-faced ridge to the south. North Traveler is across Howe Brook Valley to the north.

The trail rises less steeply for the next 0.5 mile, in and out of scrub birch and pine, sheep laurel, blueberries, bunchberry, and

The author on The Traveler

rock tripe. The last mile is a steep scramble over scree with occasional brief levelings among dwarf birch, mountain ash, sheep laurel, reindeer moss, mountain cranberry, and Labrador tea.

At 3.6 miles, as you drag yourself to the 3,225-foot summit, notice the evidence around you that moose frequent this peak. From Peak of the Ridges you might believe you could touch the sky. Views around you are breathtaking. To the east 1.5 miles away is the 3,541-foot trailless main summit of The Traveler, beyond which lie the park's eastern boundary and the East Branch of the Penobscot. North of you is North Traveler Peak. West are two-peaked South Branch Mountain and Pogy North where Pogy Brook braids its way 10 miles to Wassataquoik Stream and Russell Pond. To the south is South Traveler peak.

Return by the same trails to the South Branch Pond Campground.

The Traveler is barren as a result of the Great Wassataquoik Fire of 1903, which swept from north to south, funneling through Pogy Notch into the Russell Pond area. The fire burned every trace of life, even consuming topsoil. This makes climbing The Traveler difficult and slow, as every step must be well placed. Allow plenty of time, and be cautious, especially over the scree, to avoid spraining an ankle on your descent.

45

Howe Brook

Location: Near South Branch Pond in Baxter Park, northern end

Total distance: 6 miles (a return hike)

Hiking time: 3 hours

Vertical rise: 700 feet

Maps: USGS 7.5' Wassataquoik Lake; USGS 7.5' The Traveler; USGS 15' Traveler Mountain; Baxter Park Map; DeLorme map 51

Howe Brook is a small mountain brook with pools and cascades near South Branch Pond Campground in Baxter State Park. The hike is a beautiful walk for a small amount of effort.

How to Get There

From the Matagamon Gate, drive 7 miles west on Park Perimeter Road and turn left (south) down South Branch Pond Road, continuing 2.3 miles to the South Branch Pond Campground. (This turn is 36 miles north of the Togue Pond Gate to Baxter Park.) Park your car at the South Branch Pond Campground.

The Trail

To reach the Howe Brook Trail, leave South Branch Pond on the Pogy Notch Trail, skirting Lower South Branch Pond. At 0.1 mile, pass on your left the North Traveler Peak Trail, which leads 2.6 miles to that summit (Hike 43). Continue, passing under the sheer North Ridge, and come out onto the flat land separating Upper and Lower South Branch Ponds. This flat land is a delta of Howe Brook that has gradually filled in and changed South Branch Pond from one lake into two. The trail passes a canoe landing and turns left away from the pond, paralleling the left bank of Howe Brook. This brook is also called Dry Brook, because it filters down into the delta 50 yards before it enters Lower South Branch Pond. Only during spring high water is the brook visible all the way to the pond.

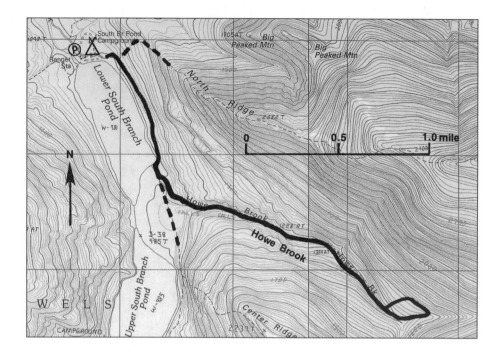

The area where the brook flows out into South Branch Pond from underground is a good fishing spot for brook trout.

At 1 mile, you reach a trail junction. The Pogy Notch Trail turns right and crosses Howe Brook. You continue straight ahead on the Howe Brook Trail. The brook originates from a spring in The Traveler and flows down the valley between North Traveler and Center Ridge. Walk upstream 0.2 mile where the falls and pools begin. A series of chutes here are fun to slide through on a hot day. These pools and chutes can entertain me half a day. The water is always *very* cold. There are smaller pools to splash in. Farther up the trail are some well-polished potholes hollowed out by centuries of water-swirled gravel. The water in these pools is crystal clear and emerald tinted in the deepest places.

After leaving the falls, you cross and recross the brook and then begin a gradual

ascent. You'll notice several stumps of large white pines, old and rotting, victims of the 1903 and 1914 fires. The Great Wassa-taquoik Fire of 1903 swept this area clear of all life—even the topsoil. These huge stumps are the only remains of the fire. The young woods are still open and sparse, but sandy-soil plants such as hawkweed, gold-enrod, asters, and meadow rue have begun to flourish. This sunny openness, resulting from the fire, gives a sparkle to the water and a sense of freedom to the hike.

At 1.8 miles up the Howe Brook Trail, the trail forks into a final loop. Take the right fork, cross the brook, and climb a rough trail through a deep ravine until you pass a set of hidden, almost secret falls. They are step falls and flumes through dark woods. At 2 miles from the stream's outlet, you come to the bottom of a 20-foot vertical cascade falling into a small pool. The spruce at the head of Howe Brook are noted as being

Baxter State Park's only virgin timber (besides those in the Klondike) to escape the axes and fires of the 19th and 20th centuries. In the upper reaches of the brook where the virgin timber begins, I've found many bleached skulls and bones of moose. The beginning of Howe Brook is either the location of or the outwash place for many moose deaths. Their antlers are found in a different location in the park.

From here, the Howe Brook Trail climbs out of the ravine and loops left to rejoin the path you took out to the falls. Retrace Howe Brook Trail to the Pogy Notch Trail and then back to the South Branch Pond Campground.

Both the falls at the end of this trail and the cascades and pools near its beginning are perfect lunch spots. This is one of my favorite hikes. I can easily spend a whole day on this trail and not even go to the end.

Aroostook County

Introduction to Aroostook County

Aroostook County, referred to within the state as "The County," is Maine's largest county in area but smallest in population. Much of eastern Aroostook County is covered with potato farms, while the central and western parts are mostly forest. Most of the timberland is within an area designated as the North Maine Woods (NMW), a 2.5-million-acre tract of land that covers most of Aroostook and some of Somerset, Piscataquis, and Penobscot Counties.

NMW is the administrative wing of the landowners of this area, mostly paper companies, and is responsible for managing public access for hunting, camping, canoeing, fishing, and hiking. Organized in the early 1970s, NMW checks people in and out at checkpoint gates and charges minimal fees for use of the land. This large section of Maine encompasses two entire river systems—the Allagash and the St. John—over 2,000 miles of permanently maintained gravel roads, dozens of campsites, and a system of gates, permits, and access control to minimize confusion and prevent people from getting lost. For advance information, a map, and a camping permit, write to North Maine Woods, P.O. Box 421, Ashland, ME 04732-0421. It is also acceptable to register at the gate. Reservations are not taken.

The terrain and topography of Aroostook are different from the rest of the state. The area is largely a flat expanse of sedimentary shales, left fairly undisturbed by the mountain-building that folded, warped, and changed the rest of Maine. It remains much the same as when Maine was laid down as sediment at the bottom of a shallow sea over a span of about 50 million years, during the Devonian period. Some variation in rock type and terrain occurs in the southeast, closer to the action that rumpled and peaked the rest of Maine. Some of these variations, namely the few mountains in The County, offer the best opportunities for views, both for fire wardens and for hikers.

The easiest hike to reach is Hedgehog Mountain, located beside ME 11 just 4 miles south of Winterville and 13 miles north of Portage. The trail begins at a picnic area on the west side of ME 11. The well-used, 1.5-mile trail leaves from the parking lot, passes the Maine Forest Service (MFS) ranger cabin, and rises easily to the 1,594-foot summit, an elevation gain of 500 feet. Although the fire tower has been removed, views are good south to Round and Peaked Mountains, St. Froid Lake, Fish River Lake, and Portage Lake. To the northwest, Deboullie and Black Mountains form twins.

In the Presque Isle area are two mountains of yellow rhyolite, the remains of volcanoes: Quaggy Joe and Haystack Mountains. Both mountains offer easy hikes. Quaggy Joe, altitude 1,213 feet, is located in Aroostook State Park. The 2.25-mile, round-trip hike takes less than 2 hours, with an elevation gain of 600 feet. Of the twin peaks, South Peak is higher, but North Peak has better views: west to the cone of Haystack Mountain, with Chandler and Squapan behind. On a clear day, you can see the outline of Katahdin to the southwest.

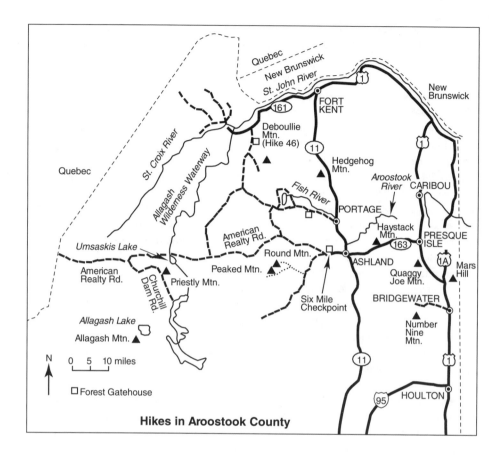

Hikes in Aroostook County

Haystack Mountain, the other volcanic remnant, is located at the roadside of ME 163 halfway between Presque Isle and Ashland. The trail starts on the north side of the highway and is a short climb of less than a mile to the peaked summit. Even though it has retained the shape of a volcano, Haystack is merely the eroded stump of a volcano, which has been weathering away for hundreds of millions of years.

Two other hills can be climbed in the Presque Isle area—Mars Hill, half a mile from the New Brunswick border in the town of Mars Hill (south of Presque Isle on US 1), and Number Nine Mountain, 1,638 feet in altitude, with a fire tower. Number Nine is accessible by road about 15 miles west of US 1 in Bridgewater.

A four-wheel-drive vehicle or a canoe is necessary to reach Priestly Mountain and Allagash Mountain (both actually in northern Piscataquis County). Both can be hiked as side trips on a canoe trip of the Allagash Wilderness Waterway. Allagash Mountain, with its fire tower, is located at the shore of Allagash Lake. Do not attempt to reach this mountain on logging roads; save it for the canoe trip. Priestly Mountain can be hiked from Umsaskis Lake on the Allagash Waterway, a round-trip of 7 miles, or it can be reached with a four-wheel-drive vehicle, making the hike a 4-mile round-trip. To reach the latter trailhead from Ashland, drive west on American Realty Road to Six Mile Checkpoint, pay fees, and confirm directions to Priestly Mountain. Follow the Realty Road to the intersection of Churchill Dam Road, 67 miles west of Ashland. From the intersection, it is 7.5 miles on Churchill Dam Road to a small sign on a tree on your left indicating the trail. The trail follows an old road to Drake Brook, the outlet of Priestly Lake, which is nestled among low hills. Here the trail from Umsaskis Lake joins your trail for the 0.75-mile climb to the 1,900-foot summit.

Aroostook's two highest peaks, Peaked Mountain (2,270 feet) and Round Mountain (slightly lower), stand 2 miles apart west of Ashland. A four-wheel-drive vehicle may be needed to reach these mountains. Round Mountain's fire tower, presently not in operation, offers close-up views south to Peaked Mountain and northerly views of the northern Maine woods and waterways. The trail to Peaked Mountain is difficult to find and directions should be obtained at the MFS office in Portage. Then drive west from Ashland on American Realty Road. Just

beyond Six Mile Checkpoint, take the left fork and drive about 11 miles to the Machias River. Cross the river and turn right onto a logging road. At 5 miles from the river crossing, a road to your right takes you 5 miles to Round Mountain. Or, if you continue until you are 10 miles from the river, you will come to a trail on your right to Peaked Mountain. Neither of these trails should be attempted without updated information from Six Mile Checkpoint or from a MFS station, since the trails are not frequently cleared of brush.

If you are fortunate enough to have time to spend in Aroostook County, you might want to find out about some of the many interesting canoe trips on the Allagash, St. John, St. Croix, Aroostook, and Fish Rivers. With a DeLorme *Maine Atlas and Gazetteer,* you should be able to find places to camp with a fireplace, picnic table, and tent site.

The one hike written about in detail in this section, Deboullie Mountain, is in a state recreation area with plenty of campsites, fishing, hunting, and even sporting camps.

46

Deboullie Mountain

Location: Aroostook County in northern Maine, about 20 miles south of St. Francis and Quebec province

Total distance: 6 miles (a return hike)

Hiking time: 4 hours

Vertical rise: 850 feet

Maps: USGS 7.5' Deboullie Pond; USGS 15' Fish River Lake; North Maine Woods Map; DeLorme maps 62, 63, 66, 67

Deboullie Mountain gets its name from the French past participle for *fallen,* which refers to the fallen rock in the Deboullie Slide. It is the highest of a small cluster of mountains in the wilderness south of St. Francis on the New Brunswick border. Owned by the state of Maine in a 15,000-acre tract, the mountain is surrounded by (Bowater) Great Northern and International Paper Company lands, whose roads provide the lengthy approach. This area is part of the North Maine Woods (NMW), explained in the introduction to Aroostook County.

How to Get There

The approach to the hike, or combination canoe paddle and hike, begins in St. Francis on ME 161 between Fort Kent and Allagash. From the St. Francis Post Office, drive 5.9 miles southwest on ME 161 to Chamberlain's Market on your left. (This is also 22.6 miles southwest of the junction of ME 11 and ME 161 in Fort Kent.) Beside the market, the Pelletier Brook (Negro Brook) Road leaves ME 161 for the North Maine Woods. At 0.1 mile, fork right, leaving Pelletier Brook Road on the Red River–Togue Pond Road, and at 7.5 miles check in at the gate, pay an entry fee, and obtain a *North Maine Woods Map of Roads and Campsites.* At 8 miles fork right, and at 8.5 miles fork left, following signs to Red River Camps. At 15.3 miles, you pass on your right the NMW Togue Pond Campsite. Park off the road at 19.3 miles, by a sign that reads THIS ROAD DEAD ENDS AT RED RIVER

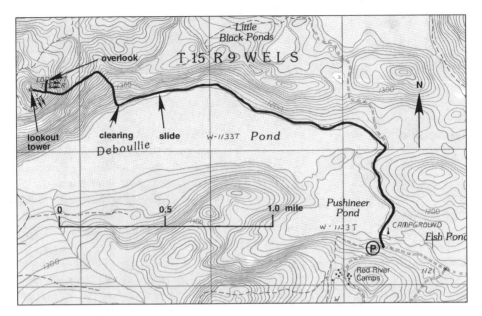

CAMPS. You may first want to visit the attractive Red River Camps and confirm trail instructions or rent a canoe or camp. Return to the dead-end sign to begin the hike.

If you are starting by canoe, put in at Pushineer Pond below the dead-end sign, follow the right (east) shoreline through the thoroughfare into Deboullie Pond, and canoe two-thirds of Deboullie's right (north) shoreline, past a rock slide to a break in the alders leading to a campsite. The mountain trail leaves behind the campsite at a sign that tells you it is 1 mile to the tower.

The Trail

If you are hiking all the way, walk northeast down to the old dam between Pushineer Pond and the Red River. Wade across the river or walk over the old dam, skirting the NMW Pushineer Pond Campsite on your left, and continue walking the woods road. At 0.4 mile, pass on your left the NMW Thoroughfare Campsite, and at 0.5 mile, pass on your left the NMW Deboullie Campsite (no sign). From all three camp-

sites you can see the tower on Deboullie's summit. At 0.8 mile, look carefully on your right for the remains of a rotting, abandoned boat, and shortly on your left is a small, abandoned dump with a wooden sign that says TOWER. The trail leaves from behind the dump, follows the shore of Deboullie Pond, and crosses the Deboullie Slide, where lichen-patched rocks are sprinkled with spears of fireweed, making a green and pink color combination in August. There is a place in the Deboullie Slide called the "ice chest," where the ice never melts, even in summer. The trail stays near shore beyond the slide until shortly, at 2 miles, it runs into a campsite with a sign to the tower.

The last mile leaves the rear of the campsite and climbs steeply west up the mountain. Halfway up, avoid a right fork, and ascend through large birches and maples. At 0.3 mile from the summit, pass a spring on your left and then a spring on your right (both have good water). The trail then climbs very steeply through spinulose wood fern, wild sarsaparilla, wood sorrel, bunchberry, clintonia lily, and asters. Just before you reach the summit, a short trail on your right leads to a view of Black Mountain. One last effort brings you to the open summit, with fire warden's cabin, fire tower, and helicopter launch pad. Mountain ash decorates the dooryard with white flowers in spring and red-orange berries in summer and fall.

Views from the tower stretch south to Katahdin (Hike 35) and north to New Brunswick. Northeast, the sheer cliffs of Black Mountain drop into Little Black Pond with Black Pond behind. In the distance, you can see Eagle Lake and Square Lake. Eastward lie Deboullie Pond, Pushineer Pond, and St. Froid Lake. Southeast, behind Fish River Lake and Portage Lake, are Haystack and Squapan Mountains near Presque Isle. South-southeast, Whitman and Chapman Mountains, named after the original owners of the Red River Camps, hide the camps on

Island Pond. South, behind these mountains, Round and Peaked Mountains are Aroostook County's two highest. Southwest beyond Gardner Pond is Gardner Mountain, beyond it to the right is Togue Pond, and in the distance is Long Lake. South-southwest are the Rocky Brook Mountains, of which Horseshoe Mountain with its tower is the highest. Deboullie's ridge continues northwest over Fifth Negro Brook.

Return by the same trail to your car.

I had a startling experience while gazing from the tower ladder one afternoon. A Maine Forest Service helicopter landed on a launch pad a dozen yards away, bringing fire warden Marilyn Kenyon to work. The warden's cabin was as unusual as her transportation to work: The windows were boarded to keep out bears. Although the tower is not currently in operation, it is maintained so it can be reopened at a moment's notice.

Backpacking Trips

47

Bemis Mountain Loop

Location: Overlooking Mooselookmeguntic Lake near Rangeley

Time allowed: 2 days, 1 night (a circuit hike)

Total distance: 14 miles

Vertical rise: 2,900 feet

Maps: USGS 7.5' Metallak Mountain; USGS 7.5' Houghton; USGS 15' Rangeley; USGS 15' Oquossoc; MATC map 7 (1993); DeLorme map 18

Bemis Mountain and Bemis Stream valley offer striking beauty in the heart of the western Maine mountains between Rumford and Oquossoc in the Rangeley Lakes region. This 14-mile backpacking circuit covers rugged ground, especially on the first day's ascent of the four main summits of Bemis Mountain. The Bemis Mountain Lean-to makes a good place to stop over in spring or fall. In midsummer, however, you should carry a tent or plan to sleep on the ground in case the lean-to is filled. The 7-mile exposed ridge of Bemis Mountain is not the place to be in bad weather.

How to Get There

Drive north on ME 17 from Rumford toward Oquossoc. At 26 miles, look carefully for the Appalachian Trail (AT) crossing at a scenic turnout at Height of the Land, 11 miles south of Oquossoc. From here you can see the long, many-peaked open ridge of Bemis Mountain falling into the vast spread of Mooselookmeguntic Lake. Backtrack 0.6 mile to the Bemis Valley Trail (former AT), and park in a gravel pit at the Bemis Valley trailhead. This is where your trip will begin and end.

The Trail

Day 1: Height of the Land to Bemis Mountain Lean-to

Total distance: 5.2 miles
Hiking time: 6 hours
Vertical rise: 1,500 feet

Begin with 2 to 3 liters of water per person. From the Bemis Valley Trail walk 0.6 mile

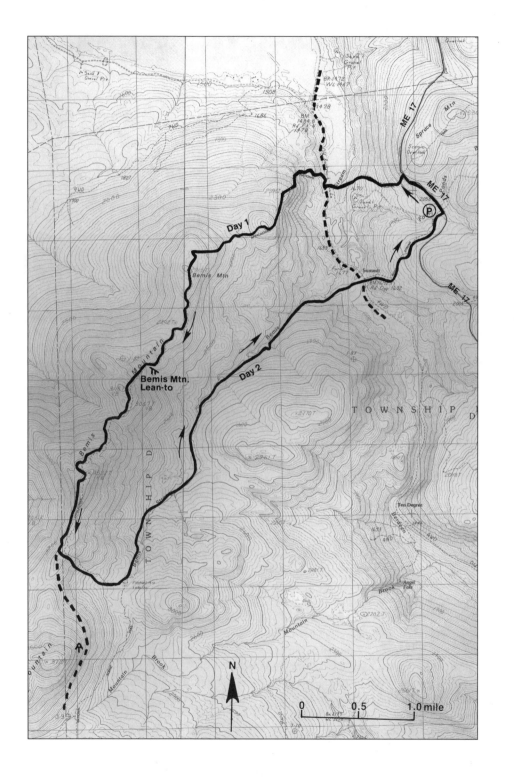

The view to Bemis Mountain from the summit of Old Blue

north on ME 17 to the AT crossing at Height of the Land. (To your right the AT goes east to Four Ponds Mountain and Sabbathday Pond.) Hike mileage begins where the AT crosses ME 17. Follow the white blazes left (west), dropping straight down to Bemis Stream for 0.8 mile. Cross the stream on a footbridge and ascend to a dirt road, which used to be the Rumford and Rangeley Lakes Railroad bed. (From here, it is 1 mile north on the road to the southeast shore of Mooselookmeguntic Lake.)

Follow the AT across the road and very steeply up the northeast shoulder of Bemis Mountain. At 1.2 miles, you reach a spring that is the last sure water for the entire Bemis Ridge. The next 0.5 mile will find you grabbing trees and pulling yourself up a very steep trail, but by the time you have gone 1.6 miles, the most difficult ascent is over. Leave the woods and ascend over ledges to the first of many knobs or false summits. There are five false (apparent) summits, but only three are named:

First, Second, and Third. The "Fourth" (really the sixth) is not a false summit but the actual one. Cross a ravine and rise over quartz-swirled granite through blueberries to the First Summit of Bemis Ridge (2,604 feet) at 2.2 miles.

Follow cairns and white blazes past clumps of juniper, sheep laurel, and cranberries. At 3.1 miles you come to the Second Summit of Bemis Ridge at 2,923 feet. Cross more ledges with increasingly beautiful views north to Mooselookmeguntic Lake, east to Height of the Land, and west toward the rest of the Bemis summits. At 4.6 miles, in a small sag, you come to Bemis Mountain Lean-to, built in 1988. This spot with its nearby spring is a good place to rest from the strenuous assault of Bemis Mountain and stay overnight.

Day 2: Bemis Mountain to ME 17

Total distance: 8.8 miles
Hiking time: 6 hours
Vertical rise: 1,400 feet

Continue hiking south half a mile to the Third Summit of Bemis Mountain, 3,110 feet high. Blueberries, bunchberries, reindeer lichen, and other lichens garnish the exposed trail here and there. After descending into another sag, the trail climbs at 1.7 miles to the "Fourth" and, at 3,532 feet, the highest summit. It has two knobs. At this point you have completed all but 150 feet of the vertical rise for the entire two-day trip.

Views are outstanding south to Elephant Mountain and Old Blue Mountain (Hike 6); west to Metallak Mountain, which rises over the Richardson Lakes; northwest to Aziscohos Mountain (left, Hike 8) and Observatory Mountain (right); north to Bald Mountain (Hike 7) over Mooselookmeguntic Lake, and behind to Cupsuptic Lake; north-northeast to Rangeley Lake; northeast to Saddleback Mountain (Hike 10); and southeast to Tumbledown (Hike 1) and the Jacksons (Hike 3).

From the summit, begin a steady descent onto the long connecting ridge between Bemis and Elephant Mountains. You are likely to see spruce partridge along the trail and possibly partridge (ruffed grouse). At 2.7 miles the AT comes to a junction with the Bemis Stream Trail, which runs 6.1 miles back to ME 17 where you parked.

Turn left onto the Bemis Stream Trail, following blue blazes from now on. A half mile from the trail junction, you cross the headwaters of Bemis Stream. Follow the blue blazes carefully, as recent logging has confused the trail. Dense evergreens begin to open into sunny mixed woods as the trail crosses and recrosses Bemis Stream. Look for wildlife (deer, raccoon, bear) along this trail. When you come to a gravel road, take a left across the bridge, picking up the trail across the bridge to your right.

The trail descends gently into predominantly birch woods with various kinds of hardwood ground cover: Canada mayflower, bunchberry, clintonia lily, wild sarsaparilla, wood sorrel *(Oxalis),* and doll's-eye (white baneberry). The trail follows old lumber roads for short sections and slabs a steep bank above the stream.

At the last crossing of Bemis Stream, the widening stream tumbles through boulders. The trail then continues on the other side of the stream, ascends a high bank leaving the stream, and descends through raspberries to a logging road. Turn right on the logging road, walk 0.2 mile, and follow the trail left back into the woods a short distance until you cross another dirt road. This is the old railroad bed that you crossed yesterday.

Continue in the woods for the last mile, rising gently from Bemis Valley to ME 17. Much of the Bemis Stream Trail has been relocated through recent logging slash and is not scenic at present. The trail ends at Bemis Stream on ME 17 where you parked your car.

48

Crocker Peaks and Sugarloaf

Location: Near Sugarloaf Ski Area, 15 miles north of Kingfield

Time allowed: 2 days, 1 night (a one-way hike)

Total distance: 12.6 miles

Vertical rise: 6,300 feet

Maps: USGS 7.5' Sugarloaf; USGS 7.5' Black Nubble; USGS 15' Stratton; MATC map 6 (1993); DeLorme map 29

Between Kingfield and Stratton and south of Flagstaff Lake stand three of Maine's twelve "4,000-Footers": Sugarloaf, North Crocker, and South Crocker. Sugarloaf, at 4,237 feet, is Maine's second highest mountain. The Crockers are close behind: North Crocker is 4,168 feet and South Crocker is 4,010 feet. The Crockers are separated by a deep col, and Sugarloaf is separated from the Crockers by the Carrabassett River Valley, so there are tremendous gains and losses of elevation for hikers. For this reason the trip is divided into two days of climbing. Rugged terrain, dramatic views, and the hand of nature make the trip very rewarding.

How to Get There

When hiking the three peaks, you almost make a circuit. To end where you began requires 4.5 miles of road walking (not included in the distance of the hike). By spotting a second car or bicycle at the hike's end at Sugarloaf Ski Lodge, however, you can avoid the road walk. You can reach the lodge (in Carrabassett Valley) by driving 15.4 miles north of the center of Kingfield on ME 27, or 8 miles south of the junction of ME 16 and ME 27 in Stratton. Turn south off ME 27 at the SUGARLOAF USA sign and drive 2 miles to the lodge parking lot.

The beginning of the hike is farther north on ME 27 at the Appalachian Trail (AT) crossing, 19 miles north of Kingfield, 2.5 miles north of the Sugarloaf road, and 5.3 miles south of the junction of ME 16 and ME 27 in Stratton. A parking area marks the trailhead.

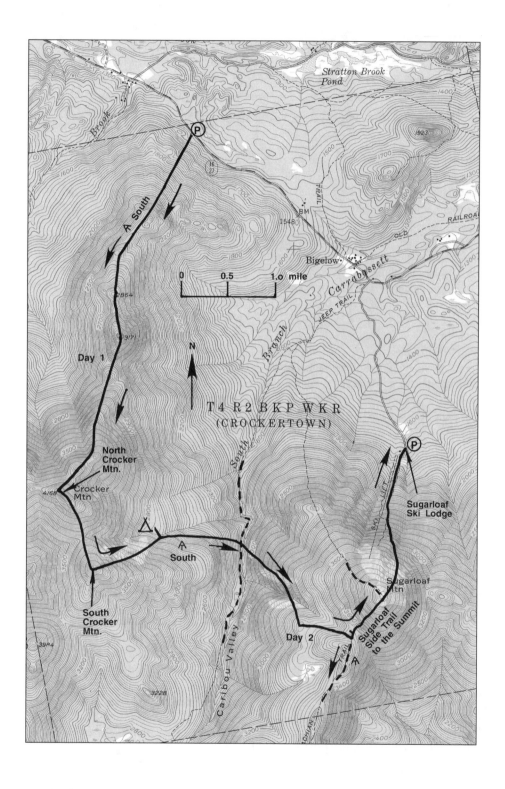

The Trail

Day 1: ME 27 to Crocker Cirque

Total distance: 7.3 miles
Hiking time: 6 hours
Vertical rise: 4,200 feet

Begin with full water bottles. From the parking area on the southwest side of ME 27, begin following white AT blazes south on the 5-mile, gradual approach to North Crocker Peak. The trail passes through a low area of large white and yellow birches, climbing on an even grade toward the north–south ridge that makes up the Crocker Peaks. At 1.4 miles, you mount the first of several knobs of North Crocker Ridge. The trail levels for a short distance and then rises gently for another mile.

With the elevation, the woods change gradually from predominantly white and yellow birches to predominantly spruce and balsam. Spruce grouse inhabit the upper reaches. They are bold birds that do not run from people. This trait gives them the nickname "fool's hen" and has made necessary a law to protect them from hunting. They can be distinguished from ruffed grouse by their darker plumage and red eye markings.

At 4 miles the trail crosses a small tributary to Stoney Brook, not always reliable and the last water for 3 miles. The 0.8-mile ascent from here is very steep to the crest of North Crocker's summit. The trail has eroded, exposing roots of trees that will eventually die. At the crest of North Crocker summit, turn southeast. A short walk brings you to the partially wooded summit of 4,168 feet. Views are limited to a glimpse northeast to Bigelow through the trees.

The trail descends steeply 0.5 mile into the col between the peaks, levels briefly to cross the sag, and then shoots up 0.5 mile to South Crocker Peak. When the trail reaches its high point on South Crocker, a short blue-blazed side trail leads 50 yards to your right to a rocky outcrop at the 4,010-foot summit. Views are limited, but to the south you can see Spaulding Mountain with Mount Abraham (Hike 11) behind it.

Return to the AT and begin descending the east shoulder of South Crocker 0.5 mile to a small, intermittent spring. Shortly, at a rock opening, the trail opens, swings off the shoulder, and plummets steeply toward Caribou Valley and down to the floor of a glacial cirque between the two Crocker peaks. Be careful; the descent is steep and rocky.

A cirque is formed when a glacier cuts down from the top of a ridge, carving a large round hollow with a vertical rounded headwall. Crocker Cirque has an unusual added feature. Beavers have dammed a small tributary to the South Branch of the Carrabassett, flooding the cirque floor into a pond, which reflects the cirque walls bordering it. A quiet morning or evening can be spent in this sanctuary, watching birds, beavers, and clouds mirrored from high above the cirque walls.

At the floor of the cirque, a blue-blazed side trail leads left past the beaver pond 0.2 mile to the Crocker Cirque campsite. You will find here a wooden tent platform and one improved tent site, but no lean-to. The brook has plenty of water, which should be boiled or filtered.

Day 2: Crocker Cirque to Sugarloaf Lodge

Total distance: 5.3 miles
Hiking time: 4½ hours
Vertical rise: 2,100 feet

Follow the blue-blazed side trail from the Crocker Cirque campsite back to the AT. Turn left on the AT and begin a 1-mile descent to the South Branch of the Carrabassett. Soon after you start, you pass a small beaver pond on your right and descend gradually through white birch with numerous wildflowers beneath: wild sarsaparilla, Canada mayflower, purple wakerobin, and starflower. At 0.9 mile, cross Caribou Valley Road. This gravel road ends 2 miles south (right) at Caribou Pond. It is a good exit route north (left) 4.5 miles to ME 27, if you are unable to complete the climb to Sugarloaf.

At 1 mile, cross the South Branch of the Carrabassett, quite a large mountain brook. In high water, the stream can be difficult to cross. You may need a stick for balance, and you may have to remove boots and pants. Running shoes make stream crossings less painful. They dry quickly and are much lighter to carry than sneakers. On the other side the trail runs upstream for a short distance and then climbs away to the southeast, ascending Sugarloaf's steep western spur through birch and poplar. The trail opens and sends you scrambling up a series of slate ledges. Climbing is slow in this steepest section. At 1.7 miles, you reach the rim of Sugarloaf's vast glacial cirque and begin skirting the rim on a precipitous trail to the top of the cirque headwall. This is a dramatic stretch of trail.

At 2 miles, the trail sees you safely back into woods of well-spaced, beautifully shaped spruce in small alpine meadows. The trail levels for 0.5 mile, a welcome respite. At 2.6 miles, cross a small mountain brook (last water), and at 2.8 miles, you reach the Sugarloaf Summit Side Trail. Leave the AT and follow blue blazes left uphill for 0.5 mile to Sugarloaf's 4,237-foot summit. This was the route of the AT before it was rerouted away from the developed summit. Now it is relatively unused, and you are likely to see spruce partridge and other wildlife. The 0.5-mile spurt to the top does

not seem as steep as earlier ascents of the day. (Knowing it is your last ascent helps it seem easier.) With this last elevation gain, growth reduces from spruce-pine to scrub spruce-pine, to blueberries and bunchberry, and finally to lichen-splotched black scree at the pointed bare summit.

A few buildings on top might detract from your feeling of isolation, but you will never have any more dramatic views than from the summit of Sugarloaf. The peak is small, giving the feeling that you can almost jump off in any direction. Most of the other 4,000-Footers in Maine are close around, and Bigelow looks as if you can touch it. Due south is Spaulding Mountain with Mount Abraham (Hike 11) behind it. Southwest over Redington Pond are Poplar Ridge, Saddleback Junior, Saddleback (Hike 10), and the Horn. Far in the distance, Mount Washington in New Hampshire is visible on a clear day. West are the Crocker Peaks with Crocker Cirque between. North are the many peaks of the 17-mile Bigelow Range: left to right, Cranberry Peak (Hike 14); the Horns, West Peak and Avery Peak (Hike 12); and Little Bigelow (Hike 13). Behind Bigelow due north is Coburn Mountain. North-northeast behind Little Bigelow are Little and Big Spencer Mountains (Hikes 31 and 32), with Big Moose (Hike 28) to the right. Northeast is the Barren-Chairback Range, behind which you can see Katahdin (Hike 35) on a clear day. To the east rises the barren cone of Burnt Hill.

Notice the very dark rocks at the summit. Sugarloaf is made of Devonian gabbro, an ultramafic (dark) rock. Gabbro is formed when molten magma wells up from the earth's interior like an underground "blister"— the same way in which granite is made. Whereas granite is light colored because of its particular mineral content, gabbro is very dark or black because it contains dark feldspars, amphiboles, and other mafic minerals. Sugarloaf was created in the Devonian period, which dates it at 350 to 390 million years old. It was a much larger formation back in those days, but erosion has gradually worn it down to a fraction of its former size.

The old AT used to cross over the summit and descend to the northwest, dropping away from the gondola station. In winter this is a ski trail. The old AT is no longer blazed or maintained and is not advised for a descent.

The ski lifts and gondola descend the north side of Sugarloaf. Choose a ski trail and walk down a very steep 2 miles to Sugarloaf Lodge. From the open slope you can look at Bigelow during your entire descent to the lodge, where you spotted a car or bicycle. If you did not spot a car, walk 2 miles out to ME 27, turn left, and walk the remaining 2.5 miles to the AT crossing where you parked at the trailhead. This adds 4.5 miles and 2½ hours to the hike.

49

Webster Brook Trail

Location: Northern Baxter Park near Matagamon Lake

Time allowed: 3 days, 2 nights (a one-way hike)

Total distance: 24.3 miles

Vertical rise: 1,000 feet

Maps: USGS 7.5' Trout Brook Mountain; USGS 7.5' Frost Pond; USGS 7.5' Webster Lake; USGS 15' Telos Lake; USGS 15' Traveler Mountain; Baxter Park Map; DeLorme maps 50, 51, 56, 57

You are not likely to see many people on this trail, and wildlife is abundant. This is the only trail through the extensive northern wilderness of the park, featuring Matagamon Lake to the northeast and Webster Lake to the northwest. You will find solitude and silence in this little-explored lake country.

This 24-plus-mile trail—among streams, brooks, ponds, and bogs—is often wet and muddy. Rain chaps and waterproof boots could enhance your hiking. In the mud on the trail you can count the tracks of numerous animals: moose, deer, coyote, bobcat, raccoon, and some very large bear.

The first 18.3 miles of the hike follows the old Freezeout Trail—part of which is a 3-mile return—and the last 6 miles, the new Wadleigh Brook Trail. The hike ends on Park Perimeter Road, 5.5 miles west of Trout Brook Farm where Wadleigh Brook meets Trout Brook and Park Perimeter Road. A car or bicycle should be spotted here in advance, because walking back to Trout Brook Farm would add 5.5 miles to the hike, for a total of 29.8 miles.

Water is plentiful along the way but, as always, it should be treated. I have seen bear tracks along this trail, so packs should be hung in trees at night.

How to Get There

The Webster Brook hike in the northern wilderness of Baxter State Park begins at Trout Brook Farm Campground, 2.6 miles west of the Matagamon Gate entrance from Patten. For driving directions, see the Baxter State Park introduction.

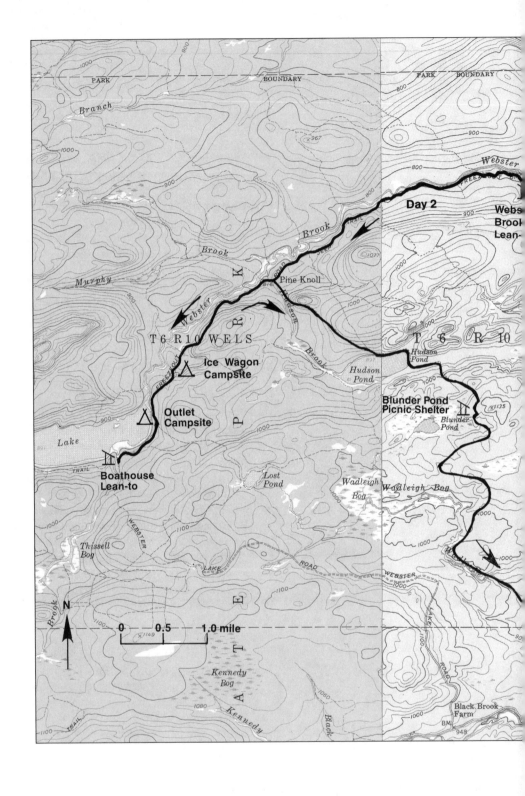

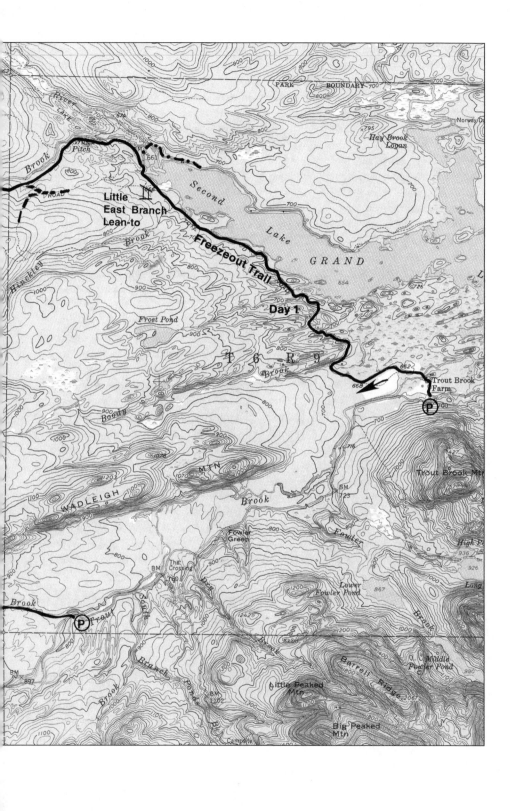

Day 1: Trout Brook Farm to Little East Branch

Total distance: 6 miles
Hiking time: 3 hours
Vertical rise: 180 feet

This is a half-day hike, which allows you some driving time to the park, along with car-or bicycle-spotting time, before setting out on the trail. Leave the park perimeter road at the FREEZEOUT TRAIL sign at the Trout Brook Farm Campground, following the dirt road down to Trout Brook. Behind you to the south is a view of Trout Brook Mountain. At 0.4 mile you reach a footbridge at Trout Brook. Cross the bridge and begin walking the old road in a northwesterly direction. The Freezeout Road provided winter access to Webster Brook. Logs were hauled and stored along this road. At "freezeout" time in spring, soon after thaw, high water carried logs downstream.

At 0.6 mile, you enter a field (now being reclaimed by alder and beautifully shaped spruce) with meadow flowers such as goldenrod, pearly everlasting, and fireweed. This field was part of the old Trout Brook Farm Operation, run by a succession of companies from 1837 to the early 1950s and based at the campground. At one time there were barns, blacksmith shops, storage houses, and quarters for crews. The camp was destroyed by fire three times. Old foundations can be seen in the fields and in the campground. The operation harvested timber south and west of Matagamon Lake. Logs were then driven into Matagamon Lake and down the East Branch of the Penobscot.

At the far end of the old field, follow tire tracks into the woods. This is the old Burma Road, abandoned since 1950 and named for its ups and downs as it crosses a series of slate ridges. At 1.5 miles, you cross two branches of Boody Brook. In autumn, the entire trail is lined with large, colorful mushrooms, puffballs, and bracket fungi. At 3.3 miles you cross Frost Pond Brook, where the trail begins to level out. At 3.5 miles, the trail swings close to the shore of Second Matagamon Lake by an extensive spread of sawdust—the only remains of a lumber mill. The trail skirts the lakeshore for the next 2.3 miles, cutting around a cove and across two brooks, the second of which is Hinckley Brook.

At 5.4 miles, you cross a raspberry clearing on the lakeshore. (An overgrown branch of the old Freezeout Road used to enter this clearing from the left.) A clear, cold spring on the left of the trail provides good water. At 5.6 miles, an obscure trail forks left away from the lakeshore, but you should bear right, staying next to the lake. In another 0.3 mile you reach a small clearing on Webster Brook. (Burma Road used to cross the stream here.) The trail turns sharply left off the tote road and onto a woods trail by Little East Branch Lean-to on the shore of the stream.

The lean-to accommodates three, and there is room for tenting in the vicinity. Webster Brook Lean-to is 2.5 miles farther on, but in a less scenic location. Little East Branch Lean-to is more open (important during bug season) and has a view of the confluence of Webster Brook and the smaller East Branch of the Penobscot.

Day 2: Little East Branch to Webster Lake

Total distance: 9.3 miles
Hiking time: 5 hours
Vertical rise: 380 feet

From Little East Branch Lean-to, the trail turns west and trends west-southwest all day, dipping down to Webster Brook and back. The old Freezeout Trail has been made more scenic by side trails that run along the stream bank, so when you come to forks, always choose the right fork along the stream.

At 0.8 mile you come to Grand Pitch, the largest falls on Webster Brook. At the falls, Webster Brook narrows into oblique walls of slate, forcing a great volume of water through a narrow gorge. Above the falls, the stream is a quiet flatwater. A rusted old sign on a tree here reads, MANY FRIENDS REGRET THE DEATH OF JOE HOWELL, KILLED HERE BY AN EXPLOSION OF DYNAMITE, APRIL 1, 1912. Webster Brook and Webster Lake were yet another watercourse used for log driving from Telos and Chamberlain Lakes. Originally, these lakes flowed north through the Allagash River into the St. John and into Canada. To avoid paying taxes to Canada, in 1841 lumber companies blasted the Telos cut through the narrow piece of land between Telos and Webster Lakes and built Churchill Dam on Heron Lake (part of Chamberlain Lake). This reversed the flow of water, from north to south, and logs could be driven more directly and less expensively to Bangor by way of the Penobscot.

The trail turns away from Grand Pitch and back into the woods. Along the shore, vegetation is lush: cedar, alder, spruce, balsam, hardwoods, mosses, polypody ferns, and mushrooms. One mile before Indian Carry, the trail crosses the red-blazed town line from T6 R9 to T6 R10. After passing several clearings it arrives at 2.3 miles at Webster Brook Lean-to at Indian Carry. Indian Carry was recorded by Thoreau in *The Maine Woods* as a place where Indians carried their canoes around rapids, but the lean-to is situated on a quiet bend in Webster Brook. The woods here are a mixture of young hardwoods, with typical hardwood floor vegetation—starflower, long beech fern, wood sorrel, bunchberry, clinto-

nia lily, Canada mayflower, Indian cucumber, and trillium. Here and there ancient rotting stumps stand witness to the huge white pines that once covered the state and burned in the great fire of 1903.

At 5 miles, you cross a field growing up in raspberries. At 6.3 miles you cross Hudson Brook. Here the trail turns left (south) to return to Park Perimeter Road. But first you want to continue straight ahead on a side trail to the Ice Wagon Campsite. One mile later you pass the outlet of Webster Lake and take a side trail to the Webster Lake outlet campsite, a beautiful place for lunch or to pitch your tent if you do not want to hike the last 0.6 mile. Lake water should be boiled 1 minute before drinking, cooking, or washing dishes. Beyond the campsite you'll find the remains of an old lumberman's dam and the Webster Lake outlet into Webster Brook. On his 1857 canoe trip through Moosehead, the Allagash, and return by Webster Brook and the East Branch of the Penobscot, Thoreau ate lunch at this outlet. While his Native American guide searched for navigable waters on Webster Stream, Thoreau and his companion proceeded on an old path on the south side of the stream. From the campsite you can see an island, with a campsite that can be reached by canoe. (Canoes are not provided.)

At 9.3 miles you will come to Boathouse Lean-to and Campsite, an equally enticing location with a panorama of Webster Lake and a dry roof overhead. This is my choice for a place to spend the night. You will probably see loons floating on the lake and perhaps eat a supper of brook trout.

Day 3: Webster Lake to Hudson Brook and Wadleigh Stream
Total distance: 9 miles
Hiking time: 4 hours
Vertical rise: 420 feet

Leave Boathouse Lean-to on Webster Lake and return to the main trail at Hudson Brook, a retrace of 3 miles. From here you have 6 miles to go. At the brook turn right and hike a short distance downstream before crossing it. The trail now leaves the brook, runs east-southeast, and skirts the northeast shore of Hudson Pond before dropping south to a picnic shelter on Blunder Pond. It skirts Wadleigh Bog before picking up Wadleigh Stream, which it runs along all the way back to Park Perimeter Road and Trout Brook. From here it is 5.5 miles back to the Trout Brook Farm Campground, where you started.

I have rarely seen another human along the trail on this three-day trip. Wildlife makes good company, and the summer and fall flowers are good friends. The hike is remote but not dangerous, because it keeps to low elevations. It is a wonderful way to spend some time alone, or with a friend.

50

Russell Pond

Location: Baxter Park interior

Total distance: 40 miles

*Time allowed: 5 days, 4 nights
(a return hike)*

Vertical rise: 3,200 feet

*Maps: USGS 7.5' Mount Katahdin;
USGS 7.5' Katahdin Lake; USGS 7.5'
The Traveler; USGS 7.5' Wassataquoik
Lake; USGS 15' Katahdin; USGS 15'
Traveler Mountain; Baxter Park Map;
DeLorme maps 50, 51*

One of the nicest vacations an outdoors lover can plan is a few days at Russell Pond in Baxter State Park. The hike-in campground is 8 miles from the nearest road and situated among many fascinating geological and natural wonders. This backpacking trip requires that you carry your backpack 8 miles to Russell Pond on the first day and 8 miles back out on the last day. Since you will be camping at Russell Pond each night, the three intervening days will be spent on short day trips. You should be in good physical condition before attempting this trip. Children also need to be experienced hikers and strong. My four-year-old made this trip with a few rest stops along the way, but I doubt that many children his age could have enjoyed it.

See the introduction to Baxter State Park in this guidebook for general driving directions to the park and for more information on hiking and backpacking in Baxter.

The facilities at Russell Pond were originally built early in the 20th century for an outlying logging camp of the Draper Operations and were later converted into six sporting camps. None remains, but there are lean-tos, a bunkhouse, and tent sites available for reservation. No one may visit Russell Pond without reservations, which are obtained by writing and sending fees to Baxter Park Headquarters, 64 Balsam Drive, Millinocket, ME 04462.

How to Get There

The trail to Russell Pond begins at the Roaring Brook Campground, which you can

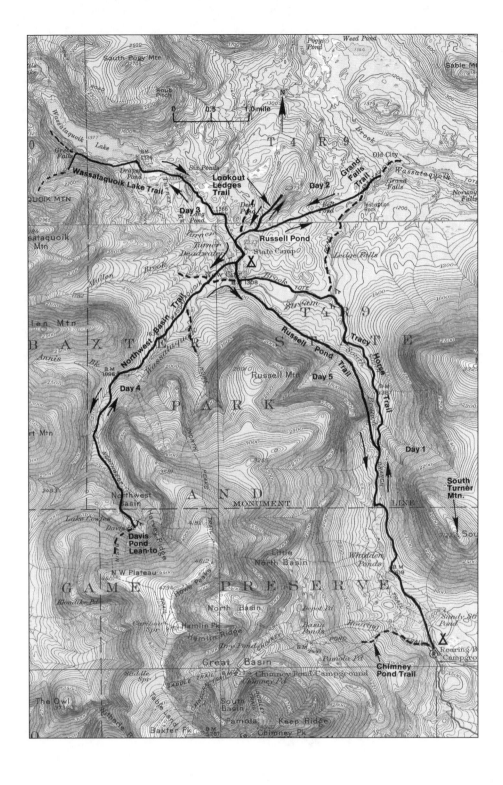

reach by entering the Togue Pond Gate, the southeastern entrance of Baxter State Park. Bear right at the fork and drive approximately 8 miles to the end of the road at the Roaring Brook Campground.

The Trail

Day 1: To Russell Pond

Total distance: 8 miles
Hiking time: 5 hours
Vertical rise: 400 feet

Get an early start from the Roaring Brook Campground. The latest departure time allowed is 1 PM; after that the rangers close the trail. (You may have to spend the preceding night there.) Even though the Russell Pond Trail remains in a valley and there is very little vertical rise, your pack is always heaviest on the first day. After signing in on the list in the Roaring Brook ranger's cabin, follow the trail to the junction of the Chimney Pond Trail (left). Stay to the right on the Russell Pond Trail and cross Roaring Brook on a bridge. In 50 yards the Russell Pond Trail turns sharply left. (Ahead is Sandy Stream Pond Trail, which rejoins the Russell Pond Trail 1 mile farther north.) Notice the decaying cavities of huge stumps of white pine, the remains of forest fires and logging that occurred in the 20th century. You ascend through large mixed hardwoods and cross a spring-fed brook.

In 1 mile, the Sandy Stream Pond Trail comes in on your right. About 0.2 mile beyond you begin skirting the east shore of the first Whidden Pond, passing on your left a short side trail that leads to its shore. Here is your best view on the trail, looking west into Katahdin's three great cirques: the Great Basin, the North Basin, and the Northwest Basin.

The trail soon bears northeast away from the pond and flanks South Turner Mountain (Hike 34). You then descend to the South Branch of the Wassataquoik Stream, which the trail follows onto an old tote road to a junction. Here the Russell Pond Trail turns left and leaves the tote road. In times of high water you should follow this trail. In drier weather, the more interesting route is the Wassataquoik Stream Trail which uses the former Tracy Horse Trail (tote road) to your right, described here. You continue down the tote road along the South Branch of the Wassataquoik approximately 3 miles, where it flows into the main current of Wassataquoik Stream. Here you must ford the main stream; this can be dangerous in high water, especially with a pack. Running shoes or aqua shoes make crossing the stream easier than with bare feet. These shoes dry quickly and are much lighter to carry than sneakers. Two Wassataquoik Stream lean-tos are located on the south shore at the ford; this is the site of the former South Branch Dam. An old lumber camp called the Bell Camps was located here on the south shore where the lean-tos are. One hundred yards north of lean-to #2, blue blazes lead you to an old but occupied beaver pond. The grass-grown dam still supports water, and beavers still live in the lodge, which is now covered with wildflowers.

After fording the stream, you pick up the old Wassataquoik Tote Road west across Turner Brook, through some old fields. In July and August you will be slowed by the bountiful blueberry bushes lining the trail. If you're quiet, you might even see a bear feasting on them. Raspberries are also abundant in the sunny fields in July and August. In the years from 1910 to 1914 these fields were cleared for a lumbering town called New City, population 800, part of the Draper Operations of which Russell

Crossing Wassataquoik Stream

Pond was an outpost. A careful look through the waist-high brush will reveal rusting implements from the town's sawmill, store, and houses. There was even a hotel in New City.

The Wassataquoik Stream Trail returns you to the Russell Pond Trail 0.4 mile from Russell Pond. Turn right and cross Turner Brook on a bridge. In 0.3 mile the Northwest Basin Trail comes in on your left, and shortly you arrive at the Russell Pond Campground.

Day 2: Grand Falls and Lookout Ledges

Total distance: 7 miles
Hiking time: 4 hours
Vertical rise: 500 feet

You can find plenty to do at Russell Pond without ever leaving the area. Fly-fishing brings many people in. Canoes rent by the hour: for floating, paddling around, fishing, and moose watching. In fact you can often see several moose on the pond at one time. The pond itself does not afford pleasant swimming, because it is too shallow and the bottom is too soft. But you can backtrack on the Russell Pond Trail 0.1 mile to the Northwest Basin Trail and follow it to your right a few hundred yards to Turner Deadwater, a pleasant and warm swimming place. For a colder swim, jump into Wassataquoik Stream, south or east of Russell Pond.

If you'd like to plan a more strenuous day, try one or both of the following hikes. Each takes no more than a couple of hours. Both leave from the Russell Pond shore opposite the lean-tos: The Lookout Ledges are 1.3 miles away, and the Grand Falls on the Wassataquoik are 2.7 miles off. The start for both destinations is the same. Walk 0.4 mile around the west and north shores of Russell Pond until you reach the junction where the Lookout Ledges Trail turns left and the Grand Falls Trail bears right.

Grand Falls. From the junction, follow the

Grand Falls Trail east through widely spaced evergreen growth, a result of forest fires in 1884 and 1903. In blueberry season, plan on taking longer than normal to hike this trail. The trail turns and leaves Russell Pond, skirting Bell Pond, where a curious beaver may swim beside you the pond's entire length. At 2.2 miles you cross a beaver flowage and walk on logs through a marsh, then up through tremendous boulders rolled by glaciers and onto the old Wassataquoik Tote Road. When you come to a large cairn, be careful. (At this point, a short trail leads right 25 yards through alders to Inscription Rock, a granite boulder at the edge of the stream bearing the worn inscription TRACY AND LOVE COMMENCED OPERATION ON WASSATAQUOIK, OCT. 16, 1883.) Turn left at the cairn and follow the stream. Shortly, at 2.5 miles, the trail leaves the tote road and climbs the stream's high bank. The next 0.2 mile offers dramatic views down into the gorge of the churning rapids and pitches of Grand Falls.

The Grand Falls Trail ends 2.7 miles from Russell Pond on a high ledge overhanging the lower end of the falls 50 feet below. The falls are a series of swirling drops rather than one large one. You can see several washed-out potholes on the opposite shore. The trail ends at the falls, from which you retrace your trail to Russell Pond. It is possible to bushwhack 0.7 mile farther downstream to the site of Old City. To do this, leave the trail at 2.5 miles on the old tote road and pay close attention, since below this point it is overgrown.

Old City, located at the fork of Pogy Brook and the Wassataquoik, was the first lumber camp within the present park boundaries. It was settled in 1883 by the Tracy and Love Operation and burned in the Great Wassataquoik Fire of 1903. This intense fire, fed by slash from lumbering operations, roared down through Pogy Notch and fanned out around Russell Pond. The fierce heat burned down through the humus, and the fire burned over 132 square miles, leaving effects visible today north and east of Russell Pond. Giant stumps stand in memory of the thousands of virgin white pines that burned. On most of the Grand Falls Trail, trees are spaced widely, and today, over 94 years later, the soil is only just beginning to support larger trees. This accounts for the acres of blueberries and sheep laurel along the trail.

On your return, 0.2 mile from Grand Falls, where the trail dips low along the stream, you can make your way down to the water and ford the stream to a smooth granite terrace on the opposite side. Here the stream eddies into a sizable swimming hole—a perfect place to swim and picnic, with blueberries and cranberries for dessert. This is also the site of former Mammoth Dam, part of the Tracy and Love Operation.

Lookout Ledges. The Lookout Ledges Trail takes you to open ledges on a small hill north of Russell Pond. (There is no water on the trail.) You ascend easily from the junction with the trail to Grand Falls. About 0.7 mile along this trail, you cross open ledges with fine views east and south down over Bell Ponds and the Grand Falls Trail. Continue to the 1,730-foot summit ledges, where the panorama includes a large part of the interior of Baxter State Park.

To your left (north) you can see the clustered conical peaks of South Traveler, behind them, The Traveler (Hikes 43 and 44) and on its left flank, Pinnacle Ridge. These peaks are remnants of a volcano 400 million years old. (Tucked behind The Traveler lie South Branch Ponds in the northern end of the park.) Northeast is lower South Traveler, and east in the distance lies Mount Chase, the roots of an older volcano of 500 million years ago. Sable Mountain is the lower ridge in front of Mount Chase. Southeast over Bell Ponds rises the scree-splotched granite summit of North Turner, with South Turner (Hike 34) behind, both on the eastern border of the park. To the south behind Russell Mountain rises Katahdin (Hike 35), Maine's highest mountain, whose Pamola Peak and Knife Edge rise behind the Howe (North) Peaks. This is a most unusual aspect of Katahdin—different from any views from locations you can reach by car. Southwest you can see the outlet of Russell Pond.

Return to Russell Pond the way you came, turning right at the junction with Grand Falls Trail. The many huge decaying stumps illustrate the size of the gigantic white pines that grew in the area before the fires of 1884 and 1903.

Day 3: Wassataquoik Lake and Green Falls

Total distance: 6.4 miles
Hiking time: 4 hours
Vertical rise: 300 feet

This is a lengthy day hike that offers swimming possibilities in good weather. You should carry a lunch, but water is available at Green Falls. From the Russell Pond Campground walk north behind the lean-tos and turn left behind lean-to #4 through a raspberry patch on the Wassataquoik Lake Trail. From the clearing you enter spruce-fir woods on a wide, easy trail of blueberries and bunchberry. At 0.7 mile, a short side trail takes you to Deep Pond, where Russell Pond campers may use a park canoe.

At 1.3 miles, you climb and pass an arm of one of the six ponds, where you can usually see a moose. A park canoe is chained to a tree at the pond, and you can borrow the key from the Russell Pond ranger. Shortly you cross first a causeway formed by a glacial esker between two of the ponds and then the connector stream between the ponds. At 2.1 miles you cross Turner Brook, the outlet of Wassataquoik Lake. Soon after, the trail descends to the shore of beautiful Wassataquoik Lake.

Another canoe is locked on this shore for the use of Russell Pond campers. If you have borrowed the key from the Russell Pond ranger, you may want to canoe around the lake. At the lower end of the lake is a small island with a cabin and campsite for which reservations can be made. The lake, 1.5 miles long and 0.7 mile at its widest, is remarkable for many reasons: Its gravel beaches and firm bottom make for good swimming, and tall peaks surround the crystal clear water, which is emerald green because of its 200-foot depth.

If you continue hiking, the trail leaves the south shoreline and goes 0.75 mile through the woods to Green Falls. This waterfall, unlike showy Ledge Falls and Katahdin Falls, is named Green Falls because it flows like angel hair over a backdrop of emerald green moss. Above the beautiful lower falls, you can climb to the upper falls, which flow through a deep cleft in the rock. At the upper falls are good views across the lake to South Pogy Mountain, with its talus slope (rock fall). Water from the falls is potable. Green Falls has always enchanted me, in summer, fall, or winter.

Return to Russell Pond the way you came.

Day 4: Davis Pond

Total distance: 11 miles
Hiking time: 7 hours
Vertical rise: 1,600 feet

This rugged hike will take you to Davis Pond in the Northwest Basin and back. Do not attempt it if you are tired or have blisters. You will be hiking all day, so pack a lunch and some snacks.

Leave the Russell Pond Campground on

the Russell Pond Trail and bear southwest 0.1 mile to a junction, where you turn right onto the Northwest Basin Trail and cross the outlet of Turner Deadwater on the remains of an old lumbering dam. At 1.2 miles, you reach a junction with the North Peaks Trail. Stay on the Northwest Basin Trail, and at 2.6 miles cross Annis Brook where another outlying camp of the Draper Operation was once located. Many logging implements can be found on the forest floor in this area. In another 0.5 mile you'll ford a branch of the Wassataquoik and continue on or near the stream through shady conifers. You'll cross the Wassataquoik again at 3.7 miles and continue along the banks of its tributary, Northwest Basin Brook.

This is a wonderful walk. For nearly 1 mile everywhere you look there are pools, falls, and huge boulders. The farther you go, the smaller and more beautiful the brook becomes. At 4.6 miles, you walk along the edge of the smooth brook bed of polished rock for 50 yards. From here you begin the steep ascent into the Northwest Basin, following the headwaters of the brook up steps of rock.

At 5 miles you reach an open knoll at Lake Cowles (elevation 2,850 feet) with excellent views. Nearby is a large stone pile marking an old survey line called the Monument Line, surveyed through the United States east to west in 1833. Lake Cowles is a large tarn, typical of ponds formed in the floors of glacial cirques. The trail crosses the lake outlet and skirts the northeast end of the lake through knee-high sheep laurel, a pink garden in July. Beyond, you climb an unusual heath-covered knoll 60 feet high, a miniature glacial "sheepback," or *roche moutonnée*. There are also two smaller ones in this basin. Descend over the far side of the sheepback, and at 5.3 miles

you reach Davis Pond Lean-to. An overnight stop here can be prearranged with the Russell Pond ranger. To the left is a short trail leading down through the sheep laurel to clear, little Davis Pond, nestled in a corner of the basin under the cliffs of Harvey Ridge. Beneath the few feet of water in the pond, moose tracks crisscross the bottom. To your left stands another sheepback, smaller than the one at Lake Cowles. You can sometimes see a tiny waterfall threading down from the top of the basin wall. I once stayed overnight in this lean-to during a terrific thunderstorm but felt cozy and protected by the high walls of the basin. You can swim in Davis Pond, but don't let the hours slip by. You have to leave in plenty of time to retrace your route to Russell Pond.

Day 5: Back to Roaring Brook
Total distance: 8 miles
Hiking time: 5 hours
Vertical rise: 400 feet

Today is the day you leave Russell Pond. But there are many things to do if you can stay longer, such as bushwhack up Russell Mountain or Tip-top Mountain. Either of these treks can make a day or half-day hike and should be discussed with the ranger at Russell Pond for best directions. Neither hike's mileage or directions are included here.

Russell Mountain is one of the two northern extremities of Katahdin known to early loggers as the "Black Hills." From the Wassataquoik Valley it is the highest peak visible, at 2,801 feet. It is trailless and may be bushwhacked from the Russell Pond Trail with directions from the ranger.

Tip-top is the westernmost of the two northern spurs of Katahdin. On its north slope you can still find the remains of two old sluices used in the Draper Operations of 1910–14. They are best reached by bushwhacking from the Northwest Basin Trail near Annis Brook. High on Tip-top are the ruins of an old lumber camp, as well as a very small pond.

For your departure from Russell Pond, take the Russell Pond Trail and Wassa-taquoik Stream back to Roaring Brook the way you came in.

Regardless of how much hiking you do at Russell Pond, you can't help but enjoy just being there. Nothing can surpass a long summer evening's paddle around the pond. Views from the pond include North Turner Mountain to the southeast, with South Turner behind; south to Russell Mountain and lower Tip-top, backed by the Howe (North) peaks of Katahdin. Southwest is three-peaked Mullen Mountain; west is Wassataquoik Mountain. To the north lie South and North Pogy Mountains, and the ridge to the east leads to the Lookout Ledges.

On a summer evening at Russell Pond I watch moose come in to feed until there are five or six in sight, grazing underwater and raising up to munch and watch. I see an evening's hatch of mayflies and the joyful looks breaking over the faces of the fly-anglers on shore and in canoes. A mother otter leads her two babies on an evening swim. A cedar waxwing darts 30 yards after a bug, and then catches and eats it. As the sun sets I watch North Turner Mountain turn reddish pink to purple and then darken in the dusk, as I slowly paddle to shore. On the walk back to my lean-to in the quiet evening I glimpse the last of the chipmunks and evening grosbeaks.

I can recall one August night, lying with my son on the canoe dock until after midnight watching the annual Perseid meteor shower located in and around the constellations Perseus and Cassiopeia. The only competition was from fireflies in the dark night.

Index

Y